WRITE THE PERFECT BOOK PROPOSAL

10 THAT SOLD AND WHY

JEFF HERMAN · DEBORAH LEVINE HERMAN

3rd Edition

TURNER

Turner Publishing Company
424 Church Street • Suite 2240 • Nashville, Tennessee 37219
445 Park Avenue • 9th Floor • New York, New York 10022
www.turnerpublishing.com

Write The Perfect Book Proposal: Ten That Sold and Why, 3rd Edition

Cover design: Maddie Cothren
Book design: Kym Whitley

Library of Congress Cataloging-in-Publication Data

Names: Herman, Jeff, 1958- author. | Herman, Deborah, 1958- author.
Title: Write the perfect book proposal : 10 that sold and why / by Jeff
 Herman and Deborah Levine Herman.
Description: 3rd edition. | Nashville, Tennessee : Turner Publishing Company,
 2016.
Identifiers: LCCN 2015047861| ISBN 9781630260828 (pbk.) | ISBN 9781681621210
 (hardback)
Subjects: LCSH: Book proposals.
Classification: LCC PN161 .H47 2016 | DDC 808.02--dc23
LC record available at http://lccn.loc.gov/2015047861

Printed in the United States of America
15 14 13 12 11 10 9 8 7 6 5 4 3 2 1

To all the aspiring writers who need a little
push to make it over the top

CONTENTS

Section 1
All Aspects of the Proposal and Some Advice Thrown In

Section 2
Proposals

ACKNOWLEDGMENTS

THIS BOOK IS POSSIBLE THANKS to the convergence of many talented people.

We are very grateful for the skills, commitment, and patience shown by the wonderful people at Turner Publishing: Todd Bottorff, Angie Lithgow, Jon O'Neal, Stephanie Beard, Maddie Cothren, Jolene Barto, Jennifer Lewis, Angela Premoe, and Sydney Mathieu.

The ten proposals included in this book were generously donated by the authors due to their eagerness to help others. Each of them is listed here with information about their respective book. Please note that the titles below reflect the "final title" each book was ultimately published with, which more often than not differs from the tentative working-titles stated on the corresponding proposals.

Adam Toprek. BE YOUR CUSTOMER'S HERO: REAL WORLD TIPS & TECHNIQUES FOR THE SERVICE FRONT LINES (AMACOM, 2015)

Susan Shumsky. INSTANT HEALING: GAIN INNER STENGTH, EMPOWER YOURSELF & CREATE YOUR DESTINY (New Page Books, 2013)

Steve Levinson and Chris Cooper. THE POWER TO GET THINGS DONE (WHETHER YOU FEEL LIKE IT OR NOT) (Perigee/Tarcher 2015)

William Seagraves. BE YOUR BEST BOSS: REINVENT YOURSELF FROM EMPLOYEE TO ENTREPRENEUR (Perigee/Tarcher 2016)

Susan Pease Banitt. THE TRAUMA TOOLKIT: HEALING PTSD FROM THE INSIDE OUT (Quest Books 2012)

Mark Anthony. EVIDENCE OF ETERNITY: COMMUNICATING WITH SPIRITS FOR PROOF OF THE AFTERLIFE (Llewellyn Publications 2015)

Deborah Sandella. Title TBA. (Red Wheel Weiser 2016.)

Perry Marshall, Bryan Todd, and Mike Rhodes. (ULTIMATE GUIDE TO GOOGLE ADWORDS: HOW TO ACCESS 1 BILLION PEOPLE IN 10 MINUTES (Entrepreneur Press 2014)

Doug Devitre. SCREEN TO SCREEN SELLING: HOW TO INCREASE SALES, PRODUCTIVITY & CUSTOMER EXPERIENCE WITH LATEST TECHNOLOGY (McGraw Hill 2015)

Theo Tsaousides. BRAINBLOCKS: OVERCOMING THE 7 HIDDEN BARRIERS TO SUCCESS (Prentice Hall/Penguin Random House 2015)

INTRODUCTION

Why is it important to write a book proposal?

THE BOOK PROPOSAL IS CONSIDERED a tool of the trade for non-fiction authors. While many authors try to skip this step in the process toward publication, they soon discover that even those with enviable followings need to conform to this publishing protocol. Traditional publishing is a "hard copy" business, which doesn't exclude a digital format. It simply means that the work exists as a written expression. No matter the subject, a nonfiction book has to have strong content to be seriously considered by publishers and literary agents. A strong book proposal is like a business plan that entices the potential investor (i.e., the publisher) to part with their cash.

This is our third edition of this book, and throughout the years we have discovered a format for book proposals that we believe works very well. While our format has been adjusted to meet the changes in the industry, and in this new edition we have showcased new book proposals, the structure of the book proposal is still basically the same. The reasoning behind it is also the same. Agents and the editors who acquire books for publishing houses are very busy people. Try to imagine the amount of written material they see every day. Before the Internet became the popular way of sending files, rooms were literally filled with boxes and stacks of manuscripts that aspiring writers would send over the transom in hopes they would be discovered.

The book proposal became a necessary tool to synthesize the important information that agents and editors need to consider at a glance to determine if a book project is worth pursuing. The book proposal describes the book but also anticipates the questions agents or editors will be asking themselves while evaluating the marketability of the book. It is a cold, hard fact that marketability is the first question that enters the minds of anyone in the business of publishing when they consider a project. It is not the worthiness of it. All authors and books are potentially worthy. The first consideration is whether the book has an audience of people who will read it.

This is the reason for the book proposal. This is your place as the writer to describe your book with supporting information that will entice an agent or editor to take a closer look. The real beauty of this system is that you may not need to write an entire book to obtain a publishing contract. If you write your entire manuscript before approaching a publisher, your effort is speculative. With nonfiction, it is probable that a publisher will like your idea but have some additional ideas of how to best position your work. This could mean some significant rewriting. With a book proposal, you can have a contract and a relationship with an editor who will help you develop a book that is better suited for the marketplace.

The publishing industry has changed since we first wrote this book in 1993. When we wrote the second edition in 2001, we never could have fully anticipated how much technology would upend the publishing world for everyone. These days there are fewer spots for nonfiction authors. This means the quality of your book proposal has to be even better than ever. If you want to be one of the chosen who can benefit from the advantages of the traditional publishing world, you will need to put great effort into this part of the process. A thorough proposal will also serve as a blueprint for writing a great book.

THE CONTENTS OF A PROPOSAL

A book proposal tells a publisher or agent what your book is about, why it should exist, and why you should be the one to write it. In addition, the proposal will address these questions:

1. Who are you and why are you writing this book?
2. Is there a market for the book?
3. What are the complementary or competitive titles already on the shelves?
4. How will you reach the market?

5. What is your existing platform, both traditional and online, that can support the book?
6. What are your plans to promote the book?
7. Do you have any special endorsements?

While the proposal format we use has evolved over the years, we have found that all proposals are expected to follow a roughly prescribed format. We think it is a logical way to provide the necessary information that works well for both the writer and the publisher. Keep in mind that no proposal format is carved in stone. There is always room for creativity, and many successful writers have taken creative license with great results. We recommend, however, that if you are new at this, you might find it best and easiest to develop good habits by working within the conventional style.

Here are the elements that a proposal is expected to contain in an order that we find works well. You can certainly alter the order, particularly if there is information in an area that may be more important to your situation and therefore needs to come earlier in the proposal. Regardless of the order, your book proposal should be formatted well, even if you will be sending it digitally. Most agents and publishers today accept attachments after responding to a well-written query letter.

1. Title Page
2. Table of Contents of the Proposal
3. Overview
4. About the Author
5. Table of Contents of the Book (optional placement)
6. Complementary and Competitive Titles
7. Markets
8. Platform
9. Promotions
10. Table of Contents of the Book
11. Chapter Outline
12. Sample Chapters
13. Collateral Attachments (optional as an addendum to author background)
14. Electronic Media Kit (optional)

HOW TO USE THIS BOOK

We originally wrote this book after discovering that the best way to learn to write a resume for a job interview was to look at sample resumes that actually landed people the jobs. We applied this logic to book proposals and saw how helpful it was for writers to see book proposals that really worked. When you see samples that clearly reveal each document's successes and failures, you don't have to reinvent the wheel.

We believe that by far the very best way for you to learn how to write a book proposal is to see proposals that have succeeded. It's a great advantage for you to see where these proposals were strongest and where they were weakest.

In this, our third edition of this book, written well into the second decade of the new millennium, we have selected and critiqued an entirely new set of ten of the finest proposals on a variety of topics. We have worked with each of these authors and have sold each of these books to traditional publishers.

In walking through these proposals with us, you will see a wide variety of formats, aesthetics, and styles of expression. But you will also see that each of them clearly shows why it deserves to be a book. This exposure to a variety of successful styles will help you eventually find your own.

Section One provides brief chapters that explain each section of the proposal and also gives advice on others issues you may encounter as a writer.

Section Two contains the actual proposals. Some have been shortened to fit in the book. At the end of the book, you will find brief appendices of book proposal terms and suggested reading.

There are so many wonderful websites that we hesitate to list them. They also change every day. We suggest that you join us at our own social network for writers, agents, and editors at www.WAENetwork.com to continue asking any questions you have or to let us know more about you and your work.

Jeff Herman
Deborah Levine Herman
The Jeff Herman Literary Agency, LLC
PO Box 1522
Stockbridge, MA 01262
www.JeffHerman.com

All Aspects of the Proposal and Some Advice Thrown In

CHAPTER 1

Birth of an Idea

THERE'S SOMETHING VERY IMPORTANT YOU must do before you decide to write a book: you must know what you want to write about. This sounds like a major no-brainer, but that's because you haven't seen thousands upon thousands of book proposals over the past twenty-five years. The most common problem is the writer's apparent lack of clarity about their own book.

Ideally, an idea will drive you to write a book, but it's common for it to be the other way around. Many professionals are advised to write a book about what they know as a form of self-promotion. They might not have any emotional or ego-driven motivation to write anything, but their intellect informs them that a book would be good for business, and that's the clincher. Frequently, these individuals will outsource the book to someone who specializes in writing other people's books. There's nothing wrong with this on any level, especially since all the content will presumably be provided by the person whose name will be on the book and simply funneled through the writer for editorial crafting. Many people have excellent information to share with the world but don't have the requisite skills, motivation, or time to write it by themselves. Countless books of high quality were not literally written by the person to whom they are attributed.

Ironically, books written for promotional purposes tend to be more conceptually focused than books derived from the writer's heart. This isn't surprising since the human intellect tends to be more organized than our primal, nonsequential emotions. But what's in our hearts tends to be more interesting and revealing than what's in our heads, assuming we are able to coherently express it.

Imagine an after-work get-together with real friends over coffee or drinks. The conversation will probably be a continuum of unplanned and fragmented nuggets, and it's possible that one or more aspects of what was said could form the basis of an entire manuscript.

Unfortunately, what you are most eager to write about might not mean much to other people outside your immediate circle of friends and family. For instance, agents and editors who agree to participate in open-door pitch events must be prepared to diplomatically respond to the occasional writer who wants to write a memoir or autobiography that lacks commercial appeal. Fortunately, traditional publishing isn't the only way to get a book published. But if you are looking to break into the traditional publishing arena, it will be incumbent upon you to propose a book that they want to publish for their own reasons, not because you want them to. Researching what has already been successfully published is a reliable way to test-market the viability of your idea.

Simply choosing a subject or theme is just the beginning, and sometimes a dead end. Publishing professionals will assess your proposal on the quality of your facts, credentials, functions, stories, and editorial skills along with comparable books on the market and market needs. They need to see beyond the benefit of a doubt what the book will be and why they should publish it. Your idea's commercial and editorial viability must be made evident by the proposal. Verbal skills are always an asset, but you will probably not be able to talk yourself into a deal, especially if your editorial presentation is lacking. You're not pitching a speaking gig or a radio show. Books have to be written, and even if you somehow muscle yourself through the gatekeepers to get a face-to-face meeting, your proposal will need to be strong to close the deal. It is your blueprint that will show not only your talent but that your work can please the marketplace in order to sustain itself.

What's most wonderful about book writing is it gives an unmatched opportunity to participate in the universal mind meld known as life. In your lifetime, there are only a handful of people who might come to really know you through work, family, and community. But you can make deep and lasting impressions with everyone who reads your books.

Here are some questions that might help you zero in on what to write: What are you most passionate about sharing? Do you understand your motives? Are you looking to grow a business, get noticed, achieve self-healing, have fun, make money, and/or contribute to others? There's no reason why you can't have plural, and even shifting, motives.

Additional questions might be: What do you have to say that others will care about, and why? What do you enjoy thinking (daydreaming) about? What do you tend to worry about with regard to yourself and others? What do you like talking about? What do you actually know about? What do you do at work? What do you do for leisure? What have you experienced in your life that most resonates?

Some self-evaluation will go a long way toward finding the topic and message that is most suited to your goals. Refining your own intentions will assure greater clarity in your work. The more you ask yourself why you are really writing a book and what is going to be in it for the reader, the better off you will be. You may have the seed of a very good book. What we find the most in proposals that do not work is that the core idea is weak or not developed enough to sustain an entire proposal.

After you have asked yourself these questions and have started to craft your proposal, return to them and see if your core ideas have shifted. You are never locked into your book, and its message should remain flexible right until the very end. You might find that the book changes as you work it through. The most difficult part of the proposal is this core idea. In film, it is often called the logline. It is the synthesized essence of the book that can be told in one or two lines. What is the book about? What is happening and how will the reader be changed by reading your work? What is the takeaway? No matter the subject, all books need to have a reason for their existence.

Exercise: A good core statement about your book can be boiled down to less than ten concise words. These words should be as intuitive, self-evident, and fetching as a good conversation with a like-minded person. Don't give yourself the false luxury of thinking you can take time to explain what your book is about. If you have to use more than ten words to covey your idea, go back and do it over again. You won't have an opportunity to give a detailed explanation of what your book is about to potential customers; they have to immediately see it and feel it for themselves, or they will move on. Ultimately, old-fashioned word-of-mouth is what sustains sales, whether via mass media, social media, or person to person. And in order for that message to spread, your concepts have to be packaged for easy and compelling conversation and comprehension.

One more thing: as much as you may not believe this, there are no more new ideas to be had. This is a very big world with human beings creating and thinking at every moment. However, you are truly unique. Your voice is your own. There are always new ways to solve a problem or better ways to explain old solutions. Whatever the public is dealing with now, you can be sure they were also dealing with it thousands of years ago in a different form and context. Our lives and pressures are always in flux, but our basic humanity has probably remained the same for at least thirty thousand years, which is more or less when we presumably became the only human species on earth.

Trends come and go. For instance, diet books will be very hot for three years every decade and then become oversaturated for a time. It is best to be ahead of a trend, but anything you write, if it has your own spin, can be successful if you learn to master the protocols of publishing.

CHAPTER 2

Choosing the Title

CHOOSING A GOOD TITLE IS the most important first step on your journey to publication for many reasons. Please keep in mind that once your book is sold, a wise editor might throw your title into the netherworld, but at this stage you need it, and you need it to be even better than good.

> *Reason One:* A good title will attract the interest of a potential publisher or agent.

> *Reason Two:* It is difficult to choose a good title, so it will force you to really focus on the core message of your book, thus causing you to thoroughly plan your perfect book proposal.

> *Reason Three:* Your great title becomes the trunk of the tree of a book proposal that you are growing. Every time you veer off your path, you will envision your tree with the title you have carefully selected, and it will lead you safely back to center.

> *Reason Four:* Having a good title will get your foot in the door, and the rest of the proposal will make sure you are invited inside for a cup of tea.

For example: *Whose Turn Is It to Push the Volkswagen?*

That was the misguided title proposed for a book about customer service pitched to Jeff many years ago. Before diving into it, he assumed it was some kind of personal narrative about a road trip. To his surprise, it was a well-thought-out commercial self-help business book by someone with superb credentials and powerful self-marketing resources. He signed it up, and the first thing he and the author did together was come up with a better title. We had little trouble finding a publisher, and the title changed a couple of times until everyone was satisfied.

SELECTING A GOOD TITLE

The first law when selecting a tentative title is: Do no harm. Take titles seriously. Bad titles are like bad suits or outfits; people will misjudge your proposal (and ultimately your book) in negative ways before they begin reading it. They will either misunderstand what it's about or become dissuaded by how it makes them feel. Harried agents and editors are looking for reasons to read a proposal. They want to find gems for their lists. Your job is to make sure you have removed all disqualifiers before they dismiss your book without a thorough evaluation. There may be imperfections in the proposal or questions raised, but if your title is bad you will be completely dismissed and taken out of consideration.

You want to choose a title that will intrigue someone without confusing them. Someone reading your proposal needs to know from the title what the book is about. It is better to have a bland, self-explanatory title than a jazzy title that is too "out there." Publishers look for creativity and cleverness, but your disadvantage is the proliferation of noise that bombards agents and editors in their day-to-day lives. This is an issue you will address when considering how to write your proposal and your book, but it is imperative that you remember this when you are deciding on a title. You do not want to make your potential benefactor work too hard. The title will be your fishing lure. There has to be something wiggling in front of the editor's face that will entice him or her to bite down on the hook.

Keep in mind this perhaps overused saying when you determine your book structure and choose your title: readers choose a book that conveys clearly what is in it for them. Editors and agents are people, and they often choose to represent or advocate for projects that resonate with their own interests. Therefore, the WIIFM factor must be clear, and the first opportunity to do that is with your title.

WHAT DO YOU NOW KNOW ABOUT TITLES?

1. They should be clear.
2. They should make it clear what the book is about.
3. Sacrifice the "jazzy" factor for blandness if it means clarity.
4. Balance this with an effort to be clever.

When choosing a title, you are endeavoring to offer readers, and the editors and agents who can help you reach them, what they need balanced heavily with what they want, which is the entertainment factor. Bland is good as a base, but then you can add other ingredients to spice things up a bit. Spend some time on this and don't get married to the first title that looks right. The typical approach to book proposals is to want to get them over with. Change your mind-set about this. Make this a part of the good things you are doing for yourself. You are increasing the possibility of a successful sale of your book by spending the extra energy on this stage of the process.

SOME EXAMPLES

Let's say you are a reader looking for a book about selling. You'd probably pass over a book titled something like *Never on Weekends* because you won't know it's about selling. The book may be about how to double your sales without having to work over the weekend, but you can't know that from the title, even though you may be the perfect market for this book because you like your weekends free. This is why a better title might be *Double Your Sales Without Ever Having to Work on Weekends*. It is clear and will immediately conjure an image of an overworked man or woman lying in a hammock or gardening or reading a book instead of slaving away in an office.

Titles create visceral reactions. If you are a salesperson looking for a book to improve your output, you will likely run from a title like *Stop Losing Sales*. This title gets to the exact point of what you might need, but it will create a sense that you are a loser and a failure. It will feel like a criticism instead of a helping hand with solutions. This is why a title like *Double Your Sales Without Ever Working on Weekends* is a better choice all around.

Titles create feelings and also expectations. So the book attached to the title needs to directly address the promises made . No one wants to buy a book that only remotely relates to what the title implies.

NOW WHAT HAVE YOU LEARNED:

1. Titles need to be simple and understandable.
2. They can conjure images and create visceral reactions that will spell the difference between a sale and a rejection.
3. Make sure the title is a reflection of the promises you will fulfill in your book.

We try never to give authors absolutes. There are many examples of successful books named for concepts that only became apparent by reading the book. The most famous that is used to disprove the rule is *What Color Is Your Parachute?* This book was originally self-published by Richard Nelson Bolles in 1970 but has been commercially published since 1972 and has sold over ten million copies worldwide. It is a career-development book and was actually an offshoot of what we like to refer to as a relatively well-established platform for its time. The book will always stand as the exception to the clear-title rule, but with so many books sold, Bolles can make up any title he wants.

The more someone has to figure out what your title means, the more likely they will look for other books that may be similar to yours or could even be inferior. A reader, agent, or editor will grab the book to which they can most readily relate. There are many places for you to show your writing chops in the book and book proposal. The title is not the place to be overly creative. Use your business acumen when selecting your title so you do not miss out on consideration.

Have we confused you enough yet? Books like ours make it look easy. You can work with this book or with one of our workbooks or even work with one of us as a writing coach, and you will still find this part of the process to be one of the biggest challenges. But when you have the right title, combined with clear structure, everything will fall into place. You will be very happy with the result.

Keep this in mind: Consumer product companies like Proctor & Gamble invest vast resources toward conjuring and researching names for mundane household products like laundry detergent. Marketing, psychology, and common sense are powerful skills when combined. If you understand what touches people on a gut level, you'll be more adept at getting them to buy what you are selling. For instance, Tide is a strong title for detergent because it provokes visceral images of pristine waves of water. But if the same product were named something like Fungus, sales would collapse. Or at least we would hope they would.

Here is another important point to consider. Consumer product companies invest resources toward names because they know they will need to market them in order for people to buy their products. They want to raise awareness of what they are selling. There is no real trick to this concept. However, it seems writers resist the idea that what they are creating is not only a work of art, it is a product. Writing for oneself is a rewarding endeavor. If you want others to read it as well, they have to know it is there. So you need to give it a name or title that will garner some attention.

HOW TO CREATE A GOOD TITLE

We wish there was a directory of every possible great and effective title of a book so we could remove any of the effort for you. This does not exist, nor should it, as title creation is part of the fun. It will also give you more ownership of your own process. Here are some considerations:

Humans think in terms of pictures and are dominated by feelings. It's best to reserve your energy for reinforcing what customers are already seeing and feeling instead of trying to explain what you want them to see and feel. Unpopular governments are likely to fall unless they can overcompensate through various forms of mind-control, coercion, and fear. Fortunately, American writers don't have access to those kinds of tactics, though some people might say that mind-control does propel some books.

One of our favorite titles ever is *Thinner Thighs in 30-Days*. Nothing needs to be explained, and the customer either cares or doesn't. Another good one is *Wealth Without Risk*. Obviously the concept is a fantasy. The only way we know of to make money without risk is to inherit it. This might explain why the author was legally compelled to stop teaching his popular and profitable (for him) classes with the same name. Nevertheless, it's a great title because it promises what everybody wants, even though it's a fallacy.

CHAPTER 3

What is a Book Proposal?

IN THE WORLD OF PUBLISHING, nonfiction writers aren't required to generate an entire manuscript prior to pitching their work for publication. In fact, most nonfiction book deals are made before the manuscript is written. All that's required in order to have a contract and an advance payment in hand is the nonfiction book proposal. It has been this way for a very long time, and there's no indication that it will change at any point in the near future, nor is there any reason why it might change. Writers who learn how to effectively generate proposals can test-market their ideas without having to write entire books on spec. Even better, they can secure partial payment for the book before writing it. Knowing how to write a powerful book proposal is a profitable skill.

WHY ARE THE PROTOCOLS DEFENDED? AND WHY DO FICTION WRITERS NEED TO FINISH THE MANUSCRIPT BEFORE PITCHING IT?

Before responding to these excellent questions posed by yours truly, we wish to give some context. The publishing establishment doesn't care if writers don't like the way the system works. This doesn't mean you can't attempt to avert the rules, but it does mean that rule breakers are at a disadvantage because they're expecting people to think and act outside well-rutted comfort zones. Sometimes rule breakers succeed by becoming the proverbial "exceptions to the rule," and once in a while they become the new rule makers and trendsetters.

All established businesses are modeled to keep doing things the same way they already are. This doesn't mean changes can't or won't happen, but it does portend that there will be blood when change does occur. Change comes in clumsy increments. It starts with a few early adapters who see something new they like and start using it. The majority will initially be dismissive, derisive, or apathetic. If the new technique is a dud, it will disappear like a bothersome virus that only infected a few. But if it gives its users decisive advantages over nonusers that can be replicated again and again, permanent shifts are in the wind. For instance, publishers were very slow at transitioning from electric typewriters to word processors, but resistance was futile. This single shift significantly altered the way offices functioned, and not everyone was happy about it. Tasks were recalibrated, and some people no longer fit in.

Publishers want fiction writers to finish the manuscript before pitching it because fiction writing is much more fragile and unreliable than nonfiction writing. It's too easy for a novel to begin strongly and end weakly, or not end at all. The only way to be sure that a novel will be good enough from beginning to end is for it to be finished. Conversely, nonfiction writing tends to be reliably consistent. A well-written and organized proposal, with one or two finished chapters, is usually sufficient evidence that the book will fulfill its editorial promise when finished.

Why is there such a large dichotomy between fiction and nonfiction writing? Frankly, nobody has the definitive answer, but the evidence is decisive. A pop-psyche theory, or maybe it's just my theory, is that not all writing is managed by the same part of the brain. It's plausible that more creative forms of writing engage a more "fragile" part of the brain, whereas more fact-based writing derives from a more "solid" part of the brain. This would help explain why many commercial nonfiction writers are unable to write commercial fiction no matter how much they want to. It also might explain why some creative fiction writers are unable to organize their thoughts into a coherent nonfiction book. It's also possible we don't know what we're talking about.

WHO IS THE PROPOSAL FOR?

First and foremost, the proposal is for you, the writer. By focusing on writing a strong proposal, you will ultimately write a better book, because it will structure you to know where you're going before you depart. Proposal writing can feel like a hassle, but it will discipline your brain to be more efficient and productive when the real writing begins.

Second, the proposal is for the people you need to sell yourself to in order to procure a contract. If an agent likes your proposal, she will want to represent you, and if an editor likes your proposal, he will want to publish you. The better your proposal, the better your contract terms are likely to be.

WHAT DOES A PROPOSAL LOOK LIKE?

The proposal is like an extended sales brochure; it's meant to attract interest, answer questions, and make people want to close a deal with you. Content is king and queen, but style and aesthetics are powerful princes and princesses. Make your proposal pleasing to look at and easy to read. Frankly, only idiots or self-destructive people would screw up this part. You simply need to choose a traditional font and print style. Err on the side of what's conventional and standard. Eccentricity is a two-edged sword; some people might see brilliance while others perceive high-maintenance or extra work.

If you envision your book as being out-of-the-box, then attach a prototype showing how you want it to be seen while still adhering to the usual proposal protocols. Doing something the same way as everyone else is counterintuitive for some people. However, agents and editors are conditioned to follow similar templates; if you stray from what's easiest for them to deal with, you risk shooting yourself in the foot. On the other hand, nothing changes for the better unless some people take risks.

In the interest of readability, it's probably best to use 1.5 spacing and short paragraphs and to clearly indicate where sections begin and end. You want your best points to be easily discovered. Why? Because agents and editors have to read too many proposals, and are unhappy when something is difficult to read and comprehend. You don't want to make them unhappy. Getting a gatekeeper to say yes is a competitive process; please avoid all the avoidable mistakes you possibly can. If a proposal looks tedious to read, it will already have an emotional strike against it before the first sentence is reached. If it looks inviting, the reader won't feel resentment or fatigue at the outset. Also keep in mind that your proposal must be screen and hard-copy friendly, even if it's digitally delivered.

There's no getting around the fact that people are dominated by feelings first, intellect second, if at all. If someone doesn't like what they feel and think they see, they are unlikely to do business with you unless you manage to overcome those initial roadblocks. During the days of the Soviet Empire, there was no reason for consumer marketing to exist (though ideology was heavily marketed) because nothing was competing for market share. Usually there was a single product for each primary purpose. For instance, toothpaste was named

Toothpaste without any fancy packaging or branding. There was no competition, and the factory didn't have to worry about people not buying it. Today, Russia gets to be like the rest of us. Cuba will soon join the club, and North Korea can't avoid destiny forever. The human mind demands to be entertained, romanced, and seduced, or it becomes sullen, depressed, and unmotivated.

HOW LONG DOES IT TAKE TO WRITE A PROPOSAL?

Different books require different proposals, and writers write at a large spectrum of paces. For instance, a memoir or narrative will be largely judged on the quality of the writing, so an expansive outline and at least one full chapter will probably be necessary. On the other extreme, a basic how-to book will be more reliant on the quality and organization of the prescriptive information than on the actual writing, and a relatively brief outline will probably be sufficient, especially if the author has a successful publishing track record. The first time you write a proposal will probably consume at least twenty to forty hours, but you will surely become progressively more efficient and confident over time.

The more clear and focused you are in your head before you begin, the less time you will have to spend. You are likely to keep getting stuck, frustrated, and unsatisfied in the absence of mental decisiveness about the book you presumably want to write. If your cloudiness isn't resolved before or through the proposal process, it will also infect your ability to write the manuscript. Writing the proposal is a golden opportunity to defrag your mind; it's common for writers to frequently reorient their intentions as they write the proposal. Of course, more time and energy will be consumed if you alter your vision, but you'll more than make up for it when you write the manuscript.

When writing the proposal you shouldn't allow how long it takes to bother you. In fact, good writing can't be measured by time. Yes, deadlines must exist and delivering on time is crucial, especially if you're a journalist. But in most instances you should gift yourself with more than enough time to do it right. But don't become paralyzed through perfectionism; anything can be excellent, but nothing can be perfect. Focus on getting it done, review it a couple of times over a forty-eight-hour period, and then consider it done.

ARE THERE DIFFERENT KINDS OF PROPOSALS?

Yes, just as there are many different kinds of nonfiction books. Basically, books that are more reliant on the quality of writing and storytelling will need long-form outlines, whereas books that are more information oriented can get by with relatively condensed outlines. Memoirs, narratives, biographies, and histories are prime examples of books that require strong editorial skills. Books about how to invest money, use software, or write a book proposal aren't as dependent upon "great writing." However, some nonfiction categories can't be adequately assessed on the basis of a proposal alone and will require a large portion of the manuscript to be written on spec. These include humor, coffee table, young children's, gift books, illustration books, and books combined with nonbook products.

CAN I SKIP THE PROPOSAL AND JUST WRITE THE MANUSCRIPT?

Yes, and many people do, especially if they are prepared to quickly self-publish as an alternative to the traditional method. No one is commanding you not to write the manuscript. The point to all of this is that you don't have to write the manuscript in order to get a contract, which is obviously a huge advantage. However, even if you have a finished manuscript, agents and editors will still want to see an abbreviated proposal because it's the only way to assess important information beyond your content, and they will want to see each chapter at least briefly summarized. Importantly, agents and editors will be wary about jumping into an un-vetted manuscript, whereas the proposal is a way to efficiently determine whether the project is even something they should be considering in the first place. Also keep in mind that what you consider to be a finished manuscript might not be acceptable as is to a traditional publisher. Often I've seen publishers insist that the work be significantly shortened, expanded, or revised in specific ways in order to be accepted for publication.

IS THERE ONLY ONE WAY TO WRITE A PROPOSAL?

There's no absolute way to write a proposal, and whatever works in the end was the right way. However, don't take this as a license to stray too far off course. Most effective variations tend to be marginal, such as the sequence of sections or perhaps a deletion of one. Anytime you go off the beaten path, make sure you're moving in a carefully calculated direction and aren't making your proposal overly burdensome to read.

Any proposal that more or less follows established protocols will be given due consideration by virtually all agents and editors, which is why the usual way is also the safest way. Out-of-the-box proposals that trigger confusion are more likely to be abruptly rejected, no matter how clever the proposal might be. This doesn't mean that outliers can't or don't succeed, but it does mean that more risks are being taken. Keep in mind that the current template has been the universally accepted method for many decades and isn't considered to be broken or worn out. If you leave something out because you think it's too obvious or unimportant, it's likely that interested editors and agents will want you to provide the missing information before they can make a final decision. The decision-making process follows a fixed structure, and the proposal template exists to match the structure.

It is a good idea to break up your content in an organized way. We use this format for proposals because it is the easiest way for you to make sure the end reader, the agent or editor, will see the information that is most important. Another good idea is to break up sections with headings and subheadings. You want the reader to be able to digest your proposal in easy bites. Otherwise, they will skim. They may even glaze over, and it is not because your proposal is not a good one. Think about their experience and present your material accordingly.

We think this format is not broken, so with the exception of making it your own, don't fix it too much. This is our third edition of this book. The first one was in 1993, the second in 2003, and now this one in the second decade of the 2000s. There are many new pieces of information. What has not changed is the format. Go figure.

CHAPTER 4

How Are Proposals Structured?

THE BOOK PROPOSAL IS CONSIDERED a tool of the trade for non-fiction authors. While many authors try to skip this step in the process toward publication, they soon discover that even those with enviable followings need to conform to this publishing protocol. Traditional publishing is a "hard copy" business, which doesn't exclude a digital format. It simply means that the work exists as a written expression. No matter the subject, a nonfiction book has to have strong content to be seriously considered by publishers and literary agents. A strong book proposal is like a business plan that entices the potential investor (i.e., the publisher) to part with their cash.

DO I NEED TO SEQUENCE THE SECTIONS IN THE SAME ORDER THEY ARE PRESENTED HERE?

No. We've seen successful proposals organized all kinds of ways. However, we don't recall ever pitching a proposal that didn't begin with the "Overview" section and end with the "Chapter Outline" or "Sample Chapter(s)." What's presented below is how we would organize our own proposal, but our way isn't the only way, which will be made apparent by the ten sample proposals that follow.

SECTION 1: THE OVERVIEW

The overview is the proposal's "Genesis," though it shouldn't be nearly as long as the biblical Genesis. First and foremost, the overview needs to be an abundantly clear and precise statement about your vision for the book. In fact, a short 100-word overview is perfectly acceptable if it accomplishes this crucial goal. Agents and editors should be able to easily and quickly understand what your proposed book will be about on the basis of your overview. One of the most common mistakes is burying what the book is about in a rambling overview. If agents and editors can't decipher your overview, they might presume your ideas are equally muddled and press the reject button.

A good exercise is to imagine you only have thirty seconds to describe your book. You will be compelled to condense your description down to its most revealing and magnetic aspects or risk sounding like a babbling brook. The overview is meant to serve as a seductive invitation to read the entire proposal. You don't want the overview to be a maze, quicksand, or Death Valley. It's a doorway, a portal, a promise that a happy ending is in store for all who keep reading.

We prefer short and sweet overviews. However, we have successfully represented proposals that had overviews of more than 1,000 words, which is about ten times our preference. We tolerate long overviews if they don't break the cardinal rule of overshadowing what the book will be about. A long overview can occasionally effectively reinforce and reaffirm the author's vision and why it matters.

SECTION 2: ABOUT THE AUTHOR

Imagine a laudatory press release explaining why you are qualified to write the book in question. The document would be written in the third person because someone else has written it about you. In order of their relevance, it would present impressive facts about your professional and personal credentials, achievements, experiences, education, special honors, and blah blah blah. It might conclude by saying things of an entirely personal nature in order to show off what a well-rounded person you are.

The above is exactly how you should write this section. Don't be modest, but don't be boastful. Leave nothing out that might look good, but don't say anything that can't be supported. If you have an abundance of accomplishments that would overwhelm this section, it's best to make reference to and attach a stand-alone addendum to the proposal where you would insert impressive documents like a formal resume/vita; a list of published articles and perhaps some of the actual articles, or articles written about you; your professional brochures; or, to save space, the links to the sites and videos. An "About the Author Addendum" provides space to extra-sell yourself without cluttering the main body of the proposal.

SECTION 3: AUTHOR PLATFORM

Go back two hundred years and imagine yourself in a crowded public park and that you have something important to say for everyone to hear. In order to be seen and heard by the crowd, you will need to stand on a tall, sturdy wooden platform that rises above everyone. Without such a platform, it will be difficult, if not impossible, to get most people's attention. If such a platform doesn't already exist that you would be allowed to use, it follows that you will need to provide your own platform. In today's noisy and cluttered environment, authors need to have meaningful platforms and/or the ability to access other sturdy platforms. Except now it's about how to connect with your targeted audience from your keyboard or mobile device.

How will enough people find out about your book in ways that both cause them to buy it and tell others about it? Your answer to this deceptively basic question is your platform, so be very careful about how you answer it. As we will explain in our chapter on this topic, this is your brand or online footprint. Publishers won't give you a platform or allow you to use your book as your platform after the fact (there are always exceptions). You need to introduce yourself to publishers with a preexisting record as a neo-celebrity within the specific tribes relevant to your proposed book. In the alternative, you need to have a solid way to reach that audience that is already underway. If your book is unique and you know how to reach your audience, a developing platform can potentially put you in the running. But this means all the elements of your proposal have to be top notch.

This vexing section might easily be the most important part of your proposal, which was much less often the case a mere ten years ago. Frankly, mediocre content can be overcompensated for with a powerful platform, but the reverse scenario is much less likely. You must understand that the platform goes way beyond your resume, no matter how impressive it might be. The Internet has made the world ever more noisy and busy, and those who are best at getting the most attention aren't necessarily the best at what they do. For better or worse, "the best people in the room" are often deemed to be the ones who are most noticed because they can sell the most products and generate the most revenue. This troublesome bias makes perfect sense in the context of a commerce-dependent universe. University and other nonprofit presses are exceptions because they're subsidized to publish brilliant books even if no one buys them. For-profit publishers must at least break even or heads will roll. Revenue precedes quality; author platform precedes content. Period.

Publishers need to leverage the author's marketing infrastructure, resources, and skills for the purpose of selling copies. Unlike in other consumer-product industries, publishers don't have high-quality in-house marketing departments, and never did. The industry never quite adjusted to the fact that most people can read and can afford to buy books. In its heart of hearts, publishers still primarily serve the tiny elite of overeducated and high-wealth individuals who are perceived as a captive market. It follows that publishers are compelled to piggyback their author's resources in order to achieve mass-market level revenues.

If you're well known in your field or are the proverbial celebrity, your Internet traffic might preclude your need to have any actual traditional self-marketing skills; the publisher can simply plug into your highly charged platform and reap the benefits. This dependence and expectation understandably conflicts with some writers' preconceived notions about what publishers actually do. Well, guess what? Publishers provide many benefits, but selling and marketing tend to be their most anemic skill-set. The author's inaccurate assumptions are reinforced by the industry's endemic lack of veracity about what they can't and won't do. However, this isn't a deliberate deception; publishers don't think they should be expected to do these things in the first place. The bottom line is that publishers depend upon their authors for two crucially important things: (1) They need the author to provide all content (no surprises there). (2) They need the author to bring the resources (platform) upon which the marketing will happen.

Platforms are largely measured by tedious nuts-and-bolts items like social media networks (friends, followers), the Internet, and general media visibility within relevant communities (tribes), speaking events, and public appearances. The importance of what happens when your name is Googled can't be overestimated. For publishers, authors with lively SEO-magnet websites that generate revenue are manna from heaven. Look, you don't have to be famous, but you do need to be a recognized "brand" within the communities of potential customers relevant to your book's subject.

What if you don't have much of a platform? First, keep it to yourself; don't ever concede to an agent or publisher that your platform sucks, or that anything about you sucks. Don't be deceptive either. But sometimes people have more than they realize. We have successfully represented books where the authors had zero platforms. In each instance, the author did have a subject and/or experience that would trigger an instant platform upon publication. Examples are true crime, newsworthy narratives and memoirs, or just old-fashioned fascinating stories that people would talk to each other about. If you fall into this category, then show how the book itself will create a spontaneous platform.

Don't attempt to plug holes with dubious promises about what you will do when the book comes out. Publishers won't see much currency in these commitments unless you can guarantee them sales in tangible ways, like purchasing thousands of copies yourself or spending thousands of your own dollars on promotions.

Finally, if you just don't have any kind of public standing to speak of and your subject isn't a natural media magnet, then you might want to consider building a platform before pitching or self-publishing your book. Self-publishing in the absence of a platform is equally unwise, because how will people find out about the book? There are many low-cost books focused on how to build platforms that are worth investing in.

SECTION 4: AUTHOR MARKETING PLAN

This is sort of an extension of the platform section in that it will show specific ways your platform will be used for promoting your book. It helps to organize this section in an easy-to-follow, numerically sequenced list of action points. For instance, the first one might be a promise to send compelling alerts to your qualified list of 50,000 e-mail subscribers/customers. The second point might be leveraging your influence with a list of important bloggers. Number three might be sending comp copies of your book to an impressive list of "cultural influencers" you personally know or can get to. Additional action points might include soliciting companies to buy hundreds or thousands of copies for in-house staff distribution or selling copies back-of-the-room at a list of events where you will be appearing. If it's something you can possibly do but can't guarantee, then it's best to disclose it and say you will make vigorous good-faith efforts to make it happen. Don't bother including anything you know to be a long shot.

The power of this section will have an undeniable bearing on the number of offers you receive and the level of advance you can negotiate. If a publisher can securely see that a certain quantity of books will likely be sold within a measurable period of time, the level of your advance will reflect that confidence.

SECTION 5: WHO IS THE BOOK FOR (THE MARKET)?

Obviously, your book won't be acquired by a publisher unless there are enough findable people who will presumably buy it. It's your job to show and convince the publisher that one or more sufficiently sized and seeable communities exist for your book, and you might need to provide sources proving your case. Don't make the mistake of assuming that the publisher already knows, or should know, what you know about your customers. It's safest to assume that the publisher is from another planet, which then gives you an extra opportunity to show off your expertise. For instance, if your book is about book proposal writing, you will want to show how many nonfiction writers there are. This information can be made self-evident by referring to the huge number of new nonfiction titles published each year, both self and traditional. You can then reasonably suggest that for every book that gets published, there's at least one writer (probably more) who aspires to be published. Don't stop at only stating the most obvious customers; you should also mention all the plausible secondary populations, such as the constant flow of college professors who must publish or perish, or the number of print journalists at risk of losing their day jobs.

There are several common and potentially damaging mistakes that can be made in this section. For instance, be specific. You don't want to say, "My book is for all hundred-million-plus American adult women." That kind of blanket statement won't track; you have to break it down into identifiable nuggets and explain why your book will appeal to a specific market.

Sometimes a huge market clearly exists, but publishers know from experience that no one in that group will buy the book. For instance, it can't be assumed that American men will buy a nonbusiness self-help book no matter how obvious the need is unless they have done so in the recent past. By the way, guess how many successful books there are about how to plan a funeral? The answer is zero, even though millions of people are forced to plan a funeral every year. Ironically, books about probate and estate planning perform reliably well. Human psychology is a wild card, which is why "sure things" are few and far between.

SECTION 6: THE COMPETITION

Frankly, this is usually one of the least important and easiest sections of the proposal. There are two opinions about this: (1) You want to be aware of the competition because it is possible the publisher you are seeking has a title just like yours. (2) However, as long as your title is complimentary, not competitive, the publisher might be happy to keep serving a proven profit zone.

The purpose of this section is to distinguish your book, not denigrate other authors. You can also call this section "Comparative Titles" if it helps you play nice. This section can become a destructive trap if improperly handled. Basically, the publisher wants *you* to tell them about existing books that are most likely to compete for your readers' dollars and the shelf space. You can't possibly list all books on the subject, and you are only expected to refer to approximately six of the most viable competitors. You shouldn't list books that are poor sellers because that might suggest that your topic isn't commercial. It's to your advantage only to list the most currently successful titles. Though you are allowed to use Amazon's real-time sales rankings for your research, you're also expected to know which titles matter the most as part of your self-claimed expertise.

The next trick is to turn your competition into a cross-marketing opportunity. Underneath each listed titled you need to provide a brief description of the book, who it mostly serves, and what's strongest and weakest about it, followed by how your book will fill neglected needs. Your mission is to show how these other books only paint part of a much fuller picture that your book will help complete.

Strong competition and a cluttered bookshelf are actually an advantage. It shows that a lot of people are buying a lot of books or the books and the sales revenues wouldn't exist. People are buying these other books because they need constant information, which is a great opportunity for you to provide more of what they need.

What if there truly isn't any or much competition for your subject? Tread carefully here. You don't want to inadvertently give the impression that no market exists for your book. You might need to simply broaden your category to include books that are peripherally competitive, and/or prove that you are a true visionary and that an unfulfilled need exists. The people who wrote the first self-help computer and software books obviously lacked directly competitive titles they could refer to.

SECTION 7: OPTIONAL SECTIONS

Potential Endorsers/Contributors

If you have access to important people who might agree to endorse your book, or even write something more expansive (Preface, Foreword, Introduction), it will add value to your proposal to list these people in a dedicated section. Make sure to include a brief description about each person, and be clear that you will attempt to get their endorsement but don't yet have any guarantees (unless you actually do).

Time Needed

Stating this in the proposal isn't a requirement because it's the first question interested parties will ask anyway. Nevertheless, it doesn't do any harm to include this information, and nothing is binding until you sign the contract. In my experience, most nonfiction manuscripts require six to nine months of serious attention, and this assumes that the author is maintaining her day job. Biographies, histories, and similar research-laden books can require years to write, and the kinds of publishers who handle these books know that.

Estimated Word Count

This is important information, but it doesn't need to be stated in the proposal under its own section unless you envision a wide variance from what's customary (50,000 to 80,000 words). If you feel your book needs to be extra long or extra short, you obviously need to explain this in the proposal so there's no misunderstanding later in the process. Your book contract will include an approximate word count that you'll be expected to comply with.

Special Format, Packaging, Style, Permission; Illustrations or Photos

Unless said otherwise, agents and editors will assume you're proposing a conventional book, meaning it will only consist of words and will look like most other books. If your book has "special needs," it's important to describe what's needed in detail. Examples include gift books; unusual shape, size, or paper; and illustrations or photos, especially if permissions are required. Children's books are a prime example of books that probably have a lot of extra production requirements to be worked out prior to contract. Unconventional or highly illustrated books are likely to cost much more to produce, so the publisher needs to assess what that entails before making an offer. Another example is a book that needs to license the rights to reprint other peoples' work. Most of the time these costs range from nominal to zero, but popular works can be expensive.

SECTION 8: CHAPTER OUTLINE (Often Preceded by a Table of Contents or TOC)

This is the nucleus of your proposal, and could easily consume most of your attention and space. Because you're not being asked to write the manuscript on spec, the outline's importance can't be overstated. Agents and editors will use the outline to assess your ability to organize and write the book. Anything that undermines their confidence will be a reason to reject you. They obviously don't want to go through the trouble of issuing a contract and paying an advance if there's a serious question about your ability to write and deliver an acceptable manuscript. Therefore, don't blow it.

It's best to begin with a simple TOC listing the chapters in numerical order with a tentative title for each. This should only be one to two pages, depending on how many chapters are planned. Most nonfiction books have seven to ten chapters, but this isn't a rigid rule; you have the parameters to propose whatever makes sense.

The outline is nothing more or less than a lucid, content-rich description of each chapter. You want editors and agents to easily absorb the essence of what each chapter will be and get an affirming sense of your editorial style and skills. If upon reading the outline they still don't know what your book is about, or are unsure about your ability to write it, then you have failed, not them. Yes, everyone in this business makes more mistakes than smart decisions, but if more than one professional is expressing a lack of comprehension or confidence, you need to think about that. The outline needs to close the deal from an editorial perspective. Even if your platform and credentials are pristine, the book still needs to be a product that people won't regret buying and reading.

The type of book you're writing determines how expansive your outline should be. Memoirs, true crime, and biographies, for instance, require strong editorial skills in addition to organizational abilities. The world doesn't need yet another book about Gettysburg unless you have a unique and compelling way of telling the story. Buried in the previous sentence is what's most valued in these kinds of books: good storytelling. Obviously, the accuracy and quality of information is equally paramount; but if you can't write it in a way that people will enjoy, then you probably need to forego mass-market expectations. Your outline will need to capture and project all of these qualities. For these kinds of books we have seen outlines that run anywhere from 5,000 to 10,000 words for a book that will probably need to be at least 100,000 words.

Basic reference and how-to or self-help books are more dependent upon the novelty and usefulness of the information than the editorial quality. In fact, too much expression can sometimes get in the way of the book's lessons and content. In this context, the outline doesn't need to be long; it simply needs to present what each chapter will deliver. However, brevity cannot be an excuse for leaving any questions about your writing style and ability.

Another important factor affecting the outline is how many sample chapters you have or whether you have a finished manuscript. If you've already written the book, then your outline will mostly need to show how the book is organized and themed; reading the manuscript will answer the larger questions. The quality and number of sample chapters will probably accomplish the same purpose and supersede the need to write an expansive outline.

SECTION 9: SAMPLE CHAPTER(S)

Generating at least one sample chapter is a good idea because it's the best way to prove that you can really write the book, especially if you've never been published. An outline without a sample chapter is essentially asking people to take a leap of faith that you can do as promised, and it puts extra pressure on the quality of your outline. If you're serious about writing the book, even to the point of self-publishing in the absence of a traditional deal, then writing one or more chapters on spec won't be wasteful, and your commitment will be noticed.

Sometimes writers will gain a whole new perspective on their book once they begin writing the sample chapter, which gives them a valuable opportunity to go back and revise other parts of the proposal before it's pitched to agents and editors.

CHAPTER 5

Building Your Digital Footprint and Platform from Scratch

BY @DIGITALDEBORAH AS SHE IS CALLED ON TWITTER, BECAUSE SHE ENJOYS TECHNOLOGY.

NO ONE LIKES THE WORD *platform*. We started to hear it overused in the early part of the decade, and it has been the bane of the existence of writers ever since. Back then, digital marketing was in its infancy, so the focus was on traditional publicity. Authors needed to show that they had an audience, and these numbers were typically derived from speaking engagements or radio and television appearances. These things are still important, but the true advent of the Internet has leveled the playing field.

We discovered this after we launched our social network Writers, Agents and Editors Network, www.WAENetwork.com. We created it with an entrepreneur who saw how many writers there are who want to be published. What I didn't know was anything about social networking. I had a Facebook page and tweeted a bit, but I still thought of it as a bird. I was thrown into doing the social media for the site and discovered that the Internet to the novice is akin to the Wild Wild West. I was barraged with snake-oil and get-rich-quick schemes. I truly tried to understand it but was baffled and frustrated.

Thank goodness for Rutgers University Mini MBA program. I highly recommend it. They have intensives on Digital Marketing Strategy, Social Media Strategy, and even Entrepreneurship. I took all three at different times and gladly drank from the firehose. You can do it too if you'd like to, but I will share some of the relevant things I learned so you don't have to attend. Since I just saved you a lot of money, make sure to follow me on Twitter @digitaldeborah and join www.WAENetwork.com so I know my education is not going to waste.

The first and most important thing I learned and for you to keep in mind is that the entire paradigm of marketing has changed. Push advertising and marketing where you barrage people with messages does not work. Here is a paraphrased story from one of my professors:

Before any kind of mass media, people asked each other their advice on what they should buy or who they should hire to help them with things. A neighbor would say things like, "Yeah, old Zeke is a very reliable handyman."

Then when newspapers became popular to the common person, someone decided that you could create a need and place an ad to fill it. You could tell people they smelled bad and then advertise a type of soap that would make them smell better. So even old Zeke could place an ad to say that he was a very reliable handyman. The more you saw the ads, the less you asked your neighbor.

Then came radio. Someone came up with the clever idea that if you were selling soap, you could become a sponsor of a radio show. Since people liked the people in the radio shows and gave them authority, you could have the radio personalities say they even used the soap. Sales of soap would soar, and people wouldn't smell bad anymore.

Then came television. Everyone would be fixated in front of the small screen to watch people like Lucy and Ricky every week. Lucy would light up a cigarette and give it to Ricky, and they would say something about how great it tasted. This was also the beginning of product placement and direct advertising. As people associated their own realities with that of the sponsors, they would create brand loyalty and buy more products. Television advertisers loved that they could know where people were on any given night. That is when the Nielsen ratings that measure viewing habits became more important. The quality of the shows was significant, but only if it meant they could maintain enough ratings to satisfy advertising.

Then advertising hit a snag. With the development of cable television, it became more difficult for advertisers to determine where their potential buyers might be. They were having all kinds of choices, so it would not be so easy to mesmerize them.

Then an even bigger snag occurred: the Internet. When social media really took off, a very strange thing happened. People started spreading out and finding each other according to their own interests. Advertisers tried to push stuff at them, but they didn't count on the fact that the users of the Internet could talk to each other about stuff.

Now the tides have changed back to the time of neighbor asking neighbor if old Zeke is a good handyman. And this is why if you want to be effective in building a platform, you have to change your strategy.

Here is something for you to put on your wall: People are sick of hype! People are now more suspicious than ever and will trust their peers far more than people who are trying to sell them something. This is why your online marketing strategy for your book has to follow this new line of thinking.

Online marketing is now all about relationships. You have to build trust with your potential readers before you can expect them to ever want to buy something of yours. Of course this excludes those authors who have already established a following. They may not even need an online footprint. And if you are a celebrity, you may want to understand how all of this works, but it is not a necessity. Traditional publicity still works, but the ideal is to use it in combination with online techniques.

So where do you begin? Believe it or not, for many years my son had to turn on my computer for me. I was an early adopter of word processing, but I remember the days when hitting the wrong key would format your computer, which simply meant everything would be gone. There is nothing more tragic than watching your work disappear into nothingness.

Today this doesn't happen so easily. There are things to watch for like viruses or spilling water in your keyboard, but computers are pretty user friendly. So here's the first step:

GET COMFORTABLE WITH TECHNOLOGY

If I can do it you can do it. I had an advantage of having learned to type as a teenager. So if you can't type, learn. There is software that will teach you.

No one will force you to adopt the tools of technology. If you really don't want to learn and you are comfortable with your yellow legal pad, that is fine. However, don't let anxiety over technology stand in your way of accessing your audience. The Internet is for everyone. If you like to research things and are not a Googler, you are missing out. Take a class if you have to. Most local colleges offer beginning classes in using computers.

IF YOU ARE COMFORTABLE WITH TECHNOLOGY AND THINK YOU HAVE A DIGITAL PRESENCE BY HAVING A FACEBOOK PAGE AND A WEBSITE, LOOK AGAIN

People will often dismiss what they do not understand. Facebook is not stupid. Yes, the younger set is using Instagram and even Snapchat, but for the most part Facebook is vibrant. Who knows, by the time we do the next edition of this book, it might be replaced by something even better. But as of now, you need to determine of all the social platforms, where are the people who are your people?

There is an important step before this. You need to be clear about why you are writing, what your core message and mission are, and who your potential tribe is. If you can answer these questions without hesitation, you are ready for a comprehensive digital marketing plan.

The next step is to list topics you feel relate to your core message so you can come up with a plan for making yourself an information expert. Then you will know what to post and what to share to your potential audience. Your clarity will be felt throughout everything you do, and that is what will build your relationships. You need to be clear about your own authenticity so the people, potential readers, will know what to expect and will trust you.

Once you have your own core message and have clarity about who you are, you can think about your personal brand. All writers need some kind of personal brand. You can think of this as a type of persona. You are a person in your personal life, but as a writer you share a part of you that belongs to the world. This is the persona that will become your brand. It will have the thick skin you might not have as a person, and it will have the courage to put itself out there for the world to see. You the writer can stay in your private room with your dog or cat and your keyboard. But you the brand, published author and persona, will have a presence that is open for others to see.

When you are building a platform and an online presence, it is important for you to keep this in mind: the biggest problem people have is tooting their own horn. They become flummoxed and don't want to do it. They don't know what to say. "Why would anyone want me to tweet about what I had for breakfast?" They don't. At least not right away.

What you are doing is promoting your persona and brand. This will create relationships that will lead to people wanting to buy your books. You the person put your underwear on like anyone else. But you the writer are a wordsmith and the spinner of tales. That's the case whether you are writing nonfiction, fiction, erotica, or children's books. Readers don't want you to be up front and present. They want to experience your writing without you. They want their personal experience of you. Even if it is a memoir, they want to experience what they imagine of you. This really takes you off the hook if you think about it. It is much easier to promote someone else than it is to promote yourself. The same rules apply to celebrities. For instance, even in these so-called socially liberal times, it's not uncommon for an actor's true sexual orientation to be shielded so that they can still be presented as a traditional, unblemished leading man or femme fatale in the public's mind.

Although some of us may do this well, it is usually not very effective to walk into a room full of strangers and announce, "Buy my book." They will look at you askance and then go on with whatever they were doing. If that makes you bristle, it should. That is what push advertising is. Now, if you went to a party and met everyone and found some common ground, an opportunity might arise to mention that you are a writer when someone asks what you do. Then you can bring up your book in an appropriately humble way, and perhaps they will ask you to tell them about it. This is one possible scenario.

The idea is to get to know people first before you try to sell them something and to allow them to get to know you. The "you" they are going to get to know is the "you" you carefully calculate. You choose what they will know about you so it benefits your ultimate goal. You can develop friendships as well. That is fine. But for the most part you want to have more readers than you could ever possibly claim as friends.

SO HOW DO YOU BEGIN BUILDING A PERSONA AND ONLINE FOOTPRINT?

WEBSITE

Claim your real estate. Every author should have a website, and you shouldn't pay thousands of dollars for one. Your money is better spent on other things like hiring editors for your work. Websites used to cost exorbitant amounts because they had to be custom made. Now, with content-management systems like wordpress. com, you can do your own posting without needing a web master every time you want to upload a blog. For the uninitiated, a blog is simply a web log. It is the easiest way to drive traffic to your website, but that is getting a bit ahead of ourselves.

There are so many ways for you to build a website. Today my preference is wordpress.org, but who knows the future. It has a learning curve, so you might want to have a designer do it for you. Just make sure you are given access and are taught how to post. It is like using a word processor. You always want to be able to access your own website. Wordpress.org is a self-hosted platform that does well in the search engines. In other words, Google, the largest search engine as of today, likes it. There are many YouTube videos explaining how to set up your own site. People have said they like drag and drop sites, but I have not used them. Every day, technology becomes easier to use.

You will need to register a domain name for your site. Keep it relevant. You may want to simply use your name. People try to be fancy, but the most important thing is that you want to make it something that people will be able to find when they look for you.

WHAT TO INCLUDE IN A WEBSITE

Your website can serve many functions. It can be an online media kit, or it can focus on your blog. You can have many pages and should carefully write your descriptions to be relevant to your goals.

You want it to be visually appealing and want it to be shareable. What this means is that you want to add, or have your web designer add, what are called plugins, which are pieces of code that will allow those people visiting your site to share your content on social media.

In the early years of websites, they used to be what is called static. There would be information on the site and nothing would change. While you still want some parts of the site to be static, you also want your website to be engaging. You want to encourage traffic and build your fan base. There are many opinions about the usefulness of websites with the proliferation of social media platforms. However, in my opinion it is good to have a base of operations, so to speak.

You should make sure your website links to your own social media and that people can easily follow you.

Make sure you have a way to capture e-mail addresses on your website. People often forget the importance of this. When you create relationships and have a book to promote, you can use these addresses to send out newsletters or announcements. I don't believe that anytime too soon e-mail will become obsolete. As long as you do not overdo it, your list is invaluable. These are people who are indicating that they want to hear from you. How great is that?

You can provide incentives for people to sign up for your list like offering them some free content, but for now make sure you at least have a place for people to sign up.

SET UP A BLOG

Have a blog and utilize the category feature of your blog to highlight topics that people might search on the Internet. While this is a much more detailed discussion than the scope of this book, a blog is only as good as the people it reaches. If you write what are called optimized blogs regularly, you will be utilizing one of the best ways to build your ranking and recognition in the search engines. This is called "organic SEO." The search engines exist for good content. You are a writer. If you have determined your core message, it is advantageous for you to write regular blogs on those topics to draw in your audience.

The key is "regular." The best way to blog is to have a set schedule. Keep your blogs short and on one topic, similar to a short opinion piece. You can also write your own opinion of topical subjects if they relate to who you are and your audience. Sometimes you can just write what inspires you. It is good to associate an image with your blog because it will show up when people share your material. Readers on the Internet are highly visual, so images are valuable.

Your website can have a share plugin to allow you to send it out to many online outlets for blogs. Be patient. Your blog may take time to build an audience. Consistency will help.

SOCIAL MEDIA

Remember that you are building a persona. With your core message in mind, try to determine who your people are. Then figure out where they congregate and where they find the information they want to read.

Become a curator. You can subscribe to blogs or online alerts so you have information to select for your followers. Social media is a marathon, not a sprint. There are many opinions on where to post and what to post. In my opinion, Twitter is viable now, and the more posts, the better. Keep in mind time zones so you can post late at night. There are algorithms for Twitter. You can follow up to 2,000 people, but once you hit that 2,000, the number of people you can follow depends on the number of people who follow you.

Twitter is not just a way to blast out of your daily routine or talk about your book. Twitter is a way to engage with people. Retweet something that catches your eye. and tweet to people with whom you would like to connect. As long as you are polite, the worst that can happen is they will say no. Don't spam with too many of the same thing. Sometimes people go overboard. Hashtags are useful if there are trending topics because people will look for them and find you. Hashtags are the words that follow the symbol #. Watch out, because you can drive yourself crazy with this if you are just starting out.

If you are using Twitter, you should set up a nice account with a cover image, follow like-minded people, and tweet relevant, 140-character tweets on a regular basis. You can automate through many great apps, but to begin with you should do it by hand until you have a sense of your audience and the response you are receiving. Then you will know right away if you are being effective.

You do not need to be on all social media platforms. Choose the ones that you feel are relevant to you. There are also many platforms for authors that can be overwhelming. My opinion is to focus on places where you will stand out for your own message and persona.

If you provide value for your followers such as carefully selected information and you share theirs, you will be successful. Look at quality, not numbers. If you have a smaller number of engaged connections, those are far better than large numbers of fake connections. The people who have hundreds of thousands of followers are usually already celebrities. Focus on building a good list. And never, please never, buy followers.

Choose things you will stick to, but don't perceive social networking as a time suck. Many jobs and business connections have been cemented through LinkedIn alone. As long as you are not using social networking as a distraction from life, it is useful and recommended. For business, it should be strategic. For life, it should be fun. And for business, adding some fun and humor is recommended as well.

You should add a smattering of personal information on your social networking sites, but don't let it get too personal. Don't overshare. This is why Facebook has a personal page and allows businesses to set up their own page. However, many personal pages with the maximum amount of friends are certainly a combination of business and personal. People do want to know about you. But don't be negative and whiny. Don't rant unless it is your persona to do so. People have so much competition for their leisure time that you want to show gratitude if they pay attention to you. Remember to acknowledge them as well.

DON'T FORGET YOUTUBE OR OTHER VIDEO PLATFORMS

YouTube is the second-largest search engine, only surpassed by its parent company, Google. What this means is that this is a great opportunity for you to promote yourself. However, most people do not optimize their You-Tube videos. This means that they do not strategically set them to build their online platform.

YouTube gives you the opportunity to be the star of your own channel. What many people do not realize is that the important thing to consider is the number of subscribers you have to your channel, not the individual views of a particular video. It doesn't hurt if a particular video goes viral, but if it is not also capturing subscribers, you are missing an opportunity.

Do not randomly upload videos. Set up your YouTube channel with some marketing strategy. Encourage people to subscribe, and if you are doing videos, make sure you are posting regularly, just as you would on any other social media platform.

You can also increase your views by optimizing. This means using keywords in your titles and other "tags" in your description that will make it easy for people to find. Then you also can embed your video or links to your videos on your personal website. So the videos drive traffic to your website, and the website drives traffic to your channel. Everything works in tandem.

Many people are now creating book trailers. This is a great idea, but there needs to be a context. You need to make your trailer easy to find by using the proper descriptions. Think about your audience and what they might be searching, then name and tag accordingly. When you look at your YouTube channel setup, you will see where to tag your videos. The proper use of YouTube changes so rapidly that you are better off having this marketing mind-set and keeping up with the changes by following news and blogs about YouTube. I try to post any changes on my @digitaldeborah Twitter feed, but it is best to focus on the simple aspects.

- Try to increase your subscribers.
- Be consistent.

Another tip: People prefer to have good sound quality even if the picture is not top-notch. You don't need a lot of money and an expensive camera to be a successful user of YouTube, but it is wise to know your market.

CONCLUSION

This chapter is an overview of what is available at your fingertips. These are tools for you to use to build relationships, which is the key for you. The idea is to create relationships because people trust each other more than they trust hype.

It makes sense that if you are providing good content in a consistent way, they will like you. It is that simple. Of course, it is the "persona" you. This takes you out of the overwhelming limelight and allows you to focus on what you are writing and the information you are sharing. You can promote your persona with abandon, but the new definition of promotion is to build relationships by building trust.

This is the essence of platform building. If you always focus on "what is in it for them," you will eventually be able to fulfill the need they express with your writing. Whether it is to entertain, transport, or provide tangible tools, you are providing content. You will have your accolades, but this strategy will help you build an audience.

CHAPTER 6

Write the Perfect Fiction Synopsis

THERE IS SUCH A THING as a fiction book proposal. It is very much like a nonfiction book proposal because it serves the purpose of anticipating the concerns of the editorial committee who will be considering your book for publication. Whether it is an agent or an editor, the person evaluating your proposal knows that even if they like the book, there will be a sales force at some point looking at it as some kind of product that will either bring profit or loss. This is just the reality of traditional publishing. So the proposal allows you to anticipate the questions they will have. The items to consider are:

A query letter, which differs from a nonfiction query only in that it contains a few paragraphs of plot and character description.

Some comparison of your book to others if there is a direct comparison by style and genre to give the agent or editor a good sense of where your book fits. If it does not fit nicely into a category, don't worry about it.

An author bio, where you list your previous publishing experience, relevant qualifications, and awards. In fiction writing, this is only relevant to get someone to read your synopsis and book. The book will have to stand on its own. You can be well connected, but if the book is not well written, unless someone owes you a big favor, it will not make a difference.

Chapter outline: You will need some writing sample, usually the first three chapters or the first fifty pages. Some authors choose to do an annotated outline with descriptions of each chapter. You can also do character and plot summaries. You want the potential agent or editor to see the book in its finished form. Fiction relies on good storytelling.

The most important thing to have ready is the synopsis, and it is often the thing writers like to write the least.

THE FICTION SYNOPSIS

Many people like to write a fiction synopsis even before they write their book because it gives them a good roadmap to follow. Unlike with a nonfiction book, a novel needs to be completed before you begin to contact prospective agents and publishers. The worst thing is if you gain interest and do not have the book. No agent or editor is willing to take a chance on a book that may or may not live up to its promise. You can write the synopsis before writing the book, but for our purposes, let's assume that the book is written and you are writing the synopsis to presell your novel.

You want to entice someone to read your book, but unlike in a movie trailer, you do not want to hold back the best parts. An agent or an editor wants to know what happens to your main characters and your story line complete with the whodunits and who gets the girl.

A synopsis should not be longer than three pages, which means that you cannot include a vast amount of detail. Spend time perfecting it because a good synopsis can go a long way in getting you through the door and onto the desk of the right reader. Agents and editors screen books for a living. They are looking forward to liking something. So don't put all your energy into writing the book while giving short shrift to the synopsis. The most important task for you in writing the synopsis is knowing what details to leave in and what details to leave out. The essence of a synopsis is that of a sales tool. You only have a short period of time to hook your reader into wanting to know more about your characters and your story.

INTRODUCTORY PARAGRAPH

Your first paragraph should make a clear statement of who your characters are, what they are doing, and what the story is about. This is a good place to mention the genre of your book and the word count. Keep in mind there is a big difference between a 50,000-word book and a 150,000-word book in time commitment alone. An agent and publisher will want to know what they are considering. Also, make sure the first sentence of your actual synopsis is engaging. You want to keep the person reading.

MIDDLE PARAGRAPHS

This is where you do what you never do in writing a good novel: you tell instead of show. You get to the main points of your plot without flowery description and minute details of what the book is about. You give a sweeping view from beginning to end so the agent or editor has a clear picture of what the big plot points and turning points of your story are. Only name essential characters and keep your focus narrow. Use good writing in your synopsis. You can make it lively and descriptive, but make sure you are able to get through the important points of the book. Don't waste your limited space with claims about the book and how much of a bestseller it will be. Agents and editors don't pay attention to those. They are looking for good books. They want to be engaged. Let your writing and plot speak for themselves. The synopsis should be written in third person present tense narrative style so the reader can experience the book as something that exists. You are creating your own world. Allow your reader to escape into it and imagine how wonderful the book will be.

CONCLUSION

In this last paragraph or so reveal the ending. The temptation is to think if you write a big build up and then leave a cliffhanger the reader will be dying for more. What will happen in reality is an agent or editor will probably hit Delete or file it in the circular file. This is a set up for rejection as it is seen as amateurish. It is also a matter of time constraint. There are many people vying for a few minutes of the attention needed to determine if your book will be requested. Don't hold back anything. You want your agent or editor to be practically presold by the time they have read all or part of your manuscript.

Fiction authors are also subject to the rules of the marketplace. You do not have a straightforward ability to market the same way nonfiction authors have, but you can do a lot of networking to build a fan base. You can blog about your characters and what inspires you. If you are writing about something historical, there are many blogging opportunities to describe the history and backstory of your book. Put it into context. Draw in your readers as fans of your work and begin that process before you even put finger to keyboard. The suggestions in the platform-building chapter apply to you if you are creative about it. Writing can be solitary, but publishing involves showing that others will read your work.

There are wonderful organizations for genre fiction writers. Look at these gatherings as opportunities to get to know what is succeeding for others. Don't look at them as places to increase your anxiety and self-loathing because you have not been writing every day or do not have an agent yet. That becomes silly. It is the most counterproductive thing you can do. Don't forget that you also write because you enjoy it. Don't let the publishing climate deter you. Believe passionately in your story.

Proposals

CHAPTER 7

Critiques for 10 Sample Proposals That Sold

ALL OF THE PROPOSALS IN this section were sold to traditional publishers by the Jeff Herman Agency, Inc. This does not mean that they were "perfect" book proposals. We both have differing perspectives of what makes a good book proposal, but for the most part we agree.

When you look at these proposals for guidance in writing your own, look at what is really great and what we believe could have been better. There are always things you will see after the fact when you are really drilling down to explain how something is done. We think all of these proposals were worthy of publication, and they are now great books. However, we do believe there is always room for improvement. By reviewing these proposals, you have an opportunity to make your proposal that much better. The world of traditional publishing is shrinking. You want your proposal to be a true stand-out and as perfect as it can be.

Take your time with your proposal. It may look like a formula, but a lot of time and energy goes into each one. It represents a snapshot of your work. Make sure it is completely in focus so your potential agent or publisher sees clearly what you are offering them.

Proposed Title:

EMOTIONAL PHYSICS

7 Organic Ways to Manifest What You Want

By Deborah Sandella

published by Red Wheel Weiser.

Jeff's Comments

1 The author and I had quite a few discussions about how to title this intriguing work, and we finally agreed to what you see here.

Deb's Comments

a The title did not say much to me, but I do think the concept of emotional physics is provocative and would make the right editor or agent want to read more.

47

Jeff's Comments

2 This is an interesting way to combine and format the overview and author bio sections. It's sharp looking and gives the impression that the author knows how to market herself (which she, in fact, does).

Deb's Comments

b Good opening paragraph for the overview. This overview is visual and integrates the "about the author" information effectively. This format does not work for every kind of book. However, the author's previous work and connection with a bestselling author is a strong plus that this author has made sure won't be overlooked.

c "A sense of awe is inspired" is passive voice. Whenever possible, especially when writing persuasively, you will want to use the active form, such as "it is awe inspiring how quickly and effectively ..." Better yet, use "awe inspiring" as the description of the program. This "awe-inspiring program shows how quickly and effectively we can use emotion to accelerating ..."

d While it is good to mention how many people use the program, I find this

---

2

Your Feelings Are Smarter Than You think

b Emotions are invisible, taken for granted and dismissed much of the time, a paradox given they are some of the most powerful forces on earth. They inflame wars, induce death, inspire invention and control stock markets. What is more important, each of us has them—constantly!

*Your Feelings are Smarter...*provides 7 extraordinary ways for the everyday person to appreciate and use their feelings as a gift rather than a curse. Additionally, the process is as fast as Google, as fun as imagination and as easy as 1-2-3.

c A sense of awe is inspired by how quickly and effectively we can benefit from the intelligence of our feelings; it's like having an emotional self-cleaning oven. However, we need to know how to turn it on. Enlivened with convincing scientific findings and tender real-life stories of emotional and physical healing, this book empowers readers to "try it" themselves with self-guided activities.

e *Your Feelings are Smarter...* is founded on eighteen years of remarkable client results by this author and trained facilitators across the United States and around the world in Australia, Czech Republic, Egypt, Singapore, Denmark and Canada. This book goes far beyond others and teaches how to sense the form of feelings and intentionally reshape them for better health and more love.

CONTACT INFO:
Deborah Sandella PhD, RN
303-229-8686
Denver, Colorado
drdeb@RIMinstitute.com

Co-author with Jack Canfield of
Awakening Power
Author of *Releasing the Inner Magician*

f **Dr. Deborah Sandella** has been helping others find themselves for over 40 years as an award-winning psychotherapist, university professor and originator of the groundbreaking RIM Method. It wasn't till she faced her father's imminent death did she experiment with an inventive way of engaging physical and emotional challenges. His miraculous recovery inspired her to close her psychotherapy practice and discover how to harness this power.

The result is the seminal RIM (Regenerating Images in Memory) **d** work, which has benefitted thousands over the last eighteen years and been featured on radio, television and in print. Deborah frequently shares the stage with Jack Canfield, and their co-authored audio program *Awakening Power* is considered a popular life-changing tool for achieving greater success. She gets rave reviews when she speaks because she adeptly demonstrates this inherent healing power right before our eyes.

Foreword by JACK CANFIELD

(g) *"I'm so excited to share the work of Deborah Sandella with you! She's been my co-author and worked with my students for years, producing dramatic results. Her original, ground breaking technique just magically dissolves what is blocking us—and accelerates more success in every facet of our lives. Deborah is the BEST of the BEST! And I'm so glad she's now providing this extraordinary resource to the world. Grab this book now, if you want more success in your life!"*

—Jack Canfield, *NY Times* Bestselling Author

paragraph confusing as to whether it is the author's program that others are using or she is using the results of other's work to prove the effectiveness of her program. For greater impact, I recommend separating the two thoughts. First, make a strong statement of how emotional physics, based on sound neuroscience principals, is derived from eighteen years of remarkable client results. Then add the supporting information of the data from trained facilitators. What is their training? Neuroscience? Is there something actually called "emotional physics" or is this the author's term? When you are submitting a book proposal, you are the expert. Your editor or agent is not expected to know this. You have to explain it so they understand it without needing to be neuroscientists. If you have developed your own concept or technique, make sure that it is clearly stated, even if there are others in the field using similar techniques.

(e) This is a good place to put contact information. You want to make it easy for editors or agents to find information, so keep in mind the visual layout of the proposal.

(f) In the author bio, it is a bit confusing if her origination of the RIM Method is what she is using for this book. If so, it would be good to mention that in the overview. Anything that is important to your credibility can be worked into several parts of the proposal.

(g) The use of the conjunction "she's" here is not the best choice. It seems too informal compared to the rest of the proposal. Use "she has."

Jeff's Comments

❸ I never discourage a writer from wanting to generate a TOC showing how the proposal is organized, nor do I generally require it. Anything that helps the editor read your proposal is a positive.

Deb's Comments

 It is good to create a table of contents for the proposal. The proposal is often divided and given to the appropriate members of the editorial board at the publishing house. If your book is under consideration, the sales people will look at the marketing section while the editors will focus on the substance of the book. You want to make it easy for them to find what they are seeking.

 This book proposal is structured a bit differently from our typical format, but that is fine if the strengths are found in the author's platform.

This author has a strong marketing plan, so she is putting that up front. I am a stickler for logic and structure in an outline, so my preference would be to put the book's table of contents before the chapter summaries. You won't be marked down a letter grade if you don't do it this way. However, it does make more sense.

Proposal Table of Contents

I.   One-Page Overview & Endorsement by Jack Canfield

II.   Book Marketing Platform
   A. Author Platform
   B. Marketing Plan
   C. Speaking Schedule

III. Target Audiences
   A. Primary Market
   B. Secondary Market
   C. Tertiary Market
   D. Look and Feel
   E. Competition
   F. What's Unique About this Book?
   G. Foreign Sales Potential

IV.   About the Author: Deborah Sandella
   A. Biography
   B. Testimonials

V.   Special Book Features
   A. Workshop Coupon
   B. Potential Themes and Accompanying Product Sales/Gifts
   C. Monthly Teleconferences
   D. Potential Future Books for Other Target Audiences

VI.   Manuscript Overview
   A. Introduction

VII. Chapter Summaries
   A. Chapter 1: *Flow & Go*
   B. Chapter 2: *See & Free*
   C. Chapter 3: *Unstick & UpWick*
   D. Chapter 4: *Repel & Attract*
   E. Chapter 5: *Squeeze & Breeze*
   F. Chapter 6: *Redo & Renew*
   G. Chapter 7: *Me & Thee*
   H. Chapter 8: *Dip See Do*

VIII. Table of Contents (Book)

IX.   Sample Chapter: "Chapter 2: *See & Free*"

■ Book Marketing Platform

Author Platform

- has been working with Jack Canfield for 9 years & we have co-authored a product

- speaks and facilitates at 4 Jack Canfield events annually

- is friends with many bestselling authors who can send this book launch to their lists and offer endorsements e.g. Marci Schimoff; Tama Kieves; Jean Houston; Marilyn Suttle; Pete Winarski; Cynthia James; Sheri Fink

- speaks at Nursing Conferences

- speaks at Psychiatric Nursing Conferences

- speaks at **ISSSEEM** (International Study of Subtle Energy Medicine) Conferences bringing together well-known scientists and healers; this book launch can be sent to their mailing list of 8,500 members

- speaks at CampExperience (annual luxury weekend for 250 women)

- speaks at Science of Mind Events

- has experience with local **TV** (**ABC**; **NBC** and **CABLE**) and numerous radio interviews

- reviews articles for *Holistic Nursing* Journal (would submit an article to them)

- has experience with doing an amazon book campaign

- writes regularly for *Science of Mind* Magazine

- has submitted workshop proposals to Esalen and Kripalu (would include book signings onsite)

- has a **RIM** community of 60 people who can market the book in their areas and to their clients

- has given workshops at Mile Hi Church (Denver) with over 13,000 members

- has email list of 3,000 subscribers

Jeff's Comments

4 This is a well-formatted platform statement with many valuable details.

Deb's Comments

j The author platform has good content, but the structure could cause the reader to briefly skim it. Don't take any part of your proposal for granted. It is your job to organize the material into categories. Put all the speaking engagements under a headline and then add bullet points. Put all the writing under a headline with bullets. And definitely put a bold headline that says "Endorsements" before putting the sample endorsements from the people you hope will push your book proposal into a sale. This author is impressive and needs to make the most of her credentials.

k It is also a good idea to separate the "have already done" from the "will dos." One is the platform and the other is the marketing and promotion plan. From the list here it isn't clear that she will be presenting a separate marketing plan later in the proposal.

Jeff's Comments

5 It can be helpful to generate several YouTube segments showing off your knowledge and presentation skills that can be easily linked. Just be sure that your presentations don't show you in a less-than-wonderful context and end up doing more harm than good.

6 When possible, it's a smart move to separate your marketing plan from your platform. The platform should show your potential, whereas the plan should reflect what you intend to actually do. However, you should be aware that the publisher might assume it's okay to attach your plan to the book contract, thereby obligating you to do what you have stated in the proposal. So don't promise more than you are prepared to deliver.

Deb's Comments

1 When referring to YouTube Videos, make it clear what your purpose is in including them. If you are including them so the editor or agent can see you in action, say that in a headline or subheading. If it is to show your audience, you need to look at how many subscribers you

- has celebrity endorsements from Jack Canfield; Larry Dossey; and Joan Borysanko:

"I'm so excited to share the work of Deborah Sandella with you! She's been my co-author and worked with my students for years, producing dramatic results. Her original, ground breaking technique just magically dissolves what is blocking us—and accelerates more success in every facet of our lives. Deborah is the Best of the Best! And I'm so glad she's now providing this extraordinary resource to the world. Grab this book now, if you want more success in your life!"
—Jack Canfield, *New York Times* Bestselling Author

"Deborah Sandella is a masterful guide who can help uncover the core of peace, creativity, compassion and delight that resides within you."
—Joan Borysenko, Bestselling author

"Dr. Sandella offers a practical, down-to-earth method of realizing the immense potential that lives within everyone."
—Larry Dossey, Bestselling author

- has several YouTube videos of workshops and interviews about RIM. There is a sampling below. You can search youtube for Deborah Sandella to find more: **5** **1**

Radio Show Episode 25 - The Power of Visualization ... - *YouTube*
▶ 53:03 ▶ 53:03
www.youtube.com/watch?v=5ERP4AglhzY
Nov 27, 2013 - Uploaded by Richard Levy
YouTube home ... You need Adobe Flash Player to watch this video. ... 25 - The Power of Visualization ...

Introduction & How did RIM get started? - *YouTube*
▶ 1:49 ▶ 1:49
www.youtube.com/watch?v=S9SELz4vLfI
Mar 28, 2013 - Uploaded by RIM Institute
Interview with Dr. *Sandella* about The RIM® Method (Regenerating Images in Memory)

RIM Institute - *YouTube*
www.youtube.com/user/DrDebRIMinstitute
Deb Sandella 1 3 mov. 6 hours ago; 4 views. Dr. *Deborah Sandella*, founder of the RIM Institute, shares the power of experience and connection. RIM Institute ...You've visited this page 2 times. Last visit: 12/16/13

Focus Forward - Dr. Deb Sandella - Meditation for the ...
- *YouTube*
▶ 26:54 ▶ 26:54
www.youtube.com/watch?v=R7VlsnCRink
Apr 21, 2013 - Uploaded by Lauri Flaquer
Meditation and what it can do for the entrepreneur. Tap into the universal knowledge and guidance for those ...
More by Lauri Flaquer - in 75 Google+ circles

Marketing Plan

- will coordinate with Jack Canfield's marketing director because he is willing to support this book through his social media with 500,000 and rising Facebook fans

- will travel to book events in strategic bookstores and on strategic dates to gain NY Times bestseller status. These events would be 1-2 hours long and done in Katie Byron style: a facilitation with someone from the audience conducted in front of the group... seeing is believing

- will purchase Facebook ads to market to the audiences in the areas of book events in addition to the traditional advertising e.g. newspaper, radio etc.

- will pitch media interviews in towns of book events

- will create a dedicated website

- will launch an Amazon bestseller campaign

- will invest $10,000-15,000 to finance a publicist　**o**

- will purchase 400 books　**p**

- will write articles and submit to Psychology Today, Huffington Post and others

- will pay to attend the Publicity Summit for 3 days of pitching book to 100 top journalists/producers who do stories and shows for major media like: ABC's *The View*, CNN, *Today Show*, Fox News, *Fox & Friends*, *48 Hours*, ABC's *20/20*, USA Weekend, *Dateline NBC, Inc.*, Health magazine, Entrepreneur, Family Circle, O the Oprah Magazine and many other top outlets (Steve Harrison's Program)

have and how many views. If you do not have impressive numbers, then use them as a reference. For your own marketing benefit, look at how you have your YouTube channel set up. Are you optimizing your use of YouTube?

m It is impressive to mention that someone with over 500,000 Facebook fans will support your book. However, it is even more impressive to explain how. Will he be posting about you? Will he be mailing information about your book? The more tangible you can be with this information, the better.

n If you are planning to sell a book, you should create a dedicated website before you submit your proposal. You should be building your audience for the book well before you type word one. Saying that you are going to create a website does not add to the marketing plan.

o Not everyone has the money to invest in a publicist. If you have it, this is a definite bonus for the traditional publisher.

p Purchasing your own books is easier for most writers so look into this first. Publishers like this.

- will send book launch to **ISSSEEM** (International Study of Subtle Energy Medicine) email list of 8,500 members

- will travel to present at several nursing conventions

- will ramp up the social media presence

- will travel to present at various Centers for Spiritual Living across the United States (450 possibilities in total)

- will approach the Centers for Spiritual Living Practitioner Programs (global community of 450 centers worldwide) about using this book as their annual course book

- will subscribe to Steve Harrison's Radio and TV Report to advertise for interviews

- will send press releases to media contacts

(q) • will pursue concept of a documentary-style TV show that demonstrates how people can heal more quickly than we thought; it would follow a series of people in different walks of life and economic levels who are suffering with emotional/physical pain. The show would include clips of how these individuals are operating in their lives, segments of their **RIM** process and scenes of the evident changes. Marci Schimoff who has done something similar has offered to share her wisdom regarding this project

- will arrange speaking at Denver chapter of International Coaching Federation (The RIM Institute is a certified provider of continuing education for ICF)

(r) • will encourage the community of **RIM** Facilitators to speak at their local ICF chapters; I will have book promo fliers prepared for facilitators to distribute to their audiences.

- will personally communicate with each **RIM** Facilitator to engage their support e.g. social media, email lists and clients

- will have Louie Sharp an eloquent and passionate speaker attend select media events to share his personal story of how his **RIM** experience changed his life forever after his mother had given him up for adoption at the age of 5. He is creating a non-profit to support abused kids with **RIM** sessions. He also is working to bring **RIM** training to school counselors/nurses in the Chicago area.

Deb's Comments

(q) It is better to have a documentary in the works than to say that is something you will pursue. If you know how to make a documentary, that information is important. Otherwise it becomes another item that does not add weight.

(r) Here the author mentions that there is a community of RIM facilitators. In my opinion, it would hold more weight to provide information about how they are certified to use her program, how many there are, and what their credentials are. This adds strong credibility to the book and the marketing, and should be described more thoroughly somewhere in the proposal.

- will ask Peyton Manning (neighbor although we have not met) and Alan Arkin (participated together in a workshop) for endorsements

- will ask bestselling author of *Emotional Intelligence* Daniel Goleman for an endorsement

2014 Speaking Schedule:

Event	Date	
Jack Canfield Seminar Long Beach, CA	February 10-14, 2014	Guest Speaker & Facilitator
Center's for Spiritual Living Annual Convention Orlando, Florida	February 18, 2014	Speaker: "Healing with Imagination"
Advanced RIM Techniques Denver, CO	March 5-9, 2014	Teacher and Facilitator
4-Day Life-Changing Retreat San Diego, CA	March 13-16,2014	Facilitator
RIM Master's Class Denver, CO	March 28-April 3, 2014	Teacher and Facilitator
RIM Community Reunion Sunrise Ranch, Longmont, CO	May 30-June 1, 2014	Facilitator
RIM Master's Class Denver, CO	June 9-13, 2014	Teacher and Facilitator
RIM I Facilitation Program	June 18-21, 2012	Teacher and Facilitator
Jack Canfield Seminar Scottsdale, AZ	June 23-27, 2014	Guest Speaker & Facilitator
RIM Basic Facilitator Program Sydney, Australia	July 2015	Teacher and Facilitator
Jack Canfield BTS Seminar Phoenix, AZ	August 11-15, 2014	Guest Speaker & Facilitator

Jeff's Comments

7 Not everyone has a speaking schedule they can brag about, but if you do have one, even if it includes speaking to a room of five at your local library, then you should make the most of it as shown here. Back-of-room sales can be a valuable source of revenue for you and your publisher, and some events generate valuable publicity.

Deb's Comments

s I recommend writing a paragraph about the type of speaking and the frequency followed by the schedule. This will give it more meaning. This author is teaching her method at many venues. This translates into real numbers of people who will be potential book buyers and who can also become a tribe of supporters who will tell others about the book.

Event	Date	
CampExperience Colorado Springs, CO	September 19-20, 2014	Guest Speaker
RIM II Facilitator Program San Diego, CA	October 1-4, 2014	Teacher and Facilitator
Jack Canfield TTT Seminar San Diego, CA	October 6-12, 2014	Guest Speaker & Facilitator
Jack Canfield Advanced San Diego, CA	November, 2014	Guest Speaker & Facilitator

Jeff's Comments

8 I have no complaints about how the "Target Audience" section is organized and presented. But in hindsight, it might have been even more effective to separately label the numerous market segments throughout the section, such as "People who feel overstressed" or "People who feel tired or burned-out much of the time."

Deb's Comments

t There is an opportunity in this description of the market to tie it directly to the practice and methods in the book. The anecdote in the third paragraph would be more effective in the first paragraph to describe the market, then follow with the statistics. Remember that you want to maintain the interest of whoever is making the decision about acquiring your book. The information in the third paragraph is the first place in the proposal where we see a tangible description of how the technique works.

Target Audience

Primary Market

Let's face it—there is a lot of stress in today's world. Feeling whole is more complicated; yet, everyone wants it more than ever. The market audience who will love and credit this book with changing their lives are adults who do everything they can to be healthy, happy and successful, yet continue to experience anxiety, self-doubt, missed opportunities, loneliness and illness. They don't understand why their lives aren't working better, and they are stressed and fatigued from all the effort. According to a report from the U.S. Department of Health and Human Services in 2000, stress-related and stress-induced illnesses account for 70-80% of the annual1 billion visits to the doctor. They estimate stress contributes to 50 % of all illness in the United States, and the cost of job stress rides around $200 billion.

People unsuccessful in securing long-term relationships and those leaving marriages through divorce and spousal death are a large group in this target audience. In 2005, the U.S. Department of State reported that roughly 40% of the workforce is unmarried. These Americans contribute more than $2 trillion annually to the economy according to the Consumer Expenditure Survey of 2006.

Further, Jennifer Baker of the Forest Institute of Professional Psychology in Springfield, Missouri reports that 50% percent of first marriages, 67% of second and 74% of third marriages end in divorce. The CDC recorded 1,163,000 divorces in 1997 alone, which means there are around 2.5 million new divorcees every year. With second and third marriages reflecting increasing rates of failure, it is apparent many don't understand what went wrong, thus change is unlikely.

I worked with such a woman who at fifty had not dated for ten years since her husband's death. To her surprise, she discovered her body was immobilized in the shock of seeing him on the kitchen floor on Christmas Eve so long ago. As she was able to sense these feelings stuck in her body, she used imagination to complete her relationship with him. A month later she had her first date and a year later she was in a long-term, committed relationship that continues. There is hope for more successful relationships, yet deeper insight and healing is necessary for a shift to happen.

Secondary Market

Therapists, life coaches and helping professionals also are a strong market audience. Some 10,000 life coaches are working in the US alone, according to a review in the current *Psychotherapy Networker*, a professional magazine. APA's Center for Workforce Studies estimates that there are 93,000 practicing psychologists and the Bureau of Labor Statistics calculated 1,811,660 counselors, Social Workers, and Other Community and Social Service Specialists employed in the United States in 2012.

Traditional methods can be slow and produce mixed results. Clients frequently have hidden blocks, which unconsciously express as defensiveness and resistance to move forward. These factors frustrate helping professionals and leave them vulnerable to caregiver fatigue. I know because I experienced it during my 25 years as a psychotherapist. *Emotional Physics...* provides a new effective tool that makes a therapist's life much easier because it goes under clients' intellectual defenses into the heart of the problem. Thus, clients actively do the work without complaint or convincing. Helping professionals in the RIM Facilitator Program are amazed at the resourcefulness that expresses from their clients during the RIM process. A psychologist recently called it, "pure genius."

Tertiary Market

People suffering from Traumatic Incident Stress and Post Traumatic Stress Disorder (PTSD) are very specific audiences who can benefit significantly from *Emotional Physics* The Sidran Institute estimates 70% of adults in the U.S. have experienced some type of traumatic event at least once in their lives. That's 223.4 million people.

The number of people estimated to be experiencing trauma stress is increasing now that we know the side effects extend to first responders, survivors and even those watching events on television. A study published following the Boston Marathon Bombing in the Journal Proceedings of the National Academy of Sciences found, "Acute stress symptoms increased with each additional hour of bombing-related media exposure via television, social media, videos, print or radio." The U.S. Department of Veteran Affairs Center for PTSD concludes there is a link between watching news of traumatic events, such as terrorist attacks, and stress symptoms. They also found people who have experienced previous trauma suffer a cumulative effect with intensified reactions. This University of California Irvine study challenges the key assumption that direct exposure is necessary to develop stress-related problems.

Such is the case for Julie whose story is shared in *Emotional Physics*. As a first responder to the Aurora theatre shooting in 2012, she gained weight and increased glaucoma eye pressure although her diet and physical routines remained the same. During a RIM process, she unraveled the horror of talking to the grandparents of the six year old child among the dead, which was stuck in her body. The result was an immediate drop in weight and eye pressure.

An Effective way of mastering stressful feelings is a priceless tool desired by many people in our country today. *Emotional Physics* is a timely, inventive and user-friendly, "How To" guide to successfully manage mental and physical symptoms of stress more quickly than we've thought possible; it's like bringing together *The Wizard of Oz* with Dr. Mehmet Oz. We can run, but we can't hide from our emotions because they will show up spontaneously in our bodies, mood and outcomes whether we like it or not. It's time to bring hidden feelings out from behind the curtain so we can realize, like the Wizard, they aren't in charge; it only looks that way.

Look of the Book

Combining the above target populations means the look and feel of this book must be clever, engaging and simple to attract the everyday person while credible enough to convince professionals of it's value.

- convenient size 5.5x8 or 6x9 in hardcover to increase credibility among professionals

- brilliant cover design

- built-in "Practice it Yourself" workbook sections at the end of each chapter

- glossary of terms

- index

- free online resources

Competition

Most books geared toward the described target audiences are psychiatrically oriented for therapists and their clients. The primary focus is on using logic and willpower to change our thoughts. In comparison, *Emotional Physics* is written in simple language for the lay person. It identifies the foundation of resourcefulness within each of us (distinct from willpower & logic) that is able to loosen and redo painful memories in an organic way; it demonstrates we are not limited or damaged by our past experiences no matter how horrible because we have an organic recovery mechanism, which can quickly and permanently shift us out of shock, fear and immobilization into presence, out-of-the-box problem-solving and creative action.

A sample of the competition includes: ⓧ

- *Getting Past Your Past: Take Control of Your Life with Self-Help Techniques from EMDR Therapy* by Francine Shapiro PhD (Rodale Books, 2012, $16.99) Although EMDR uses the same organic recovery system as RIM, it does so in a very clinical and therapist-as-expert way. In comparison, *Emotional Physics* elevates readers to a position of being their own expert; they

Jeff's Comments

9 It's always a good idea to clearly state your vision for the book's design, especially if you want it to have a unique look.

10 This does exactly what a "Competition" section is supposed to do.

Deb's Comments

v I don't find it necessary to include the desired look of the book. The structure should be apparent in the sample material.

w This is a very good, clear statement of what the book is about. I would like to see this integrated in other parts of the book because I was finding myself forgetting the crux of the offering.

x This information is often now referred to as "Comparative Titles" because these books can show that there is a market for yours. This is very effectively done in this proposal because it describes differences without denigrating the other titles. It shows that the author clearly understands her book.

are given instructions how to access their specific answers; they are the book's heroes.

- *Breaking the Habit of Being Yourself : How to Lose Your Mind and Create a New One* by Joe Dispenza (Hay House, 2012, $25.95). This book offers a useful way to envision a new sense of self; it relies on the readers' willpower to envision desired images until they feel real. In contrast, *Emotional Physics* guides readers into the center of emotionally charged memory, so it can be neutralized and new outcomes regenerated. Changes occur spontaneously without applying willpower.

- *Healing Your Emotional Self, A Powerful Program to help You Raise Your Self-Esteem, Quiet Your Inner Critic, and Overcome Your Shame* by Beverly Engel (John Wiley, 2006, $16.95). This Amazon self-help bestseller applies an intellectual framework to explain how toxic parents create shame and offers mirror activities to dissolve the shame and build self-esteem; it also has a therapy-orientation. *Emotional Physics* instead, demonstrates how imagination heals difficult problems in ways, which the intellectual mind does not understand.

Jeff's Comments

11 You should always assume that nothing is new under the sun while also realizing that you are a unique being. With that perspective, you can repurpose a popular subject into something relatively original. Be sensitive to the fact that your subject might be over-published. That doesn't need to be a door-closer, but it is incumbent upon you to demonstrate ways that your book will be a unique contribution to what is already on the shelves.

What's Unique About this Book?

It is FRESH, WHIMSICAL AND REVOLUTIONARY

Today's population seeks to be enlightened. Spoiled by the speed of computers, they wish transparency that allows them to see through illusions to the truth instantly and effectively. This book reduces the overwhelming qualities of "emotion" to seven simple premises, and teaches ways to work with feelings that works so quickly, internet-users love it! The almost whimsical tone in the storytelling easily neutralizes any potential intimidation and entertains.

The old assumptions about handling difficult emotion and pain no longer apply—We don't have to talk about it; we don't have to feel the old pain, and we don't have to exercise patience. Rather, a new generation of inner technology is here that's fast, fun, and effective.

Foreign Sales Potential

Regardless of the country, who doesn't want to know how to turn on an emotional self-cleaning oven. Written in a practical, down-to-earth voice without professional jargon, *Emotional Physics* is easily translatable to other languages.

In fact, there already are RIM facilitators in Europe, Canada, Australia and Asia. They have found the process equally useful in their cultures. The international RIM Facilitators would love to have this book published in their countries and their languages as it would offer them additional credibility. They would be excellent ambassadors for foreign sales by promoting the book through book signings for their family, friends and colleagues.

About the Author: Deborah Sandella PhD, RN

Biography

Deborah Sandella has been helping others find themselves for over forty years as a psychotherapist, university professor, pioneer and originator of the groundbreaking RIM (Regenerating Images in Memory) Method.

Applying her insatiable curiosity and tremendous imagination throughout her career, she consistently has originated more effective and quicker ways to alleviate pain and suffering. Driven by an inherent desire to soar above limitations, she reminds us freedom and spontaneity are the spice of life that nurtures body and soul.

Graduating with a Masters in Psychiatric Nursing from the University of Colorado and a Doctorate in Human Communication from the University of Denver, Deborah began her career in the early 70›s by creating and managing two cutting edge programs to retain mental health clients in their local community rather than risking institutionalization at the state hospital. She was recognized for developing innovative and successful programs that effectively cut the lengths of hospital stays from 2-3 weeks to 3-4 days and allowed

Jeff's Comments

International licenses are sometimes an important value-added revenue source. If your subject is likely to have cross-cultural appeal, make a point of saying so.

Even though she has already stated a lot of information about herself and her platform, it never hurts to reinforce and even expand upon what's been said again, and even again, especially if the author's standing is a strong asset.

Deb's Comments

In the "About the Author" section, the description of the RIM Method should be expanded in the beginning as this is what relates most directly to the book. Then follow with the information about the author's education and experience. The purpose of this section is to show the relevance between the author's credentials and the subject matter. The paragraph about witnessing her father's recovery from cardiac arrest and the subsequent development of the RIM Method is more important than the resume.

families to become intimately involved in treatment, which success-fully lowered the recidivism rate.

Dr. Sandella has been acknowledged with numerous professional awards, such as "Outstanding Clinical Specialist," "Research Excel-lence," and an EVVY "Best Personal Growth Book" Award. Further, her prosperity curriculums have been employed successfully by thousands of people.

In addition to being an assistant professor at the University of Col-orado, a manager at Aurora, Colorado Community Mental Health Center, and a successful private practitioner, Deborah began facili-tating personal growth workshops and seminars in 1993. Since that time, her popular retreats have expanded to include Australia, Costa Rica, Maui and Peru. She is a master weaver of gentle, yet profoundly life-changing experiences, and highly values the Chinese proverb, "Tell me and I may listen, teach me and I may remember, involve me and I will do it."

On a personal sabbatical halfway around the world in Australia, Deborah discovered she was more in touch with her clients feelings than her own. Her personal walkabout spawned an inner transfor-mation and resulted in her first award-winning book *Releasing the Inner Magician, Ways to Find a Peaceful and Happy Life* with accom-panying Meditation CD.

When Deborah witnessed her father's recovery from a cardiac arrest following a profound, spontaneous inner experience, she again was inspired to seek beyond the status quo. During the last eighteen years she has developed the RIM Method, founded the RIM Insti-tute, and trained RIM facilitators from across the United States and in Australia, Canada, Czech Republic, Denmark, Egypt and Singa-pore. Thousands of people have benefitted.

Research has found Deborah's work significantly decreases symp-toms of stress-related illness and increases ones' quality of life. She has been featured in popular print, radio and local television. Arti-cles about RIM also have been published in professional journals.

Deborah has been working with Jack Canfield since 2004 as a guest speaker and facilitator. They have co-authored the life-changing *Awakening Power* home study program, which is a popular tool for creating more success in every area of life. It regularly sells out at Jack's events.

Her greatest gift is the ability to combine her adept professional skills with her keen intuitive abilities. Using her lessons as a professional, mother and wife, she teaches how to balance Head, Heart and Soul amidst the chaos of everyday life.

Testimonials

Our Son was diagnosed with a "complete paralysis," after a spinal cord injury, and his rehab doctor was adamant he would never walk again. He wouldn't be walking in braces today without Dr. Deb's belief in him and the RIM sessions.
—Peter, Oklahoma businessman

I'd never have believed you, if you told me I'd be writing a testimonial for RIM. I am THE MOST SKEPTICAL guy in the world. I am interested in NFL football, thick steaks, half ironman races and techno geek toys. Nowhere in there did you see anything about an interest in psychological self-help stuff. In fact, I don't believe in going to psychologists. I engaged with Dr. Deb at a Jack Canfield seminar because I was in excruciating pain. After she guided me through this inner sensing process, I was at complete peace, I was content, I was pain-free, and I was energized. I now know these RIM tools and I've used them successfully several times since. I believe RIM could relieve many people of suffering about their personal, physical and relationship issues.
—Ed Alberts, New York multi-businessman

When I scheduled my son to see Dr. Deb, he had Gardner's Syndrome, an inherited condition and doctors were suggesting he have sections of his intestine removed. By the end of his series of RIM sessions, 500 intestinal polyps had disappeared and surgery was unnecessary.
—Lynn Nichols, Denver

After my one RIM session, the residual shoulder pain remaining after a fall on the ice is gone! Not only that, the crippling fear of walking across ice has disappeared. Being a Vail ski instructor this RIM experience has saved my life.
—Carrie, Vail ski instructor

My son committed suicide 20 years ago. As Dr. Deb and I uncovered the tons of buried grief and guilt in one session, it felt like my heart might break. Hard to believe, but I actually was able to sense my son's forgiveness and love during that session. Rather than talking about the incident, I got to go back in time and redo my regrets--an indescribable gift of healing! Since that session, my life is changed. Now, I can enjoy remembering him without guilt.

—Jill, North Carolina college professor

For years after a teacher sexually abused me during junior high, I found myself being taken advantage by those around me. After I freed myself of this memory during RIM work with Dr. Deb, I spontaneously began speaking up for myself. I now consistently feel empowered and act assertively. RIM is the most effective work I have experienced in my life, and I have spent years trying all of them.

—Barbara, Montana realtor

I've had many sessions with various people and the RIM session I did with Dr. Deb was the single most powerful experience I've had, not over the past eight weeks… but in my life. I made more progress after our time together than I ever remember. With the deepest gratitude my heart can give.

—Linda, NYC business woman

For thirty-seven years I have trained individuals from just about every walk of life and many cultures around the world. I am committed to provide excellence in coaching, training and consulting services to each of these leaders. The RIM Facilitator Program has significantly improved my ability to provide excellence and immediate results to my clients while also renewing myself. Every day, I am grateful for the power of RIM to unleash the inner wisdom and heal.

—Anita L. Sanchez, PhD, Sanchez Tennis & Associates, LLC
   organizational consultant

After my teen daughter had her first RIM session, her younger brother commented she was more calm, confident, and "less cranky"! He went on to say, "What is with this Donna? She's actually confident. What happened to the Donna who has no confidence?" I did not ask for feedback from him and he didn't know she had a RIM session—he just spontaneously commented when she was out one evening.

—Mother of teen client, Aurora, CO

You won't be surprised, I know! My relationships with all four siblings who showed up in my RIM session have been transformed. This is awesome… THANK YOU!

—John, neurosurgeon, NYC

I consider my first session with you a turning point in my life. I began to gain a wise perspective of life. I have been working with several

healing modalities for quite some time and I achieved great results with them but RIM has been the most powerful.
—Adham Saleh Mohamed , manager, Egypt

I am a born and raised Cuban guy, and I did not even know the meaning of meditation and the idea of it made me very uncomfortable. I was, however, curious enough to buy " Awakening Power" in a meditation CD series by Dr. Sandella and Jack Canfield. Now, a year later, I can tell you, this former skeptic believes in meditation, and that Dr. Sandella is an amazing person along with "Awakening Power" being a profound experience. I found peace in my heart, I found inspiration that gave me ideas about many different projects, including a book I wrote, (I wrote a book) !!!! And the ideas came after the meditations!!!!!! I want to thank and acknowledge Dr. Sandella for an amazing work that serves and inspires even a complete former skeptic like me. I greatly recommend this work, it was been life transforming to me.
—Luis Morejon, businessman, Florida

■ Special Book Features

Gift Coupon

A gift coupon will be printed on the inside flap of the book jacket, which is good for attendance to one *Emotional Physics* weekend workshop in Denver scheduled within one year after the book release. Extra product sales during the workshop will be used to cover workshop expenses. The coupon would instruct buyers to go online and register on the website to activate the coupons; thus, allowing us to capture email addresses for future mailings. The coupon also would entitle the book buyer to receive free monthly audio meditations.

Potential Themes and Accompanying Product Sales

"You are More Than You Think"
"I am More Than I Think"
"Your Feelings are Smarter than You Think"

Jeff's Comments

15 This author doesn't let up. She keeps giving the prospective publisher more and more reasons why they should have confidence in her and her ability to sell.

- Audio home study program

- Journals (include quotes from book)

- Imprinted plastic wristbands

- Coffee mugs

- Refrigerator magnets etc.

Jeff's Comments

 Offering these kinds of bonuses actually benefits the author in the long run, because they are opportunities to up-sell readers into a range of fee-based services.

 The book's proposed TOC and the chapter summaries (I only included the first few) are excellent. A sample chapter was also included.

Monthly Teleconferences for First Year of Book Launch

Monthly *Emotional Physics* free teleconferences will be offered during the first year of book launch. These teleconferences would be bonus gifts referenced in articles, interviews and social media. Registration for these free teleconferences would require submitting an email address, which would allow us to ramp up the book email list as well as market the book on the teleconferences.

Potential Future Books for Other Target Audiences

- *Success Beyond the RIM, Finding Your Way Under & Around Hidden Blocks to Quicker Results* (Business Genre) co-authored with Jack Canfield

- *Feelings are Your Friends, An Adventure with Your Inner Magician* (Children Genre)

- *Filling the Empty Nest, How to Reinvent Love* (Couples Genre)

■ Table of Contents

Foreword by ***JACK CANFIELD***

Introduction

Chapter One: Flow & Go
  "Feelings Have a Natural Shelf Life"
      3 to 5 true-life stories
      How it Works Practically and Scientifically
      Practice it Yourself

Chapter Two: See & Free
  "Feelings Have Form"
        3 to 5 true-life stories
        How it Works Practically and Scientifically
        Practice it Yourself

Chapter Three: Unstick & UpWick
  "Intense Emotion+ Event= Sticky Memories"
        3 to 5 true-life stories
        How it Works Practically and Scientifically
        Practice it Yourself

Chapter Four: Repel & Attract
  "Feelings are Magnetic"
        3 to 5 true-life stories
        How it Works Practically and Scientifically
        Practice it Yourself

Chapter Five: Squeeze & Breeze
  "Feelings Increase with Resistance and Decrease with
        Embrace"
        3 to 5 true-life stories
        How it Works Practically and Scientifically s
        Practice it Yourself

Chapter Six: Redo & Renew
  "What is Real and What is Imagined Reconstitute as Memory"
        3 to 5 true-life stories
        How it Works Practically and Scientifically
        Practice it Yourself

Chapter Seven: Me & Thee
  "Wholeness is Greater than the Sum of Our Human Parts"
        3 to 5 true-life stories
        How it Works Practically and Scientifically
        Practice it Yourself

Chapter Eight: Do it!
  "Dip See Do"
        3 to 5 true-life stories
        3 Part Organic Process
        How and Why it Works Practically & Scientifically
        Practice it Yourself
  Instant and Effective Ways to Make Life Easier
        Regret Eraser
        Irritation Soother

■ Manuscript Overview

Foreword by JACK CANFIELD

"I'm so excited to share the work of Deborah Sandella with you! She's been my co-author and worked with my students for years, producing dramatic results. Her original, ground breaking technique just magically dissolves what is blocking us—and accelerates more success in every facet of our lives. Deborah is the BEST of the BEST! And I'm so glad she's now providing this extraordinary resource to the world. Grab this book now, if you want more success in your life!"
—Jack Canfield, *NY Times* Bestselling Author

Introduction

What are you feeling right now? Do you know? Chances are unless you're in the middle of an emotional event, you aren't aware of feeling anything. In Roget's Thesaurus there are more than 3,000 words describing possible emotions. Success or failure of your work and relationships ride on how you manage your feelings. Yet, emotions are invisible, taken for granted and dismissed much of the the time, a paradox given they are some of the most powerful forces on earth. They inflame wars, induce death, inspire invention and control stock markets. What is more important, each of us has them—constantly!

In 1995 Daniel Goleman's groundbreaking book *Emotional Intelligence, Why It Can Matter More than IQ* established the radical importance of understanding the power in emotion. He shows how "feeling" frequently trumps "thinking" as an automatic response to life experiences. This bias happens because the emotional brain existed long before the rational brain, "… which gives evolved emotional centers immense power to influence the functioning of the rest of the brain—including its centers for thought." Further, the emotional part of the brain learns in a different style than the logical thinking part of the brain.

In *Emotional Physics*, we'll look through a novel lens. Instead of the traditional approach, we'll explore the organic makeup of our feelings. Mother Nature is a great teacher, and workings of the Universe inspire awe. We, too, are created with life's inherent sense of order and urge to thrive. Since the workings of Nature mirrors our organic abilities, we can use the natural world as a metaphor to solve human problems. As early as 1452, men observed birds to understand flight; the Wright brothers gained insight from observing pigeons when designing airplanes. This idea is now a scientific discipline called "biomimicry," which comes from the Greek words *bios* for "life" and *mimesis* "to imitate." This book uses Nature as a metaphor to explain seven organic qualities of emotion so you can understand their physics.

Physics is one of the oldest natural sciences—the study of matter and its motion through space and time, along with related concepts such as energy and force. In general, it helps us understand how the universe behaves. Giving physicality and movement to feelings allows us to see them in a new light. As they become visible, the rational brain is engaged with matters of the heart and our emotions becomes controllable in ways we've never considered until now.

This book demonstrates how emotion predictably expands and contracts. As in all things, knowing how it works means we can produce desired outcomes. The big, harry, scary monster called FEELINGS can be reduced to seven organic principles, which empower you to gain a sense of emotional mastery. Further, you can use them to intentionally accelerate emotional and physical recovery,solve problems and manifest your dreams at speeds mimicking Google, yet, how it works is surprisingly different than what the logical mind thinks.

A sense of awe is inspired by the speedy effectiveness of our native emotional intelligence; it's like having a built-in emotional self-cleaning oven, problem solver and success magnet. However, we need to know how to dial it in and turn it on. Enlivened with convincing scientific findings and tender real-life stories, this book empowers readers to "try it" themselves with self-guided activities.

Emotional Physics is grounded in neuroscience and founded in eighteen years of remarkable client results by this author and trained facilitators across the United States and around the world in Australia, Czech Republic, Egypt, Singapore, Denmark and Canada. This book goes far beyond others and teaches readers how to sense the form of their feelings and intentionally reshape them for greater happiness, better health, and more successful outcomes.

■ Chapter Summaries

CHAPTER ONE

Flow & Go
Feelings have a Natural Shelf Life

Since the dawn of human time, we have been scared of undesirable feelings. Mythologically, Adam and Eve demonstrated how acting on one's feelings leads to dangerous outcomes. Socrates and Aristotle wrote noted philosophy on how we "should" cultivate an independent personality, never lowering ourself to the emotions of anger and lust. Somewhere in human history, we came to think of feelings as inviting control in order to feel safe and appear moral.

Further, we think we are our feelings; you can hear it in our speech, "I'm angry," as if to say, "I am anger." However, such feelings naturally arise as transient states and are not intended to be part of our hardware. Rather, their purpose is to provide feedback and organically pass through us as water flows through a river.

Deb's Comments

z Chapter summaries are a way to show what each chapter will be about. You want to take advantage of the opportunity to show your writing skills. You don't have to put the same effort or detail into each summary, but in this sample proposal I think it would be wise to put in some actual real-life stories. You don't know what might propel your proposal over the fence and into a sale and you don't know what might put you into a competitive advantage of receiving more than one offer. Even though it may feel like you are pushing rocks up a hill, it is worth putting in the effort to make each part of your proposal persuasive and organized with a reference to your core message.

Like water's life cycle, which moves through the atmosphere in and out of the oceans, over and under land, human feelings continuously precipitate, go underground, rise to the surface and evaporate through our life cycle. Trying to control feelings through resistance and avoidance is like constructing a physical dam that contains a pool of rejected emotional waters. This self-created reservoir of disowned feelings eddies in the same spot in the body unless released downstream to dissipate as designed by nature.

This chapter teaches how to devise floodgates to siphon off emotion from the body in safe ways that eliminate emotional flooding. Readers are given simple, user-friendly tools to navigate feelings and avoid emotional and physical damage. Chapter One explains how the full range of feeling is a normal aspect of our emotional navigation system, and each passing feeling brings valuable information with a natural shelf life that causes them to evaporate like water in a river. When we welcome feelings, we activate natural self-recovery. Since our emotional state directly influences our success in relationships, work, and health, we gain an ability to produce desired outcomes when we use them to create natural flow and momentum without flooding.

- 3 to 5 convincing real-life stories

- How it works practically and scientifically

- Practice it Yourself

**Lesson: When You Allow the Natural Flow of Feelings,
They Bring Valuable Information and Organically
Expire as You Move Effortlessly Forward**

CHAPTER TWO (SEE SAMPLE CHAPTER)

See & Free

Feelings Have Form

Unlike physical and intellectual measurements, feelings are invisible and illusive. Absent apparent substance, they seem unbounded, out of control and overwhelming. They frustrate the heck out of the quantitative left brain, which loves to measure problems; thus, we have a hard time understanding what is invisible and unpredictable.

This chapter reveals the form of feelings and how they can be measured. The form of happiness, sadness and physical pain show up with unique patterns, which are idiosyncratic and visible through your imagination. By revealing the form of emotion, your head becomes a partner with your heart in solving problems and dissolving hidden success-stopping unconscious blocks.

Setting aside intellectual resistance to subjective feelings, your head joins your heart and spirit on an organic journey of sensory discovery to find the cause. Sabotaging thoughts/beliefs, feelings and memories are quickly uprooted and a lighter more positive feeling of self-worth and confidence is naturally generated in the body.

- 3 to 5 convincing real-life stories

- How it works practically and scientifically

- Practice it Yourself

**Lesson: When you Sense the Form of Your Feelings,
You Gain Power Over Them**

CHAPTER THREE

Unstick & UpWick

Intense Emotion + an Event = Stuck Memories

Adhesives offer a great metaphor for understanding how certain painful and unhealthy memories get stuck in our bodies to create blocks to future success and vital health while others do not. Adhesives are activated by a chemical reaction with an external energy source. For example in 1839, Charles Goodyear discovered heating rubber with sulfur makes plastic. Later with the invention of the automobile, stronger and more durable adhesives were needed, and rubber was treated with strong acids to create rubber cement for bonding metal to rubber.

Similarly, memory adheres to the nervous system when the body has an intense biochemical reaction to a highly charged event. The result is a hardening of the memory in the body, which leaves it unyielding and resistant to change.

Non-emotional experiences, however remain neutral.

In Chapter Three, we apply this natural metaphor in two ways: 1) to neutralize the emotional glue holding intensely negative past events and 2) to anchor highly desirable feelings like confidence and love in new positive experiences. We contract/dissolve self-sabotaging emotions and expand self-affirming/creative emotions.

- 3 to 5 convincing real-life stories

- How it works practically and scientifically

- Practice it Yourself

Lesson: When You Unstick Sabotaging Feelings and Wick Up Self-affirming Ones, You Get an Extraordinary Boost in Physical Vitality, Clarity and Personal Power

PROPOSAL 2

Proposed Title:

INSTANT HEALING

Ways to Heal Your Body, Mind, Emotions, And Environment

Susan Shumsky

Overview

In a world of chaos and uncertainty, with a failing economy, loss of jobs, housing values plummeting, and general malaise, the population is increasingly lost, confused, and anxious. We are beginning to wake up to the reality that we can no longer depend on solid, steadfast institutions that we had previously counted on, even for our very survival. There is an increasing, sickening fear about the future, about the value of our investments, about inflation, about retirement savings, and about our mental and physical health. There seems to be no way out of this madness.

How can we find a path to greater well being? Is there a way to reverse this downward spiral of inner turmoil and frustration? *Instant Healing* provides an answer. This book can help anyone

Deb's Comments

a I like the title because it clearly conveys what the book promises.

b The first two paragraphs don't say as much as I would like them to. These are generalized statements that we see in many books that offer to solve the world's problems. It makes a bold claim that the book has real answers, so I am personally intrigued to see what the author has to say.

Jeff's Comments

1 The first paragraph needs to be read in context; the proposal was written shortly after the crash of 2008 when everything appeared to be in free fall. Otherwise this would not have been an appropriate way to introduce a book about physical health.

2 The second paragraph actually explains what the book will be about and what makes it special, and the proceeding paragraphs do a good job of reinforcing the basic premise.

Deb's Comments

c This author is confident and says that the answers found in this book are field tested. This is not a claim you typically find in a spiritual healing book. Now the book's content is taken out of the perception of "lightweight woo woo" into "perhaps this is a practical book with real takeaways." There is nothing wrong with philosophy, but agents and publishers prefer that these types of books are balanced with some grounding so they can compete with other nonfiction books.

d This paragraph is a clear statement of the book's category: "spiritual self-help." There is no question for the agent or editor how to position it. The more work you can do for your proposal readers, the better. You want to lead them easily into a "yes." The author also states her credentials here. Rather than burying them in the "About the Author" section, she integrates them appropriately in this section of the proposal so the publisher knows this is an author who is credible, credentialed, and takes her work seriously. She has a track record and continues to mention her prior publishing successes within the overview. The overview

find instantaneous transformation. By using simple prayer and affirmation formulas, readers can experience immediate healing, comfort, and solace. They can discover self-empowerment and gain self-confidence. They can heal their body, mind, emotions, and environment. They can attain a state of inner strength and wellness as never known before.

The field-proven, non-denominational, universal method of spiritual healing used in this book has changed the lives of millions of people worldwide over the past 150 years. In the New Age **c** movement, Unity Church, Church of Religious Science, Science of Mind, Divine Science, Christian Science, and Centers for Spiritual Living, this powerful method of healing has been variously named Scientific Prayer, Affirmative Prayer, Spiritual Mind Treatment, Affirmation, or Treatment.

With about 65,000 words, *Instant Healing* is a spiritual self-help book written by Susan Shumsky, D.D., professional speaker and highly-respected teacher in the spiritual community who has **d** written and illustrated seven spiritual self-help books: *Divine Revelation* (in its 15th year of continuous print with Simon & Schuster), *Miracle Prayer* (Random House), plus *Exploring Meditation, Exploring Chakras, Exploring Auras, How to Hear the Voice of God,* and *Ascension,* published by New Page Books. A completed manuscript can be delivered six months after signing the book contract.

Dr. Shumsky is committed to making *Instant Healing* successful as she continues to make public appearances in New Thought and New Age venues nationwide. She has already done over 500 media appearances and 500 speaking engagements since her first book was published. Recently she has been aggressively marketing her products on the Internet, including JV Teleseminars, a JV launch that made her recent book *Ascension* into an Amazon.com best seller, and another Amazon.com JV launch for *How to Hear the Voice of God* in February, 2012.

Instant Healing is the go-to handbook for anyone who wants to transform their state of mind or the atmosphere around them in an instant. The book provides hundreds of healing affirmation and prayer formulas, along with instructions on how to use them successfully. These methods are simple and effective, and require no background or training. All the reader needs to do is read the formula out loud and then let go and allow the magic to happen. The types of methods provided in this book have already proven very potent and meaningful in the lives of millions of people. Through *Instant Healing*, readers can now discover how the power of their spoken word produces miracles.

What Readers Will Learn

In *Instant Healing*, readers will discover how to:

- Use the mighty ""I AM"" presence for healing and transformation.

- Create their own destiny through thoughts, words, and deeds.

- Be fully responsible for their lives.

- Heal their body, mind, emotions, and environment.

- Heal others.

- Clear out dense, negative vibrations in the atmosphere.

- Heal lower vibrational energies.

- Heal and release negative thoughts and replace them with positive ones.

- Heal deep patterns and belief systems.

- Attain great self-empowerment and self-authority.

- Release undue attachments, co-dependency, and addictions.

- Improve relationships and create greater intimacy.

- Heal blockages standing in the way of fulfilling their heartfelt desires.

- Become happy, prosperous, and healthy.

is an appropriate length and doesn't bog down with too much detail or overselling.

Jeff's Comments

3 A "What Readers Will Learn" section isn't part of the typical proposal protocol since the information can be provided elsewhere. But it's an effective device in this setting and gives the author an opportunity to clearly spell out the book's most important purposes.

Deb's Comments

e This does not follow the typical format, but it is certainly effective here. The proposal format is a guide. If the material lends itself to explaining right in the beginning how the system works, it is easier for the agent or editor to keep this in mind as they are evaluating the remaining elements of the proposal.

Style of the Book

Instant Healing operates on four levels:

1. **Inspirational:** The book consists of inspiring affirmations and prayers that bring comfort, solace and upliftment, and give renewed hope to readers, even in tough times.

2. **Informational:** The book teaches readers practical information about how to heal themselves and how to solve everyday problems.

3. **Instructional:** The book trains readers in beneficial spiritual healing methods of affirmation and prayer.

4. **Experiential:** In this interactive guide, readers practice methods of affirmation and prayer to help them heal themselves, overcome blockages, empower themselves, and realize their hopes and dreams.

The book is written logically, clearly and simply, with language that can be understood without previous exposure to metaphysics. The reader is led step-by-step through each technique.

The following materials are available immediately upon your request:

- Copies of Dr. Susan Shumsky's books: *Divine Revelation, Exploring Meditation, Exploring Chakras, Exploring Auras, Miracle Prayer, How to Hear the Voice of God,* and *Ascension,* with related press materials.

- Video or audio interviews with the author.

- Audio and video seminars, lectures, meditations, or healing-prayers produced by the author.

Credentials: Susan Shumsky, Author

As the author of *Instant Healing*, Dr. Susan Shumsky brings expertise in the fields of spiritual development, teaching meditation, prayer, yoga, intuition, prayer therapy and spiritual counseling, conducting retreats, seminars and tours to sacred destinations, and skills in writing, editing, design, illustration, and public relations.

Experience in Spiritual Development

Dr. Susan Shumsky has practiced meditation, yoga, and other self-development disciplines for over 40 years—since 1967. For seven of those years she resided in remote areas of the Himalayas and the Alps on the personal staff of famous enlightened master from India, Maharishi Mahesh Yogi, guru of the Beatles and Deepak Chopra and founder of Transcendental Meditation, the world's largest meditation organization, with over six million members.

Under the tutelage of Maharishi, she spent many years in deep meditation and complete silence. She spent 20 years living and studying in her mentor's learning institutions, including Maharishi European Research University and Maharishi International University. Since then she has studied with several other enlightened masters and teachers.

One advantage that Susan Shumsky brings to her readers is that she developed her expertise through over four decades of patient daily study and practice. Having walked the path herself, she can guide others along their spiritual path.

Teaching Credentials and Experience

Pioneer in the consciousness field, foremost authority on spirituality, and highly successful professional speaker, author, and workshop leader who is greatly respected in the spiritual community, Dr. Susan Shumsky has taught meditation, self-development, intuition, yoga, and prayer to thousands of students in the U.S., Canada, Europe, and the Far East since 1970. As a skilled lecturer, teacher, healer, counselor, and prayer therapist, she has authored and promoted many seminars and classes.

In 1970 in Rishikesh, India, Maharishi Mahesh Yogi personally trained Susan Shumsky to teach meditation. She received Bachelor and Master degrees of Ministerial Science and a Doctor of Divinity degree from Teaching of Intuitional Metaphysics, a New Thought teaching founded by Dr. Peter V. Meyer of San Diego and affiliated with the International New Thought Alliance. Susan Shumsky is a lifetime member of the INTA and of Ozark Research

by offering to make available other supporting materials.

g Credentials are usually included in the "About the Author" section, but in the spiritual genre it doesn't hurt to show that you are a professional person and not someone perceived on the fringe. This is not meant to offend. However, until about fifteen years ago, there was not even a real category of spiritual writing. It was lumped into occult or New Age and did not cross over into the mainstream. Now we have many categories that will support these types of titles. Maintaining a level of authority is important to prevent the book from slipping back into the ethers.

h This author has done an exceptional job of dividing up her sections so they are powerful and easy to read. It is likely not an accident that she includes the word *experience* in the beginning of each section. Whether planned or not, this adds a layer of authority to her book. There is no doubt she has earned the respect of the publishing world. We have represented her throughout her career. She has not sold every book she has proposed, but her list of titles has gained her the reputation of being able to close most of her deals. She is even offered titles from her publisher's wish list and can choose what she wants to write. Her proposal-writing prowess has come from a lot of practice and rewriting over the years. This is a great one to follow for structure and clarity.

Institute. She is on the Board of Directors of Teaching of Intuitional Metaphysics, Inc.

Dr. Shumsky is the founder of Divine Revelation®, a complete technology for contacting the divine presence, listening to the divine intuitive voice, and practicing meditation, intuition, prayer, and healing methods. She now travels internationally, teaching workshops, seminars, retreats, spiritual tours to sacred destinations, and spiritual cruises. She also leads a weekly teleconference scientific prayer circle, teleseminars and webinars, and an online community group forum.

Publishing Experience

Dr. Shumsky has written many books teaching her own unique forms of meditation, intuition, prayer, and spiritual healing:

1. *Divine Revelation*, in continuous print since 1996 with Simon & Schuster Fireside, One Spirit Book-of-the-Month Club top-ten selection, also published in Spanish in Mexico by Editorial Patria, in German by Ansata: Econ and List Verlagsgruppe, in Russian by ETP publishers, and by Magma Press in India.

2. *Miracle Prayer*, COVR award winner, published by Random House Celestial Arts, also One Spirit Book Club selection and published in Russian by Ves Publishers.

3. *Exploring Meditation*, published by Career Press, also in India by Penguin Books and in India by New Age Books.

4. *Exploring Chakras*, COVR award winner, published by Career Press, also in India by New Age Books and in Russia by Budushcheye Zemli.

5. *Exploring Auras*, published by Career Press, also in Russia by Budushcheye Zemli, in Japanese by Tokuma Shoten, in Belgium and Netherlands by Deltas, and in India by Jaico Publications.

6. *How to Hear the Voice of God*, published by Career Press.

7. *Ascension*, published by Career Press, and in Romania by Adevar Divin and in Italy by Macro Edizioni.

8. *Instant Healing*, published by Career Press.

9. *The Power of Auras*, published by Career Press.

10. *The Power of Chakras*, published by Career Press.

Dr. Shumsky personally created all the illustrations, charts, and graphics for all of her books. She also wrote, designed, and illustrated many pamphlets and books, including textbooks for secondary education, for the most successful self-improvement organization in the world—Transcendental Meditation.

Susan Shumsky wrote and designed all the promotional posters, flyers, ads, brochures, and pamphlets for her various seminars and produced all her own graphics. She also authored and produced audio and video programs of guided meditations, lectures, seminars, and healing prayers. Her articles have appeared in numerous magazines, newspapers, and on the Internet.

Dr. Shumsky is the web designer and webmaster of divinerevelation.org, divinetravels.org, spiritualinformation.net, spiritualityproducts.com, and about 100 other domain names. She has authored all the web pages on her sites, with over 3800 files.

Promotional Experience

Since 1970 Dr. Shumsky has organized and conducted hundreds of lectures, seminars, retreats, tours, and spiritual cruises. Founder of the Denver Transcendental Meditation Center, one of the largest meditation centers in America, Susan Shumsky coordinated all the activities of the TM organization in five states. She was a professional free-lance illustrator and was a successful diamond jewelry designer in New York for over 20 years.

From 1985 until 1991 and again from 1996 until the present, Susan Shumsky tours as a professional speaker. She spends a few days in each new city, promoting, lecturing, teaching seminars, and selling her books and other products. From her motor home, her office-on-wheels, she conducts media appearances as well as speaking engagements at expos, conferences, bookstores, and New Thought churches.

Since *Divine Revelation* was published, Susan Shumsky has done over 600 personal appearances and about 675 media placements, including *Woman's World* magazine, *Cosmopolitan,* and *GQ,* "Coast to Coast AM with George Noory," "Weird or What?" with William

Jeff's Comments

6 The author does a good job showing that she's a full-time missionary for her books and products, and that the new book would benefit from everything she's already doing and will do. What's missing is sales numbers for her previous books. An editor needs to know that whatever an author does, or promises to do, will actually translate into book sales. A publisher doesn't care how successful an author is separate from sales.

Shatner, and the movie *Three Magic Words,* and interviews on syndicated radio and network television. For several years she employed a professional booking agent to arrange her speaking engagements, and she has recently hired a new booking agent.

This is the type of grass roots publicity campaign that Susan Shumsky will use to promote *Instant Healing.* She also successfully promotes her books, audio and video products, as well as her retreats, cruises, and international tours, on her web sites: divinerevelation.org and divinetravels.com. Her current itinerary is at susanshumsky.com.

Expertise and Authority

Where does Susan Shumsky gain the qualification and authority to author this book? Quite simply, from 40 years experience in the self-development field. She has developed a unique, profound spiritual teaching based on personal experience and wisdom acquired from many great teachers. Her techniques make it easy for anyone to experience genuine spiritual awakening. In this highly specialized field, she is an expert.

All of Susan Shumsky's years of research into consciousness and inner exploration have gone into *Instant Healing,* which can significantly enhance the quest for inner truth and shorten the time required for the inner pathway to God.

Competitive Books

Instant Healing is a unique, highly effective handbook that speaks to the needs of today's readers. Let us now explore a few competitive books in the spiritual category:

> *Life Prayers: From Around the World: 365 Prayers, Blessings, and Affirmations to Celebrate the Human Journey* by Elizabeth Roberts, Paperback: 464 pages, Publisher: HarperOne; (May 10, 1996).

This book is a potpourri of prayers from all over the world. Whether or not these prayers are effective or useful remains to be seen. Many of these so-called "prayers" are not really prayers. And very few of them would be called affirmations or prayer treatments. They do not have relevancy in today's world, nor do they speak to specific

Jeff's Comments

7 This is an effective "Competition" section, but I would shorten the per-title comparisons by at least one-third and use the space for several more title comparisons. This is a crowded book category, so it would have been wise to make even more comparisons, especially against recent successful titles.

Deb's Comments

i These can also be called "Comparative Books." Her subject matter falls into a competitive area right now, and there are many books that could knock her book out of the running. Therefore, the author does not skimp on this section. It is easy to rest on your laurels, especially when you have developed a following. But a new voice can always arise, so it is important to keep track of what other people are writing in your arena. Do not become intimidated by this, but rather describe how they support your voice.

problems haunting today's readers. *Life Prayers* consists of wishy-washy poetic drivel rather than something profound, powerful and meaningful that could be useful in personal healing. *Life Prayers* does not deal with negative emotions that need to be transformed. In contrast, *Instant Healing* is a useful, practical handbook that provides specific solutions to the problems of modern everyday life. The only method of prayer used in *Instant Healing* is affirmative prayer, a greatly effective method of prayer—much more effective than petitionary prayer (begging) and other methods used in *Life Prayers*. Readers can use *Instant Healing* to effect profound transformation, unlike *Life Prayers*.

Pocketful of Miracles: Prayer, Meditations, and Affirmations to Nurture Your Spirit Every Day of the Year, Joan Borysenko, Paperback: 424 pages, Publisher: Grand Central Publishing (November 1, 1994).

This hefty book is written as a 365-day guide, with one lesson per page/per day. The lesson consists of a seed thought for contemplation and an accompanying prayer or practice to help you realize or internalize the lesson. While uplifting, this book is a hodgepodge of inspirational thoughts rather than a guide to self-healing. *Instant Healing*, on the other hand, is a useful, hands-on guide for healing specific problems in the reader's life, and it provides a practical methodology for manifesting one's heartfelt desires. Unlike *Pocketful of Prayers*, *Instant Healing* classifies the affirmations and prayers into sensible categories, so the reader can find the solution to the problem he/she is working on at the moment. The reader can therefore use *Instant Healing* as a reference guide. *Pocketful of Miracles* has no rhyme or reason for assigning prayers to specific days. Readers could never find the solution to a specific problem in that book. In contrast, *Instant Healing* is a powerful guide for personal growth and self-healing, accessible and easy to use.

Affirmations for Self-Healing by J. Donald Walters, Paperback: 136 pages, Publisher: Crystal Clarity Publishers; (October 21, 2005).

This book by Swami Kriyananda is a closer competitor to *Instant Healing* than the two other books above. However, it still falls short in many ways. *Affirmations for Self-Healing* contains 52 affirmations and prayers devoted to strengthening positive qualities such as will power, good health, forgiveness, security, and happiness. Each topic includes a short description, an affirmation, and a prayer. However, the book does not deal with such issues as healing deep-seated emotions, negative forces, or addiction. In fact, it does not help readers heal anything from the "dark side." Kriyananda's book does not provide a way for readers to overcome deeply held beliefs and blockages that prevent them from fulfilling their desires. It does not include Scientific Prayer Treatments. Its prayers are simple petitionary prayers and not affirmative prayers. In contrast, *Instant Healing* offers all of the benefits that are missing from Kriyananda's book. The entire range of negative forces is addressed in *Instant Healing,* including astral entities, psychic vampires, psychic ties and karmic bonds, and so forth. Powerful, profound, healing takes place with the affirmative prayers and treatments provided in *Instant Healing,* which helps readers to truly transform their lives from a deep level.

The affirmation and prayer books available in today's market all fall short of *Instant Healing,* which helps readers to powerfully and profoundly change their deeply held beliefs, patterns, and thought-forms. In addition, *Instant Healing* addresses not only the individual, but also the environment, since we do not live in a vacuum. The energies of the astral cloud that covers the planet are also healed through the powerful affirmations and prayers in *Instant Healing.*

■ Benefits to the Publisher

Instant Healing is a book with the following assets:

- It is written and will be promoted by an experienced professional speaker, seminar leader, teacher, and author in the human-potential-consciousness field.

- The author has a successful public relations track record and is committed to making the book a success with a public relations campaign and nationwide tours.

- She will use the book to promote her organization and seminars. Therefore, the book has a strong backlist potential.

- It is expandable with potential spin-offs geared toward the author's students and clients.

• It will be endorsed by leaders in the self-help field, as were her books *Divine Revelation* (endorsed by Dr. Gerald Jampolsky, Dr. Larry Dossey, Barbara Brennan, Dr. John Gray), *Exploring Meditation* (endorsed by James Van Praagh), *Exploring Chakras* (endorsed by Yogi Amrit Desai, Dr. David Frawley, and Dr. Larry Dossey), *Exploring Auras* (with foreword by Dannion Brinkley and endorsed by Uri Geller, Dr. Bruce Goldberg, and Lucia Capacchione), *Miracle Prayer* (endorsed by Dr. Terry Cole-Whittaker, James Van Praagh, Denise Linn, and John Randolph Price), *How to Hear the Voice of God* (endorsed by Terry Cole-Whittaker and Sondra Ray), and *Ascension* (endorsed by James Van Praagh, Joe Vitale, Sondra Ray, and Leonard Orr).

CONTENTS AND CHAPTER OUTLINE

Contents

Introduction

How to Use This Book

Part 1: Changing Your Mind
> Chapter 1: Gaining Inner Strength and Empowerment
> Chapter 2: Healing Emotions and Deep-Seated Beliefs
> Chapter 3: Healing and Forgiving Relationships
> Chapter 4: Overcoming Addictions and Co-Dependency
> Chapter 5: Becoming All that You Can Be

Part 2: Lifting Your Environment
> Chapter 6: Healing Environ-mental Static
> Chapter 7: Healing Entities and Vampires
> Chapter 8: Overcoming Enemies and Saboteurs
> Chapter 9: Making Your Space into a Cathedral

Part 3: Making Dreams Come True
> Chapter 10: Living in Perfect Health
> Chapter 11: Magnetizing Love
> Chapter 12: Attracting Prosperity
> Chapter 13: Making Life a Success
> Chapter 14: Enjoying Happiness
> Chapter 15: Transforming the Planet

Deb's Comments

(k) This is a well-organized table of contents. Keep in mind that this author is experienced. Aspire to this level of clarity even though you may not attain it right away. What I like about this TOC is I can visualize the book completely. It is clearly broken up into logical sections and shows me ahead of time the journey I would be taking by reading the book. Your proposal is creating a roadmap for your reader. That is why you should focus on logic and structure before getting creative. Nonfiction needs to be well written and entertaining, or at least not boring to read. However, the more important factor is that the reader can follow where you are taking them.

Jeff's Comments

(9) I think it's usually effective to precede the actual chapter outline with a brief table of contents. It helps editors get oriented to what will follow.

Jeff's Comments

 Chapter descriptions form the proposal's editorial heart, especially when the manuscript hasn't been written yet. This is a good outline. Because the author had generated several sample chapters (more than 3,000 words), it was okay for her outline to be relatively brief. In the absence of any chapters, the outline would have needed several hundred words or more of content per chapter.

Deb's Comments

 The chapter by chapter outline is a bit skeletal for my taste. I like that each chapter outline is clear about what the content will be, but I would like to see some actual narrative in the outline before I invest time in the supporting material. If you write enough in the chapter outline, you will presell before the agent or editor even gets to the sample chapter. You will also have your blueprint so thought out that writing or visualizing the book will be easy. So in this case I would like to see some actual samples within the outline. Just a preference.

Chapter 16: Creating Heaven on Earth

▌ Chapter Outline

Part 1: Changing Your Mind

The First Part of the book helps readers to transform their own minds, realize who they really are, and thereby express their true nature of being.

Chapter 1: Gaining Inner Strength and Empowerment

In Chapter 1, readers learn and use the following affirmations and prayers: Self-Authority Affirmation, Psychic Block Prayer, Prayer for Protection, Pillar of Light Visualization, Grounded in Spirit, Let There Be Light, White Fire Affirmation, Golden Healing Prayer, Energy Healing, Self-Integration Prayer, Divine Armor Prayer, Self-Authority Prayer Treatment. (See sample chapter)

Chapter 2: Healing Emotions and Deep-Seated Beliefs

In Chapter 2, readers learn and use the following affirmations and prayers: Thought-Form Healing, Thought-Form Healing—Short Form, Thought-Form Pattern and Belief-Structure Healing, Façade-Body Healing, Past Experience Healing, Letting Go Prayer, Past Life Mental Body Healing, Prayer Before Sleep, Treatment for a Positive Mental and Emotional Attitude. (See sample chapter)

Chapter 3: Healing and Forgiving Relationships

In Chapter 3, readers learn and use the following affirmations and prayers: Psychic Tie Cut Healing, Psychic Tie Cut: Layer by Layer, Psychic Coercion Healing, Psychic Bondage Healing, Psychic Anomalies Healing, Forgiveness Prayer, Forgiveness Healing Chant, Canceling Contracts, Prayer Treatment to Heal Relationships. (See sample chapter)

Chapter 4: Overcoming Addictions and Co-Dependency

In Chapter 4, readers learn and use the following affirmations and prayers: Attaining Balance, Overcoming Addiction, Overcoming Cigarettes, Overcoming Alcohol, Overcoming Coffee, Sex Addiction Treatment, Freedom from Co-dependent Relationships Treatment, Workaholic Prayer Treatment, Freedom from Substance Abuse and Addiction Treatment, and more.

Chapter 5: Becoming All You Can Be

In Chapter 5, readers learn and use the following affirmations and prayers: Self-Empowerment Affirmation, Self-Acceptance Affirmation, Self-Expression Affirmation, Self-Love Prayer Treatment, Overcoming Shyness Treatment, Developing Self-Expression Treatment, Self-Realization Prayer Treatment, Spiritual Enlightenment Prayer Treatment, and more.

Part 2: Lifting Your Environment

The second part of the book helps readers to change the mental atmosphere around them. Thereby they transform their environment and their relationship to it.

Chapter 6: Healing Environ-mental Static

In Chapter 6, readers learn and use the following affirmations and prayers: Healing the Mental Atmosphere, Overcoming Opinions of Others, Healing Peer Pressure, Healing Familial Pressure, Familial Healing, Deceased Ancestor Healing, Healing Societal Beliefs, Healing Brainwashing from Organizations and Cults, Healing Religious Brainwashing, Healing Gender Beliefs, Healing Undue Influences,

Healing the Home, Healing the Workplace, Healing Spaces, and more.

Chapter 7: Healing Entities and Vampires

In Chapter 7, readers learn and use the following affirmations and prayers: Astral Entity Healing, Entity Universal Healing, Entity Lifting, E.T Astral Entity Healing, Mass Astral Healing, Clearing Entities from Spaces, Psychic Vampire Healing, Treatment for Healing Astral Oppression and Possession, Treatment for Overcoming Victimization, Treatment for Overcoming Psychic Vampirism, and more.

Chapter 8: Overcoming Enemies and Saboteurs

In Chapter 8, readers learn and use the following affirmations and prayers: Psychic Coercion Healing, Psychic Hook Healing, Psychic Implants Healing, Reversing Black Magic, Healing Reptilians, Healing Sabotage, Divine Justice Healing, Divine Shield Affirmation, Healing Enemies, Divine Justice Prayer Treatment, Freedom from Imprisonment Prayer Treatment, and more.

Chapter 9: Making Your Space into a Cathedral

In Chapter 9, readers learn and use the following affirmations and prayers: Lifting the Home Atmosphere, Lifting the Workplace Atmosphere, Healing Institutional Atmospheres, Healing Old Buildings, Healing Church Buildings, Divine Light Invocation, Treatment to Heal Buildings, Treatment to Lift Atmospheres and Spaces, and more.

Part 3: Making Dreams Come True

The third part of the book helps readers to overcome problems and fulfill desires through the use of Scientific Prayer Treatment.

Chapter 10: Living in Perfect Health

In Chapter 10, readers learn and use the following affirmations and prayers: Perfect Health Affirmation, Perfect Robust Health Treatment, Healing a Physical Ailment Treatment, Healing Cancer Prayer Treatment, Healing the Heart Treatment, Healing Injuries Prayer Treatment, Healing Eyesight Prayer Treatment, Healing Hearing Prayer Treatment, Healing from Surgery Prayer Treatment, and more.

Chapter 11: Magnetizing Love

In Chapter 11, readers learn and use the following affirmations and prayers: Love Affirmation, Increasing Magnetism, Being Physically Attractive, Perfect Mate Prayer Treatment, Perfect Loving Friendships Treatment, Perfect Relationship with Children Treatment, Perfect Relationship with Parents Treatment, Harmonious Home-Life Treatment, Sexual Fulfillment Prayer Treatment, and more.

Chapter 12: Attracting Prosperity

In Chapter 12, readers learn and use the following affirmations and prayers: Fountainhead of Wealth Affirmation, Infinite Supply Affirmation, Money Magnet Affirmation, Perfect Abundance Prayer Treatment, Perfect Income Prayer Treatment, Perfect Employment Prayer Treatment, Perfect Housing Prayer Treatment, Perfect Vehicle Prayer Treatment, and more.

Chapter 13: Making Life a Success

In Chapter 13, readers learn and use the following affirmations and prayers: Divine Plan Affirmation, Becoming Influential, Developing a Winning Personality, Attracting Fame, Developing Perseverance, Being of Service, Perfect Divine Order and Timing Treatment, Treatment for Optimizing Opportunities, Becoming Successful Treatment, True Plan Purpose and Destiny Treatment, and more.

Chapter 14: Enjoying Happiness

In Chapter 14, readers learn and use the following affirmations and prayers: Being Happy, Attaining Fulfillment and Contentment, Letting Go and Letting God, Accepting What Is, Treatment for Contentment, Inner Happiness Treatment, Inner Peace Prayer Treatment, and more.

Chapter 15: Transforming the Planet

In Chapter 15, readers learn and use the following affirmations and prayers: Overcoming War, Overcoming Crime, Overcoming Injustice, Treatment to Restore Ecological Balance, Treatment to Save Endangered Habitats, Treatment to Save the Rain Forest, Treatment to Protect Endangered Species, Treatment to Maintain the Food

Jeff's Comments

⑪ I would merge everything from pages 19 to 30 to page 5, which is where the author begins to discuss her expertise and marketing capabilities. In today's marketplace, good content and expertise aren't more important than the author's unilateral ability to sell the book. In fact, editors will often want to know how powerful an author's self-marketing is before they begin to assess concept and content. It's much easier to attach good content to a proven self-marketer than the other way around.

Deb's Comments

Ⓜ I would prefer to see a more simplified or organized promotions section. The author explains what she has done in the past for her previous book. But I would like to see her create a simple plan for what she will do for this one. She might want to give the bottom-line results of what she did for the other book, but perhaps hide some of how she did it.

Then she could detail a plan of what she will do for this book to drive the sales. I would like to see a bulleted list of what she is willing to spend and on what. And I would like to

Supply, Treatment to Preserve Organic Foods, Treatment to Heal the Waters of the Earth, and more.

Chapter 16: Creating Heaven on Earth

In Chapter 16, readers learn and use the following affirmations and prayers: Planetary Well Being, Planetary Brotherhood and Sisterhood, Peace on Earth Treatment, Universal Love Prayer Treatment, Planetary Harmony Prayer Treatment, Cosmic Synchronicity Prayer Treatment, and more.

█ Promotions

Word-of-mouth should be regarded as an effective means of communicating the value of *Instant Healing* to its potential readers. From 1970 to 1971, and again from 1989 to the present, I have taught meditation on a grass roots level in many cities. From decades of learning, teaching, touring and promoting my seminars, I have found that centers and churches are continually looking for new speakers, especially authors and seminar leaders such as myself. With the book's publication, opportunities for publicity and direct sale will increase, and additional venues for promoting *Instant Healing* will open to me.

In addition to word-of-mouth, I intend to employ every other means that I can manage in order to publicize *Instant Healing*.

Public Speaking Appearances

The following is a sample of the venues that I can target for lectures and workshops. By requesting my itinerary for the past few years, you can see that I speak at many of these venues regularly:

1. The top Telesummit Series, including those offered by Darius Barazandeh (You Wealth series), Jeneth Blackert (New Wealth series), Lance Hood (Awakening series), and Jennifer McLean (Healing series). Although these Teleseminars sell downloadable products, I have found that hard copy book sales increase as a result.

2. Metaphysical churches, such as Unity, Religious Science, Science of Mind, Divine Science, and Spiritualist, and mainstream churches with an open philosophy.

3. Bookstores that offer lectures and book signings:

4. Spiritual self-help and adult education centers. Bookmarket.com offers a list of 125 such centers:

5. Residential spiritual retreat centers.

6. Public libraries.

7. College campus clubs that focus on metaphysics or self-improvement.

8. Educational institutions that offer metaphysics in their curriculum.

9. Yoga Conferences and expos.

10. Yoga Centers that invite guest speakers.

11. Metaphysical conferences.

12. New Thought Church Conferences.

13. Holistic health expos.

14. Spas and other health facilities that invite guest meditation teachers, authors, and workshop leaders.

15. Book Fairs.

16. Organizations that sponsor workshops and conferences in exotic locations throughout the world.

17. Cruise ship conferences emphasizing health or self-improvement, which invite authors to present lectures.

18. My own tours, retreats, and cruises offered by my own travel company at www.divinetravels.com.

Examples of my commitment to marketing my books through personal appearances:

- Since 1989, I have lived in a motor home so that I can travel and speak at expos, centers, churches, events, and conferences nationwide.

see the promotions broken into clear subtopics such as traditional publicity with bulleted points of what she will spend, then a separate list of what she will do. There is a difference between what you will spend and hire out and what you will do yourself. I found this list to be somewhat overwhelming. Rather than referring to the great expense she went to for other books, she can talk numbers and design a blueprint for what she will do for this one.

I would like to see online media separated from traditional promotions. She gives impressive numbers for her online presence, but I almost overlooked them because they were somewhat overwhelming. Remember to make it easy for your readers to find the key information and do not bog them down with things that may not be relevant. What you have done for another project is relevant in its results. Frame it in relation to what you will do for this project. You also might want to leave the impression that the other book achieved its success also because it is a good book. The combination of strong commitment and a good book are wonderful. This author has the chops, so there is no need to oversell.

- At my own great expense, I have rented and personally manned booths and gave workshops at over 100 expos, for many years, including Book Expo America, INATS show, and Whole Life Expos: Los Angeles, New York, Austin, Seattle, Denver, Las Vegas, Minneapolis, Atlanta, Chicago, Baltimore, Cleveland, Portland, Ft. Lauderdale, and San Francisco—and dozens of other expos that were not "Whole Life" brand.

- You may request my itinerary for a list of over 500 personal appearances made since my first book *Divine Revelation* was published.

Media and Internet Publicity

In conjunction with my publisher, I plan to book radio, television, and print interviews to promote *Instant Healing*. Below are some of the ways that I have proven my commitment to promoting my books:

I have advertised many times in the *Radio-TV Interview Report* magazine (circulation: 5000 radio and television talk show producers), published by Bradley Communications. Also, at my own expense, I subscribed to the RTIR *Book Marketing Update* newsletter, with hundreds of back issues now on my computer hard drive. This newsletter publishes insider media information of interest to potential guests or interviewees. In addition, I have used the "Publicity Blitz" database, published by Bradley Communications—a database of every form of media, including tens of thousands of newspapers, magazines, radio, and TV in the entire US. I have also used the special TV database from Bradley Communications.

At my own expense, in June, 2006, I attended the Author 101 University with Rick Frishman, Mark Victor Hansen, and others, and in October, 2006, I attended the No-B.S. Glazer-Kennedy Marking seminar with Dan Kennedy, Paul Hartunian, and others. Also, at my own expense, I took Yanik Silver's "Selling Your Book Online" class. I have already implemented many of the valuable suggestions that I learned at these seminars.

At my own great expense, in September, 2006, I attended Steve Harrison's National Publicity Summit in New York City, where I was trained to create the best hooks and pitches to promote my books, and I met top journalists and producers face-to-face. This valuable training has already resulted in greater publicity than I have ever had before, including an article in *Woman's World* magazine.

I obtained Alex Carroll's radio marketing package at radiopublicity. com, including a database of all the radio stations nationwide with an audience of 100,000 plus listeners. Using his excellent list, I did a very successful radio campaign that resulted in 35 interviews on drive-time shows in major markets. Also, Bacon's online media lists at medialistsonline.com can generate customized lists to order and execute an email campaign.

I have advertised in the *Yearbook of Authors and Experts* and on the Internet at guestfinder.com and bookwire.com. My itinerary is now posted and constantly updated on the Internet at doctorsusan.org.

All these valuable resources can be used to promote *Instant Healing*.

Internet

At great expense, I hired an Internet marketer to put together a joint venture Amazon.com campaign for the book *Ascension*. As a result, that book hit the best seller list, and my publisher sold hundreds of books during the campaign. I plan to hire Hasmark Services to do a similar campaign to promote *Instant Healing*.

I have over 60,000 total Twitter followers on two accounts, and that list is growing by leaps and bounds daily. I use Twitter and Facebook daily to promote my books and other products.

I have over 53,000 members that have opted-in with a cron program on my server called Email Marketer. I use that program on a regular basis to promote my books, products, retreats, cruises, and tours, and to notify my list of prayer circles, teleseminars, and webinars.

For many years, I have advertised on a pay-per-click basis on the web sites Overture and Google. I have sold thousands of products via my web site: doctorsusan.org, and I am the web designer as well as the webmaster.

In addition, there are hundreds of holistic health and conscious living newsletters on the Internet. I have sent out several solo email blasts using these opt-in lists. Such lists can be used to effectively market *Instant Healing*. There are many conscious living web sites on the Internet now, which will be valuable resources for marketing *Instant Healing*.

Internet News Groups

I have my own online Divine Revelation Yahoo Newsgroup with thousands of members. Also, I have often been a guest on the James Van Praagh newsgroup on their online chat forums. I plan to use these resources and to also seek additional newsgroups and chat forums in order to promote *Instant Healing*.

Outlets for Book Sales

Bookstores/Libraries/Churches/Centers

My book can be sold through approximately 15,000 self-improvement bookstores nationwide as well as the new-age or self-help departments of mainstream bookstores. I have personally compiled a valuable database of 1625 New Thought churches, most of which have bookstores. In 1998 I sent all the ministers of these churches a mailing with a reply card to promote *Divine Revelation*.

In 2003 and 2004 I again sent a mailing to ministers of 600 of these churches. Included in this mailing was a CD of a sample Sunday Service to promote my speaking engagements in churches. From 2003 to 2006, I sent hundreds of emails to ministers of New Thought churches to promote my workshops. These campaigns have proven very successful. Now that sample Sunday Service can be heard on my website at drsusan.org and susanshumsky.com.

In 2007, Celestial Arts and I collaborated to send a direct mail brochure "Minister's Guide to *Miracle Prayer*" and sample CD to promote *Miracle Prayer* to the top 250 New Thought ministers. A similar campaign can be done to promote *Instant Healing*.

At my own expense, I advertised *Divine Revelation* in *New Thought* (published by the International New Thought Alliance), read by ministers and book-buyers in these churches.

I participated several times in the *New Age Retailer* flyer program to publicize *Divine Revelation*. At that time, their mailing went to 5500 metaphysical bookstores. Currently, *New Age Retailer* has a flyer insert program to place in their magazine, which I plan to use to promote my books. In addition, I will consider sending a direct mailing to New Age and other independent bookstores in order to promote *Instant Healing*.

Distributors/Wholesalers

There are 1200 distributors and wholesalers of spiritual books listed at newagereseller.com and at pma-online.org. I personally arranged for many wholesalers and distributors to carry *Divine Revelation*, and I participated in the free flyer programs that some of them offered.

At my own expense, I arranged for *Divine Revelation* to be displayed by several distributors at the International New Age Trade Show in Denver in 1997. In addition, at my own expense, I took out separate full-page advertisements for *Divine Revelation* and for *Miracle Prayer* in DeVorss & Co. catalogs.

Reviewers/Trade Publications

Dan Poynter's parapublishing.com provides mailing lists of reviewers working with personal-growth publications. In 2001, I sent out an email invitation to editors and book reviewers in 185 new age magazines and newspapers, and as a result I received over 50 requests for review copies of *Exploring Meditation*. Also, articles about my books have been featured in the *New Age Retailer Magazine* and *Publishers Weekly*.

Mail Order Catalogs/Book Clubs

Dan Poynter's parapublishing.com lists 628 catalogs that carry books, and New Editions' *New Marketing Opportunities* listed 153 self-improvement book catalogs. *Divine Revelation* was offered in the Courage to Change catalog, the Bodhi Tree bookstore catalog, and others. *Divine Revelation* was selected by the One Spirt book club and was listed on the One Spirit top-ten list. *Miracle Prayer* was also selected by this book club.

Trade Shows/Sales Conferences

Here are examples of my commitment to promote my books at trade shows:

At my own great expense, I rented and personally manned booths at the following trades shows: In June, 1997 at the BEA—Book Expo America in Chicago in the Religious, Spiritual, Inspirational section and at the INATS—International New Age Trade Show in Denver. In 1996 at both the New Age World '96 in San Diego and INATS in Denver. In 1998 at the INATS in Denver and the BEA in Chicago in the NAPRA pavilion. In 2000 at the ESO-Fach trade show in

Baden-Baden, Germany. In addition, when I exhibited at INATS, at my own expense, I arranged for flyers to be placed in the Show Bag.

New Editions New Age Marketing Specialists and NAPRA used to offer national and international trade show representation services. At my own expense, I hired New Editions to represent my book *Divine Revelation* at the Frankfurt Book Fair in 1997 and 1998 and for the Denver INATS show in 1999 and 2000. Also at the London Holistic Trade Show in 1999. I also hired NAPRA to represent my book in 1999 at the BEA and INATS shows.

I arranged for many distributors to display my book *Divine Revelation* at their booths at the INATS in Denver in 1997. In 2003, at my own expense, I appeared at my publisher's booth at two INATS shows in Orlando and in Denver to promote and sign my books published by Career Press. Also, at my own expense, in 2004, 2006, 2007, 2008, 2009, and 2010, I appeared in Denver at the INATS show and signed autographs to promote my books. In addition, in 2003 and 2004, I promoted my books at my publisher's booth and did free readings at the booth as a promotional activity to attract retailers. I am always willing to appear at any trade show to promote my books, including *Instant Healing*.

Awards and Prizes

At my own expense, I entered *Miracle Prayer, Exploring Auras, Exploring Chakras, How to Hear the Voice of God*, and *Ascension* into the COVR Awards (Coalition of Visionary Retailers). I won awards for *Miracle Prayer, Exploring Chakras,* and *Ascension.*

Personal Sales

I plan to personally sell a substantial number of copies of the book in the following ways:

- Through an amazon.com Joint Venture program with Hasmark services.
- At my lectures, workshops, and seminars.
- At bookstore lectures and book signings.
- By personal contacts with retail book outlets.
- With a direct response print ad campaign.
- At holistic health expos, trade shows, and conferences.

- By taking orders from media publicity through my toll-free number.
- Through my website: doctorsusan.org.

Subsidiaries

Articles

The format of *Instant Healing* easily lends itself to excerpts for publication in holistic magazines or newspapers, because each chapter can be a stand-alone complete article on a different subject. After an article is printed, I can send copies to several other magazines that might seek permission to reprint it.

I sent a mailing with sample articles and a reply card to 250 new age publications to promote *Divine Revelation*. Dozens of articles, interviews, and reviews were published as a result, and responses still arrived over a year after I sent the mailing.

I sent an email prospect letter to New Age magazines to promote *Exploring Meditation*. As a result, over 50 copies of the book were requested by editors for review. As a result of efforts by my publisher, *Cosmopolitan* magazine wrote an article about *Exploring Meditation*.

In order to promote *Instant Healing* and my other books, I can send sample articles on a CD to my mailing list, which I have personally compiled, of about 600 New Age/New Thought magazines and newspapers. I also can target Dan Poynter's new age magazines and alternative newspaper lists, to be interviewed for articles or to submit articles, and thereby generate more publicity for my books.

Audio Rights

According to John Kremer, in the last ten years, audio publishing has outpaced book publishing in growth. Therefore, if *Instant Healing* is successful, then an audio book can be published. I have successfully self-published and sold many audio and video products at my personal appearances and through my web site.

Foreign Rights

Several of my books have been published overseas, and *Instant Healing* will not be an exception.

Deb's Comments

🅝 This section should be moved ahead of the promotions piece. If you think logically, identifying the market should come before you explain how you plan to reach it.

▌ Marketing 🅝

According to a report by Marketdata, there is a vast and growing $8.5 billion market for motivational "self-improvement" products, programs, or services that improve one physically, mentally, financially or spiritually, such as books, CDs, audiocassettes, infomercials, motivational speakers, videos, multi-media packages, public seminars, workshops, holistic institutes, personal coaching, and more.

Here are a few statistics about the MBS (Mind Body Spirit) market:

1. 25% of Americans regards meditation and spiritual pursuits vitally important and also accept the probability of psychic powers.

2. 69% of Americans agree that, "I feel the need to satisfy the spiritual hunger that is in me."

3. 61% of Americans are open to various ways of perceiving and experiencing the sacred in life, believe in psychic and spiritual events, think the divine is both in the world and also transcendent, and believe in developing more awareness.

4. Where the growth rate for the U.S. economy as a whole is 2-4% a year, many of the industries that serve the consciousness movement are growing at 10% to 20% a year. The size of the population they serve, and the money involved, is doubling every few years.

5. 10 million American adults now say they practice some form of meditation regularly, twice as many as a decade ago. Meditation classes today are being filled by mainstream Americans.

6. The National Institute of Health plans to spend $3.5 million over the next several years on "mind/body" medicine.

7. More than 70 of the United States' 125 medical schools—from Harvard to Stanford—offer specific courses in spirituality or incorporate the theme into the curriculum.

8. Yoga is a 3-billion dollar industry. 16.5 million people are practicing yoga, or 7.5 per cent of US adults.

9. Alternative medicine is an estimated 18 billion dollar industry. More people than ever are making their own health decisions, rather than following doctors with blind faith.

10. Spiritual and motivational "gurus" are a booming business. "Gurus" such as Tony Robbins are drawing huge audiences with incomes for their products generating as much as $80 million per year.

11. 17% of the total spoken audio market today is related to self-help/self-improvement topics.

12. 95 million visits are made to spas in the United States annually, generating $5 billion in revenues. The number of spas in the United States is growing at an annual rate of 21%.

13. 46 billion dollars are spent on the whole food and health industry, with a growth of 6.9% over previous year.

14. Alternative spirituality on college campuses is booming.

15. A growing number of brides and grooms are getting married by interfaith and non-denominational ministers in settings other than churches.

16. There is an unprecedented drop in the percentage of American adults who identify themselves as Christians.

17. Interest in New Age religion is growing rapidly. Wiccans are doubling in numbers about every 30 months.

18. Jewish mysticism and Kabbalah is a hot new trend.

19. TV shows and movies are increasingly based on spiritual themes.

20. Spirituality is booming on college campuses. The variety of alternative religious groups on campus is growing, especially Buddhism.

21. Americans spend $5.7 billion a year on yoga classes and products, including equipment, clothing, vacations and media (DVDs, videos, books and magazines)—an increase of 87% over the previous year—almost double of what was previously spent.

The Mind Body Spirit movement has grown steadily since the mid-1960s, when a revolutionary spiritual awakening began in the United States. It continues to attract followers, expanding to world-wide proportions. These are the main readers for whom *Instant Healing* is written.

My personal observation of this audience, acquired through over 40 years in this field, is that these seekers have a voracious appetite for spiritual knowledge. Their primary means of acquiring this knowledge is through 1) reading books, 2) attending workshops, seminars, expos, and conferences, 3) attending New Thought churches, 4) listening to paranormal radio or television shows, 5) traveling to spiritual tours and retreats. The large number of spiritual self-help books on the market reflects a hungry readership that buys an above-average number of books.

Every major city has a variety of highly active new-consciousness groups which can be reached through a loosely connected network of personal-growth centers and metaphysical churches, alternative magazines, newspapers, and bookstores, health food stores, and the self-help departments of mainstream bookstores. The tenets of this movement have a broad appeal to general audiences, as demonstrated by the great variety of metaphysical periodicals available today.

Self-development newspapers/resource guides in every major city of the United States are proof of widespread interest in spirituality. Churches with a metaphysical philosophy are growing at a rapid rate. I have personally compiled a current date base of about 1600 New Thought churches, which I have used to successfully promote my books, and I have spoken at hundreds of these churches.

Spirituality is no longer becoming mainstream; it has become mainstream. *Instant Healing* presents unique, esoteric wisdom and inspiration unavailable in other books in the human-potential marketplace. Its unique approach to spirituality is attractive to an already plentiful, loyal readership of spiritual books. But more than anything, the personal experiences of peace, comfort, and spiritual awakening provided by this book offer fulfillment for the nation's current hunger for spiritual experience.

Proposed Title:

READY-SET-GOAL

How Dreamers Become Achievers

By Dr. Theo Tsaousides

Neuropsychologist, Assistant Professor Mt. Sinai, NY

www.tsaousides.com

Neuropsychologist, Board Certified by the American Board of Professional Psychology Adjunct Assistant Professor, Icahn School of Medicine at Mount Sinai, New York

454 Manhattan Avenue—1L, New York, NY 10026

dr.theo@tsaousides.com | 917-626-6017 | www.tsaousides.com

Neuropsychologist, Board Certified by the American Board of Profes

Jeff's Comments

1 The author and I spent almost two weeks debating the working title. I don't recall what his suggested titles were, but none of them satisfied me. As is often the case, there are many books on his subject and he isn't a celebrity. Publishers tend to focus on what's missing before looking for what's there. If the project appears to be "more of the same" by someone without a huge fan base, the author has a big hole to climb out of before anyone even begins to read his proposal. But these things need to be seen as challenges to be preempted, not as unmovable obstacles. The first thing an editor sees is the proposed title. Therefore, the title needs to be as "wow!" as possible without being absurd. A strong title creates a positive perception and helps lessen whatever biases might be embedded in the reader. Of course, the title is likely to be changed by the publisher, which happened here.

Jeff's Comments

2 Though not mandatory, it never hurts to present a table of contents for the proposal. It lets the publisher know what's in the proposal and in what order without having to scroll through the entire document. Whatever makes it easier for the publisher is good for the author.

Deb's Comments

a This should be titled "Proposal Table of Contents" so as not to confuse the reader. That being said, it is a very good outline for the proposal. It looks well organized and completely thought out.

Jeff's Comments

3 I generally discourage long overviews because I think they usually should be a concise opening statement about the book's proposed concept, with the elaboration reserved for the chapter outline section. This preference may be a holdover my days in freshman English 101 (1977), when the professor insisted upon a brief "thesis statement" at the top of our writing assignments. This was known as the Baker Formula, and I have no idea

■ TABLE OF CONTENTS

◾ I. Proposal Overview

a. Opening Statement

As a neuropsychologist, my work involves observing, learning, and applying my knowledge to help people achieve their goals and improve their lives. Time and again I come face-to-face with the same type of clients: the people who feel stuck.

These are the people who talk a lot about how much they want to improve their lives, boost their productivity, make more money, get a big promotion, be more fit and healthy, fall in love, pursue their dreams, help others fulfill their dreams, or simply enjoy life more.

But soon after they state their intentions, they forget, they get stalled, or they give up. Year after year they state the same goals, they make the same promises, and they repeat the same excuses, but they see no results.

What is the cause of this malaise? Being inquisitive and introspective by nature and by nurture, I had to get to the bottom of this. I started looking for answers in my textbooks and diagnostic manuals, hoping I would find what was wrong. But nothing fit. The people I am describing aren't suffering from depression, they aren't psychotic, and they aren't addicted to anything harmful. They don't have health problems, they are not out of work, and they aren't lonely. But they are unhappy with their status quo. They just simply want more from life. **c**

This book was written to help all those people who are stuck wanting more and getting less from life. *Ready, Set, Goal!* is a book about the mental blocks to success. These blocks are mind-sets. They are habits. They are setbacks. And most importantly, they are failures in managing our own brains. The book is a guide to recognizing the warning signs and moving the mental blocks out of the way of success.

if it's still taught. Sorry to digress … I tolerated the expanded overview in this proposal because it worked, and the author broke it up into logical segments that were easy to grasp. Most important, the author proved that he had a lot to give and would be pouring it into his book. When writing a book proposal, orthodoxy can be superseded by whatever gets the job done.

Deb's Comments

b I am not sure what this is. An "opening statement" is usually something in a legal trial. It would be better to simply title this "Overview." An overview is a short summary of what the book is about with some supporting persuasion. Subtopics are fine, but every part of a proposal should be persuasive and every title should mean something.

c This statement would be more powerful if it clearly said how the author has solved the problem. Has the author found a way to remove mental blocks? It would strengthen this paragraph to also work in the author's background again to show its relevance to the solutions in the book. Doing this would further establish the author's authority.

b. Content Overview

i. The Problem

A World Without Success Stories

Success is probably one of the most coveted words in the English language. Despite its myriad definitions, success is something all people desire. It comes in many varieties. It can be small or big, daily or lifelong, material or spiritual, humble or grandiose, and noble or lowly. Regardless of its size, scope, or intention, success invariably starts with *setting* a goal and ends with *accomplishing* a goal. But the most important part of success is what lies between setting and achieving your goal. And that is *pursuing* a goal. That's what success is: deciding what you want (setting), working to get it done (pursuing), and watching it come into being (achieving).

There is a plethora of resources and countless experts out there all intended to inspire and teach people how to set and achieve goals. Books, videos, podcasts, blogs, webinars, live events, trainings, and coaching on anything imaginable, from how to be rich or healthy to how to be cool or sexy. There is something for everyone in the self-help buffet. The self-help industry is like the Costco of good advice.

Despite the abundance of resources, the truth is that most people *talk* about things they want in life, but relatively few actually *set* goals, and even fewer *achieve* them. The proportion of people who successfully achieve their goals is similar across different settings: a meager 10%. For example, studies have shown that among all people who set New Year's resolutions, only 8% will actually achieve them. Two months after the beginning of the year, most of them barely remember *what* their resolution was!

The same 10% success rate is evident in the self-help industry. While this industry generates billions of dollars annually from products and services, statistics show a dismal 10% success rate in terms of people achieving their goals.

Imagine the impact on society if only 10% of physicians, teachers, urban planners, business owners, or judges were able to achieved their goals. What would this low level of success rate mean for the health, education, livelihood, sustenance, and legal rights of the millions of people they serve? **d**

Deb's Comments

d Carefully read your proposal before sending it. This paragraph has a typo. It should be *achieve*, not *achieved*. Read it out loud if you have to. Or use a ruler to line edit the old-fashioned way.

e This is the crux of the book, but it is not a clear comparison. What is the difference between what physicians do and their life goals? Perhaps include a better contrast between doing one's job and setting a personal goal and achieving it. This section would be more persuasive if the agent or editor could see the definition of the problem the author is solving with the book. Doing that also pinpoints the market.

What if the life goals that people set had the same fate? What would life be like if they could only achieve 10% of what they hoped for? What if 9 out of 10 things they wished to accomplish never happened? My guess is that a 90% failure rate of achieving personal, professional, financial, academic, humanitarian, or any other type of goal would very quickly make this world a very depressive, pessimistic, and bitter place to live in.

The Tough Part of Success

There are armies of experts on multiple topics offering hundreds of methods for *setting* and *achieving* goals, with promises that range from getting things done to making dreams come true.

I am one of those experts. My job is to help people set and achieve goals. For that reason, I have a big investment in their success. I teach them a broad range of skills and strategies that they can use to achieve their goals. I make sure that the techniques I choose are tested and proven. Everything I do is based on science, backed by research, and used in many contexts, including businesses, organizations, medical settings, and schools. I even use them to achieve my own goals.

But the truth is that techniques alone don't work. Regardless of how effective we, the experts, claim them to be, and despite the number of testimonials we can provide to support the power of our methods, the reality is that a large number of people will continue to fail.

And they fail because the most important factor in any success equation is not the method, but the person who uses it. The key to success is what one *does* with what one knows. And what one *does* is entirely controlled by the person, not by the experts.

I have worked with hundreds of people with a wide range of goals. Some wanted to be more successful at work. Others wanted to be better at making decisions. Some wanted others to love them more. And others just wanted to be happier. What has always been true is that some of them are able to accomplish their goals quickly and others keep struggling. After many years of observing and learning, I made an important discovery. I figured out what's different about the 10% of achievers. It isn't the methods. It isn't their genes, or their personalities, or their education. It isn't their gender or their upbringing. It is a simple and observable characteristic: they take *action*. Achievers *pursue* their goals. They *work* toward what they want. They put effort.

Deb's Comments

f This is the second place where this author mentions how many people write or talk about this topic. This is unnecessary. This is the author's book, so the focus should be on what he is bringing to the literature, not on what other people have done. This comes off a bit like a defensive oversell. It is more powerful to state what you are doing rather than saying that you are writing something better than others before we truly know who you are and what you are writing about. Stay focused on what you are selling: your book.

g The overview of this book could have been much more succinct. This is getting close to the core statement of what the book is about. The hook is that the people who do something to achieve their success are the ones who succeed. The book is about the pursuit. I would recommend a much shorter statement of what the book is actually going to do. This is the proposal; it is not the book. You want to get right to the point so the agent or editor will want to learn how you will accomplish the promise you are making.

Setting a goal is fun and inspiring. It raises motivation, it improves mood, and it fosters optimism. *Achieving* a goal is rewarding and exciting. Seeing the results of one's labor generates a sense of satisfaction and fulfillment. But while the experts will demonstrate how to set goals and they will keep their clients' motivated by reminding them what it feels like to achieve their goals, no one talks much about the most effortful and mundane part of success: *pursuing* the goal.

Pursuing a goal refers to taking all the steps necessary to turn vision into reality. It refers to the little and big tasks that have to be done on a daily basis for a goal to be accomplished. It refers to the way in which an idea becomes a plan and a plan becomes action. It refers to implementation and execution. It refers to tracking progress and making adjustments to one's approach. *Pursuing* is taking action. And that's the part that the 90% of non-achievers flunk.

Action is the essential ingredient of success. Whether the goal is to lose weight, write a book, build a dream home, or find love, the only way to get there is by doing something. Any goal requires action. And action starts and stops in the brain.

How the Biggest Asset Can Become the Biggest Setback

Our brains are hardwired for success. They are designed to set, pursue, and achieve goals. They all come equipped with a set of mechanisms that enable it to do that. These mechanisms are called cognitive functions, and they are involved in receiving, storing, transforming, and using information from our internal and our external environment. For example, attention is the cognitive function involved in focusing us on what information is relevant to our goals at any given moment. Should I be listening to the conversation between those two lovebirds sitting at the table next to me or should I stay focused on finishing this paragraph?

Achieving success involves several cognitive functions. Our ability to set intentions, to envision the outcomes, to plan and strategize, to assess risk, to initiate our efforts, to keep track of our progress, to overcome obstacles, and to eventually celebrate our successes are all a result of our cognitive functions. And while all brains (h) come equipped with these functions, not everyone knows how they work or how to use them more efficiently. For example, all people are aware that they can remember things they learned in the past, and that the brain function responsible for storing that

Deb's Comments

(h) This is a very interesting explanation about cognitive functioning, but it would be more persuasive if it were connected to goal achievement. In my opinion this author is making the reader work a little too hard in making the connections.

information is called *memory*. They also know that sometimes their memory fails and they end up forgetting things.

Think about the last time you went grocery shopping. Do you remember which grocery store you went to? Do you remember how many items you bought? Do you remember what you were wearing? Do you remember the name of the person at the register? Do you remember how much you paid? Do you remember what song was playing as you were checking out? How many of these questions can you answer with 100% certainty? One? Two? All six of them?

Here is a challenge. Next time you go to the grocery store, try to remember the name of the grocery store, the number of items you buy, what clothes you have on, the name of the person at the register, the exact amount of money you paid, and what song is playing as check out. How many of these questions do you think you will be able to answer with 100% certainty this time? Clearly, you will remember more than before. What does that mean? That your memory function improved between visits to the grocery store? Doubtful. What it means is that you used your memory function—your brain's ability to store information—differently the second time, and as a result you were much more successful in retaining the information and answering the questions.

The same is true for all of the brain's cognitive functions. The more efficiently we use them, the better we are at accomplishing our goals. The less efficiently we use them, the lower our odds of success.

Brain Glitches: How Our Brains Undermine Our Success

Our brains are extremely efficient. But sometimes they misfire. Our cognitive functions are subject to glitches. These brain glitches block our thinking, and they affect how we pursue our goals. They affect our actions. They create confusion and congestion, and as a result we stop doing and we start drifting, stalling, or retracting. Our actions become purposeless and ineffective, and no longer serve our goals.

Brain glitches happen a lot. So often, in fact, that after a while, they not only distort our actions, but they affect the types of goals we set, the kinds of outcomes we expect, and even the way we think about ourselves and others. We begin attributing successes to good fortune, good genes, or good habits, and failures to bad luck, irreversible personality flaws, or poor habits.

What we need to recognize is that how we think and what we do starts and ends in the brain. Personality traits that we traditionally associate with stuckness, inefficiency, failure, and depression are nothing more than products of brain glitches, the consequences of inefficient use of our brains. Our brains create the mental blocks to success. And only our brains, or how we use them, can undo them. 🄸

Mental blocks are the enemy of action. They turn motivation to inertia, productive to busy, and dreamers to languishers. They cause an array of problems ranging from diminished productivity and strained relationships to serious clinical problems, like depression and anxiety. Slowly and systematically, they end up killing people's dreams.

ii. The Solution

Brain Management: Removing the Mental Blocks

We have the equipment and we have the abilities; now let's put them to use and smash our mental blocks. Our brains are powerful, and knowing how to manage them better will resolve a wide range of problems. 🄹

Brain management is the ability to use our cognitive functions in the best possible way and prevent the brain glitches from becoming mental blocks. Brain management is essential for success because it aligns our actions with our goals.

Brain management is made up of two parts: *awareness* and *engagement*. Awareness is *knowing* what the mental blocks are, what causes them, how they interfere with goal *pursuit*, and how to defeat them. Engagement is *doing* what we now know is necessary to develop new ways of thinking and acting and to be able to achieve any goal we set.

Awareness and engagement work synergistically. One cannot happen without the other. To get something done, we need to know what to do. And simply knowing what to do alone does not mean we will do it. Brain management is about turning knowledge into action. Knowing the brain's tricks allows us to actually *do* something differently. For example, if we know that we tend to procrastinate, we also know that we should start working on a project much sooner to avoid missing a deadline. But *knowing* that doesn't translate into starting to *work* on the project sooner. Procrastinators do not suffer from lack of awareness. They suffer from lack of engagement.

Awareness—what people need to know:

- what are the seven mental blocks to success
- what are the characteristic feelings, thoughts, and actions associated with each mental block
- what are the brain functions involved in goal-oriented action
- what are the brain glitches and how do they create setbacks
- what is the cost of not removing the mental blocks
- what are the best strategies to remove the mental blocks

Engagement—what people need to do:

- actively search for mental blocks in their actions, thoughts, and feelings
- recognize and label the mental block as soon as they identify it
- practice each strategy consistently until it becomes second nature
- track progress toward a goal

Given how fast the brain learns, brain management can quickly change the way people approach their goals, their work, and their entire life. However, here is an important disclaimer: even with good brain management, the brain glitches themselves can never be fully eliminated because they are generated by brain mechanisms with tremendous evolutionary value. They exist to protect us and to guarantee our survival. This is why the solution is *management*, and not once-and-for-all elimination. Management is about monitoring, adjustment, and progress. We will continue to feel insecure from time to time, we may put things off till the last minute for many "last minutes," and we may keep whining about our bad luck. Such slips are normal. Managing the brain glitches means catching ourselves in the act to prevent them from becoming mental blocks. Eliminating the brain glitches, on the other hand, is unrealistic and impractical.

Deb's Comments

Although this may not be the place for this information, it should have a bold subtopic heading, and instead of raising questions, use bulleted statements to match the second section on engagement.

Deb's Comments

 This seems like a restatement of what should be the overview. Or this should be the chapter summaries since it is discussing the structure of the book.

Jeff's Comments

 This is a unique segment that I encourage all authors to consider including. It's unusual for a nonfiction author to actually have a sequenced, strategic plan for structuring the chapters.

iii. The Strategies

How to Use This Book

Ready, Set, Goal! is a guide to removing the mental blocks and restoring goal-oriented action. To do that successfully, first readers need to learn to recognize the characteristic feelings, thoughts, and actions associated with each mental block. When they are able to recognize how the mental blocks appear and affect daily life, they will be able to remove them by applying specific strategies. Each chapter includes strategies to undo the brain glitches that cause the mental blocks and to unblock action. The techniques included make *awareness* easy and *engagement* even easier.

Each chapter is dedicated to one mental block. The order of the chapters is not random. They are sequenced in a way that reflects the order in which the mental blocks interfere with goal pursuit from start to finish. Some blocks prevent people from getting started and others prevent them from completing their work.

Readers could also opt to read the chapters out of sequence and focus on the mental block that identify as the biggest obstacle in their life. However, my recommendation is to read all chapters to facilitate awareness, especially since obstacles to goal pursuit may be well hidden.

Chapter Structure

Each chapter is divided into five different sections:

- The Confessional: In this section, I share my own and other people's stories and examples to demonstrate the effects of the mental blocks in action.

- Spotting the Symptoms: In this section, I include a description of each of the seven mental blocks in more depth, including the characteristic thoughts, feelings, and actions that it creates to make awareness easier.

- The Origins: In this section, I describe what causes the mental block, and how brain science and psychology explain the symptoms.

- The Side Effects: The mental blocks can have serious consequences for our physical, mental, emotional, and spiritual health. In this section, I describe the consequences of not managing the brain glitches.

- The Antidote: In this section, I present seven practical strategies for each mental block to help readers improve brain management and prevent the mental blocks from becoming permanent obstacles.

To facilitate engagement, in the Antidote section I included exercises to make implementation of the strategies in the readers' own lives easier.

c. Manuscript

i. Manuscript Status, Anticipated Length, Completion Date

The manuscript is nearly completed. It is approximately 50,000 words in length. At this time I am going through some final revisions and editing. I am including some additional information to illustrate some points better and adding illustrations. I expect that the final manuscript will be within that length and the final version will be available by the end of April 2014.

ii. Special Features

1. The Look

Ready, Set, Goal! How Dreamers Become Achievers is a guide and a resource. It is organized in a way that makes it easy to follow and locate the different sections. Each chapter is more or less autonomous. The strategy sections are very clearly marked, so readers can return to them to review them at any time. Bullet points, sidebars, and illustrations will be used throughout to summarize and emphasize the main points. I envision an elegant cover, like Dan Gilbert's *Stumbling on Happiness*. Similar to other books that combine research, science, and practical advice, I imagine a playful, inviting look to instill hope and optimism, and to suggest positive outcomes.

2. Illustrations

Graphic illustrations will capture many of the book's key concepts and serve as visual aides.

Jeff's Comments

5 This is information every interested publisher will want to know before making an offer, so there's no reason not to state it in the proposal. But remain flexible and remember that this kind of information won't be binding until it's stated in your contract.

6 When the author has a special vision for what the book should look or feel like, especially if it will help make the book more competitive, the proposal is the right place to present the vision. But be flexible; the publisher has primary discretion in this area. In many cases, the author cannot overrule a publisher's final decisions without actually terminating the contract.

Deb's Comments

m It is not really necessary to state all of this.

n The look of the book is not a necessary section. This is something established with the publisher. Only include it if it is something very unique.

Jeff's Comments

7 In today's climate, this is a possible trap. On one hand it shows that the author has the right ideas, but on the other hand, the author has not actually done any of this yet, so the publisher may not see this information as adding much value to the proposal.

8 Frankly, it's hard to screw up this section of the proposal, assuming that an obvious market actually exists for your product. So your first consideration needs to be: do no harm. In this case, the author presents a lucid and reaffirming explanation for why his subject is exceptionally ripe.

Deb's Comments

o This belongs under promotions rather in this section of the proposal.

p The book is about mental blocks so the author might have explained the market as people who procrastinate, are perfectionists, have low self-esteem, or any of the other factors standing in the way of success. This serves the purpose of restating the problems he is solving while establishing his market.

3. Integrated Workbook

As I mentioned already, each chapter in *Ready, Set, Goal!* concludes with an Antidote section, which functions as an integrated workbook for readers to begin applying the strategies to their personal lives.

4. Development of Online Community

My goal in the next few weeks is to create an online community using social media in order to promote the book and my work more broadly. The online community will serve several purposes. First, it will provide a venue for me to talk more about the book as well as book-related events, like publication dates, book signings, speaking engagements, and training workshops. Second, it will allow readers to interact with the author and with each other, ask questions, give feedback, share experiences, and make additional suggestions for removing the mental blocks. Third, there are a lot of ideas I haven't included in the book to keep the length manageable and the information easier to remember. This information can be shared in social media, as tips of the week, or newsletters and white papers. Finally, as I dabble more with the topic and learn more from my own research, I will continue to develop ideas and create concepts that I can share with readers and followers as an additional resource.

▌ II. The Market

a. Target Audience

According to a widely cited research study conducted by John Norcross at the University of Scranton, about 50% of Americans make New Year's resolutions. About half the population, on a day designated to set goals for the rest of the year, chooses to make a statement about something they would like to accomplish. These goals range from simple and specific aims like losing weight to more idiosyncratic and global visions like living a more fulfilling life. Excluding anyone under the age of 18, this implies that about 100 million people each year are making New Year's resolutions.

This percentage reflects the number of people who, either in jest or because of the tradition, set goals around New Year's. In reality, many more people state intentions about things they would like to accomplish, and not just on January 1, but throughout the year. Some of these goals are personal, some are professional, some aim to improve looks, and others aim to improve lives.

Based on statistics from the relevant studies, assuming that the percentage of people who *fail* to accomplish their goals is common across domains, this means that an estimated 90% of people will never meet their goals. Some of them will never see their ideas translated into action, some of them will be stalling indefinitely, some will be exhausted from being locked in an infinite loop, and others will simply fail.

These are the people who feel stuck. They are everywhere. I see them in my practice, I see them in my professional networks, and I see them in my social networks. They consist of both men and women. They include people in their most productive years, somewhere between 25 and 54. They are people who are either in need of or confronted with a big life transition, such as changing careers, relocating, graduating from school, starting a business, getting married, becoming a parent, or dealing with a health problem.

They read a lot of books and blogs, hoping to find the silver bullet. They attend live events and webinars. They watch YouTube videos and go to Meet-Ups hoping to be inspired. They take a lot of first steps, and very often. Just not second and third steps. They may seem busy, but they are not productive. But they are invested in their self-improvement. These are the people to whom the book will appeal the most.

Take two of my clients, for example. Both are in their 40s, with similar family backgrounds, unmarried, and both very smart, ambitious, and entrepreneurial. Because of unforeseen circumstances, both of them lost their jobs. They both came to see me to figure out what to do next in their lives. Both of them have big dreams about completely different things, and both were able to start working on their goals. However, as soon as I started working with them, I noticed a big difference. Jason started making progress toward his goal of starting his own home-based business immediately. Even though this was the first time he was venturing into something new and outside of his area of expertise, he was following the plan we laid out step by step and used the strategies I showed him consistently. We went over the brain glitches, and Jason became very mindful of when he was actually acting in ways that were blocking his own efforts to build his new business.

Jenna, on the other hand, had made very little progress toward her goals. Compared to Jason, she falls prey to the brain glitches and the mental blocks they create every single day. For example, she spends hours looking up unnecessary information on the Internet instead of writing articles for the newsletter she manages. When I make suggestions, she shuts them down by making grim predictions about future outcomes, and she rarely tries a new approach. We began focusing on one mental block at a time. We picked the one that we both thought she should challenge first: procrastination. She began applying the strategies, and low and behold, things were soon set in motion. What got her moving is that now she became mindful of her procrastination habits and she has strategies to help her get past them. We continue to work together, and hopefully soon she will be able to be much closer to her final goal of leading a not-for-profit organization.

b. Competition

Several books exist about how to achieve goals. For example, *Goals!: How to Get Everything You Want Faster Than You Ever Thought Was Possible* by Brian Tracy, *Beyond the To-Do List: Goals* by Erik Fisher and Jim Woods, *Making Ideas Happen: Overcoming the Obstacles Between Vision and Reality* by Scott Belsky, and the *Beginner's Guide to Goal Setting: How to Get Everything You Want* by Michael Dunar. These and many other books in this genre offer goal-setting techniques and suggestions that anyone could follow. For instance, similar to *Ready, Set, Goal!*, Scott Belsky's book emphasizes the fact that most creative ideas never materialize. He provides a framework for turning ideas into executable projects. He believes that the critical ingredients for the materializing of ideas are the quality of the ideas themselves, as well as organizational skills, community forces, and leadership capability. While this framework may indeed lead to success, it does not address the biggest factor in the equation of success: the mental blocks generated by the person himself or herself.

John Norcross's *Changeology: 5 Steps to Realizing your Goals and Resolutions* offers a 5-step method of self-change. To my knowledge, this is one of the few books in this genre written by a psychologist and based on scientific evidence, something that *Ready, Set, Goal!* aspires to as well. Just like *Ready, Set, Goal!*, Norcross focuses people

Jeff's Comments

9 The "Competition" section can be a throwaway, a neutral pro forma repeat of what can be easily discovered on Amazon. In this instance, the author has used the section to further prove his expertise and bona fides. He's not only aware of the other books, but he's read them and understands what they do and don't accomplish.

Deb's Comments

q This is an effective "Competition" section because he shows how these books support his own book.

on something that they would like to change about themselves. However, the target of change is usually a tangible behavior (e.g., exercising more or quitting smoking). *Ready, Set, Goal!*, in contrast, targets the mental blocks, the ways of thinking and being that are created by brain (mal)function and become permanent entries in one's behavioral repertoire. The goal is not just "follow this method and change one aspect" but "follow this method and learn how to change any aspect."

Great books written about habits share some relevance with *Ready, Set, Goal!* as well. The most famous in this category is Stephen Covey's *The 7 Habits of Highly Effective People*. This book is prescriptive and effective because it lays out what people need to do in order to get ahead. In a way, I see *Ready, Set, Goal!* as a juxtaposition to Covey's book, as it literally describes the 7 habits of *highly ineffective* people.

Finally, *The Power of Habit* by Charles Duhigg has done an amazing job highlighting the importance of habits and how habits are formed. This book provides a good foundation for *Ready, Set, Goal!*, as it demonstrates the mechanics of forming habits, and consequently the mechanics of un-forming them.

■ III. The Author: Theo Tsaousides

a. Biography

Theo Tsaousides is a neuropsychologist, clinical researcher, and more recently entrepreneur. His academic credentials include a Ph.D. in counseling psychology from the State University of New York in Albany and a postdoctoral fellowship in neuropsychology at the Icahn School of Medicine at Mount Sinai in New York (formerly Mount Sinai School of Medicine). He is board certified by the American Board of Professional Psychology.

From 2007 to 2013, Dr. Theo was an assistant professor at Mount Sinai where he served as a researcher, clinician, and educator. His work focused on improving the lives of people who suffered traumatic brain injuries (TBI). He has worked with hundreds of patients

Jeff's Comments

10 I usually suggest that the author's bio and self-promotional items appear in the beginning of the proposal because it might be what the publisher wants to see first before investing any attention into the body of the proposal. In this instance I did not enforce my preference because the author did a good job at embedding his specialness throughout the proposal without ever making it seem as if the book was an ego trip. And the author did a fine job presenting what is undeniably an admirable and impressive background.

Deb's Comments

r This should be called "About the Author," not "Biography." Otherwise this section is very impressive and relevant to the book.

with brain injuries and their families and participated in the research and development of innovative treatments to help people with brain injuries resume their lives.

Dr. Theo has published scientific articles in prestigious academic journals and has co-authored textbook chapters specializing in assessment and treatment after brain injury.

For example:

- His article titled "Cognitive Rehabilitation Following Traumatic Brain Injury: From Assessment to Treatment," published by the *Mount Sinai Journal of Medicine* (Wiley), is often cited as a comprehensive review of best practices in the field.

- His article "Familiarity and prevalence of Facebook use for social networking among individuals with traumatic brain injury," published by *Brain Injury* (Informa Healthcare), was one of the first studies on the use of social media by people with TBI.

- His article "Delivering Group Treatment Via Videoconference to Individuals with Traumatic Brain Injury: A Feasibility Study" is under review for publication in *Neuropsychological Rehabilitation* (Taylor & Francis). This paper describes the first study to date to investigate the delivery of group therapy online in any kind of clinical population

In addition, Dr. Theo has delivered numerous workshops and presentations for professional audiences nationally and internationally. Most recently:

- In August 2013, he delivered a training workshop for psychologists on Problem Solving and Emotion Management at the annual convention of the American Psychological Associations, one of the most highly attended trade conferences for psychologists.

- In October 2013, he delivered a training workshop for health care providers on Problem Solving and Emotion Management at a conference sponsored by Contemporary Forums, one of the largest organizations in medical training and continuing education.

Jeff's Comments

⓫ The author platform is where a lot of excellent books meet the guillotine ("Go to the door marked *Self-publishing*). But it doesn't have to be that way. This author is not a celebrity and cannot guarantee a bestseller, but he doesn't draw attention to those deficits. Instead, he promotes his strong standing within his professional communities and gives a decent impression that his peers will communally promote him and

- In September 2014, he will deliver a relationship-building workshop to individuals with traumatic brain injuries and their family members in Indianapolis, IN. The same workshop was delivered in September 2012 in Charlotte, NC, with great success.

Dr. Theo is a member of several professional organizations, including the American Psychological Association, which with 10,000 members is the largest professional organization in his field, and the International Neuropsychological Society, the largest international organization in his subspecialty. Dr. Theo has also served as a reviewer for two of the most prestigious journals in physical medicine and rehabilitation (*Journal of Head Trauma Rehabilitation* and *Archives of Physical Medicine and Rehabilitation*). In 2010, he received a $750,000 grant from the U.S. Department of Education to create and run a postdoctoral training program in neuropsychology and rehabilitation research at Mount Sinai. In 2012, his proposal for the online group study mentioned above was funded as part of a larger $4.5 million grant from the National Institute on Disability and Rehabilitation Research.

In May 2013, Dr. Theo left his full-time position at Mount Sinai to devote his time to his entrepreneurial activities, including building a marketing training program for mental health professionals, authoring his books, and developing a personal development company. He is currently in private practice in New York City and remains an adjunct assistant professor in the Department of Rehabilitation Medicine at Mount Sinai.

b. Platform

Because of my profession, a large portion of my platform consists of psychologists, researchers, and other health care providers. Through professional presentations and publications I have developed a large network of collaborators, with whom I continue to work on a variety of projects, including workshops, trainings, and program development. For example, I am a consultant for the Denver VA, the Alabama Vocational Rehabilitation Services, and the Indiana Rehabilitation Hospital. All my collaborators are providers in large health care systems. As soon as the book is in its final format, I will give them access to some of the content. These are professionals who could reach a very large number of people seeking services,

his book. He also alludes to his start-up business in a way that makes it sound very successful even though it barely existed as of the writing of the proposal.

Deb's Comments

S The author calls this a platform, but he also includes what he will do to promote the book. It might have been better to separate out the things that he would do to promote the book from the existing reach he had, which could have been put under a section called "Markets."

There are three things agents and editors want to know:

a. Market: What is the intended audience and is the author connected to it directly?

b. Platform: What is the author's existing reach and how many people already exist who will want to hear what the author has to say? This includes social media statistics if they are impressive as well as mailing lists and television or radio appearances.

c. Promotions and marketing: What will the author do to expand the platform and convert his reach into sales?

and who could benefit greatly from reading *Ready, Set, Goals!* since the book is targeting non-professionals and is not written in jargon.

I continue to be an adjunct faculty at Mount Sinai, and I also teach graduate classes at St. John's University in New York. Through the academic institution communication channels, a very large number of people will have access to information about the book and the author when the book is published. For example, Mount Sinai broadcasts a newsletter several times a week to over 10,000 employees each time a faculty or staff member publishes or makes an appearance in the news. This could include press, radio, or television. They provide a short description and a link to the interview website. This medium creates opportunities for putting information about the book in the hands of thousands of people.

Apropos, I submitted an advertisement in the *Radio and Television Interview Reporter* focused on the content of the book, which is scheduled to appear in February 2014 and run for six consecutive months. I have been receiving calls from radio producers to be interviewed as a guest on their show. I am hoping that these interviews will provide more opportunities for publicity for the book and the author.

I recently created a company, The LEAP Center, whose mission is to promote personal growth, successful performance, and emotional wellness. I have partnered with other psychologists and marketers in order to create seminars, training workshops, and coaching programs for broader audiences. As one of the first projects of The LEAP Center, I developed a training program for psychotherapists, which will allow me to reach and work more intimately with a large number of mental health professionals, with whom I am hoping to create strategic alliances. People in this group could include the book in their list of recommended readings for their clients.

The next step in my marketing plan is to begin reaching a broader audience through involvement in social media. I already have Facebook and Twitter accounts for The LEAP Center and will begin broadcasting soon. My plan is to write general interest articles on the content of the book as well as other projects created by The LEAP Center.

Finally, I frequently attend personal development trainings and events, which provide ample opportunities for networking and forming partnerships with other authors, speakers, and entrepreneurs.

For example, I am a member of Steve Harrison's Quantum Leap program, a program geared toward educating authors about publishing and publicity. I also regularly attend events by Peak Potentials, as well as Joel Roberts's Language of Impact trainings. In the last Joel Roberts event, I created a promotional video about the book.

IV. Chapter Summaries

a. Introduction

The introduction to *Ready, Set, Goals! How Dreamers Become Achievers* lays out the problem, the solution, and the strategies. The problem is that across different domains the success rate with respect to achieving one's goals is disappointingly low. This leaves many people feeling stuck and wanting more from life. This high failure rate has significant consequences for both the individual and society at large.

Success is defined as setting, pursuing, and achieving a goal. The most important variable in the success equation is the person him or herself. More specifically, the problems with goal achievement can be traced back to brain function. Our brain generates mental blocks because of our failure to utilize our cognitive functions efficiently.

Brain management is the solution to preventing the mental blocks from interfering with goal achievement. There are two aspects to brain management: awareness and engagement.

Awareness—what you need to know:

- what are the seven mental blocks to success
- what are the characteristic feelings, thoughts, and actions associated with each mental block
- what are the brain functions involved in goal-oriented action
- what are the brain glitches and how do they create setbacks for you

Jeff's Comments

12 These are fabulous chapter summaries in terms of content and style.

Deb's Comments

t The author has done a nice job with the chapter summaries. Each one is thought out and shows the structure. The agent or editor will know what to expect with the book.

- what is the cost of not removing the mental blocks

- what are the best strategies to remove the blocks

Engagement—you need to do:

- actively search for mental blocks in their actions, thoughts, and feelings

- recognize and label the mental block as soon as you identify it

- practice each strategy consistently until it becomes second nature

- track your progress toward a goal

The brain glitches that generate the mental blocks can never be fully eliminated. They are biological mechanisms that have existed for thousands of years. The goal is to manage them better. Management implies monitoring, adjustment, and progress. Elimination, on the other hand, is magical thinking!

Ready, Set, Goal! How Dreamers Become Achievers is a framework to enable you to catch yourself the very moment you experience the brain glitch by recognizing its characteristic feelings, thoughts, and actions. This book provides the language to make *awareness* easy, and the strategies to make *engagement* even easier.

Each chapter is dedicated to one mental block. You don't have to read the book in sequence, but instead you can focus on the mental block that you think applies the most to your life.

The chapters are divided into five different sections:

- The Confessional: in this section, I provide examples to illustrate how each mental block interferes with goal-oriented actions. I mostly use examples from my own life to demonstrate how small manifestations of the brain glitches have caused me big problems!

- Spotting the Symptoms: in this section, I describe each mental block in more depth, including its characteristic thoughts, feelings, and actions to make it easy to recognize.

- The Origins: in this section, I describe the explanation behind the mental block, including the brain glitches that create it.

- The Side Effects: in this section, I describe the consequences that each mental block has the potential to cause.

- The Antidote: in this section, I present seven practical strategies for each brain glitch to help you improve brain management and prevent the mental blocks from becoming permanent obstacles.

The chapters are arranged in the order in which the seven mental blocks interfere with action. First is self-doubt, which may lead to perpetual second-guessing and chronic inertia out of fear of failure. Second comes procrastination, which is the perennial postponement of getting things done. Self-doubt and procrastination are both *inhibitors* of starting action. Third is impatience, which is the impulsive and premature call to action before the ducks are properly lined up. Fourth is multitasking, the false belief that attention can be spread over many things at once. Impatience and multitasking both lead to *ineffective* action with *sloppy* results. Fifth in the sequence is rigidity, which is perverse persistence when change is what's needed. Sixth comes perfectionism, which is the obsessive fussing over unimportant details. Rigidity and perfectionism keep people busy and spinning in place with no tangible results. And finally, negativity is the seventh mental block, the inability to appreciate, to hope, and to let things go. Negativity has a destructive impact every step of the way.

Before you read further, take a minute and think about your most coveted goal, something that you have been yearning for a long time but haven't yet been able to accomplish. Maybe a rerun of a New Year's resolution. Maybe a stress-free life, a job you actually love, a talent you would like to develop further, a dream-trip you have always wanted to take, a canvas waiting for you to paint on, a poem waiting to be written, a beautiful flower waiting to be planted, a game your children are waiting for you to learn how to play, a parent who is hoping for forgiveness for deeds done in the past.

What is the reason these goals have not become reality yet? What actions do you need to take that you haven't taken yet? What actions have you taken that have not yielded results?

As you read the book, filter your thoughts and actions through each brain glitch. Learn how to catch yourself in the act of blocking action. Apply the strategies and decide which ones work better for you.

And make this the last year you have to set the same New Year's resolution ever!

b. Chapter 1: Self-Doubt: *Facing the Monster Within*

Self-doubt. A lack of conviction in yourself and your potential. Self-doubt is the most fundamental of the mental block because it strikes you on your foundation. It reflects your trust in your abilities and your core beliefs about yourself.

You are the center of your experience, the agent of your own change and evolution, the energy source that fuels your actions, and the vessel that will carry you to the finish line. Without you, there is no dream, no passion, no creativity, no ambition, no excitement, no movement, and no connection to others. Your self is the most constant and familiar entity in your life. You spend more time with yourself than with anyone else.

Can you even imagine the consequences of not having faith in yourself?

Self-doubt is the habitual second-guessing of one's abilities. Sometimes it is called lack of confidence, other times insecurity, self-consciousness, shyness, or low self-esteem. Regardless of the name it is given, self-doubt determines how big the goals we set are, how high we set the bar, and how far we want to reach.

The hallmark response typical of self-doubt is hesitating. Self-doubt is due to failure in emotion regulation. Deeply engrained in the most primitive part of our brain, self-doubt is the modern version of the fight-or-flight response. Dominated by fear, self-doubters neither fight nor flee. They freeze. Their bodies declare emergency and shut down while their minds swim in a pool of self-defeating thoughts.

The consequences of self-doubt can be enormous:

- Constant fear: self-doubters live in a perpetual state of fear, which makes them lose the ability to tell apart real from imaginary threats

- Stuck in the comfort zone: self-doubters have a lifelong membership in the comfort zone, which prevents them from learning and growing

- Shrinking dreams: out of fear of failure, self-doubters dream small and as a result end up achieving even smaller

- Zero-impact: without conviction, self-doubters become no one's role model, even if they have groundbreaking, world-changing ideas hidden in their heads

The last part of this chapter provides seven strategies to pave the way out of the stagnation that self-doubt brings about. The seven strategies aimed at building confidence and defeating self-doubt are:

- *Tout your own horn*: readers will learn how to uncover and appreciate their strengths through written exercises

- *Face the monster*: knowing what we are afraid of makes the fear dissipate. This strategy will help readers identify which of the five types fears that psychologists have discovered is making them "freeze" and holds them back. Is it fear of extinction, fear of mutilation, fear of loss of autonomy, fear of social isolation, or fear of loss of their individuality?

- *If you don't know it, learn it*: one of the main reasons for lacking confidence is because of gaps in our knowledge. Knowing what we don't know is good, but learning what we don't know is better.

- *Practice makes better*: while the saying that practice makes *perfect* may not always hold, practice makes *better* is absolutely guaranteed.

- *Model the ones who can*: seeing others succeed in what we hope to accomplish is a significant confidence booster. Finding the right role models is crucial for defeating self-doubt.

- *Stay away from naysayers*: there is nothing worse than being surrounded by others, whose own negativity fuels the self-doubter's fears.

- *Talk the talk, walk the walk*: sometimes we have to fake it! Research shows that positioning our bodies in ways that exude confidence plays tricks on our minds, which in turn starts generating confidence.

■ Sample Chapter

Chapter 1

Mental Block #1

Self-Doubt: Facing the Monster Within

To accomplish any goal it is very important that you have faith in your ability to succeed. You must believe that you can pull it off, that you have what it takes to make it happen. You must be confident that even if you fall, you will get up and keep going. You must not be afraid of the unknown, you must not be afraid of failure, you must not be afraid of hard work and trying over. But sometimes the brain glitches let fear slip through. And then a big, dark shadow is cast upon you.

Self-doubt. A lack of conviction in yourself and your potential. Self-doubt is the most fundamental of the mental blocks, because it strikes you to your core. It is a reflection of how much you trust in your abilities and what you truly believe about yourself.

You know yourself better than anyone else you know or anyone else knows you. You are the center of your experience, the agent of your own change and evolution, the energy source that fuels your actions, and the vessel that will carry you to the finish line. Without *you*, there is no dream, no passion, no creativity, no ambition, no excitement, no movement, no connection to others.

Can you say with conviction that you are able to achieve your wildest dreams? To handle the biggest challenges? To push your limits and keep growing every day? To be fearless within reason? If you find yourself hesitating even a little to answer yes to these questions, then keep reading.

The Confessional

I have done a lot of writing over the years. Between papers, theses and dissertation in my school life, and textbook chapters, scientific articles, treatment manuals, and grant proposals in my professional life, I must have written thousands of pages and millions of words.

For each piece of writing there were different "gatekeepers," who had to approve the fruits of my writing labor. My college professors had to grade my papers to determine whether I should continue my academic pursuits. In graduate school, my dissertation committee (a group of three professors whose job is to read your dissertation— a very long thesis—tell you everything that's wrong with it and give you impossible deadlines to fix your mistakes) had to approve my project so I could graduate and move on with my life. Editors had to review my chapters and articles, to decide whether they were worthy enough to include in their books and journals. And a group of impossible to please people had to review my grants, to decide if the government should fund my projects! Objectively speaking, I had been doing pretty well. Passed my classes in college, finished my dissertation, published a few pieces of scientific writing, and even got some federal funding!

A few years ago, I felt it was time to share my ideas and expertise with a broader audience. I wanted to write a book to communicate those ideas with people outside my restricted professional circle. And I wrote and wrote and wrote. But I wasn't broadcasting anything. Multiple files of text lived in well-organized folders on my hard drive but never left those folders. At the slightest chance to show my writings to anyone, I hesitated. Something was blocking me. A voice in my head, a derisive hiss, kept repeating in a stern tone: "Who cares about what you write!"

When that voice makes an appearance in my head, it resonates inside my entire skull. It fills every curve and corner in my brain. Like a force majeure, it sweeps away all other thoughts, it stifles my creativity, and it amplifies other similar messages lurking in the shadows of my cortex. And the self-beating fest begins: no one will buy your book, you're wasting your time, stick to what you know, you'll be rejected before you even get published, your friends will feel sorry for you, your colleagues will laugh at you, you will join the ranks of worst-selling authors.

In the last six years I have had many book ideas. I remember very well the first time that I was struck with a book idea that I thought was decent. It was New Year's of 2008. I woke up dizzy after an evening of festivities at a rotating restaurant in one of Europe's tallest building. I don't know whether I was dizzy because of the sweet but strong German wine from the night before or because the restaurant floor kept going around and around for 4 hours. But I do know that as soon as I opened my eyes…it was there! The book idea! The topic that I should write about! I knew exactly what I wanted to say and why, and I believed strongly that other people should hear about it as well. New Year's resolution 2008.

Then the voices started singing in my head. Am I really the best person to write this book? If it is such a great idea why hasn't someone else written about it? What if no one cares about this as much as I do? Why would people even buy a book like this?

The voices slowed me down and instead of filling pages, I was filling my time with the things that I could do best: procrastinate (you will learn all about this mental block later in the book). I put off my dream of writing a book and hesitated to pick it up again. I occasionally jotted down an idea or two in my notebook or updated the table of contents of a book that wasn't being written. And the voice in my head kept shouting that I could never write a helpful and interesting book.

That's self-doubt.

PROPOSAL 4

Proposed Title:

Crazies at the Counter

Real-World Customer Service Techniques from the Retail Front Lines

By Adam Toporek

- Customer Experience Strategist **b**
- Recognized expert in customer experience and customer service
- Founder of CTS Service Solutions and of the leading website Customers That Stick™ (www.customersthatstick.com)
- Consultant, speaker, franchise developer, and retail business owner
- BBA/MBA
- Member CXPA and Global CX Panel

Adam Toporek
CTS Service Solutions
283 Crane's Roost Boulevard, Suite 111
Altamonte Springs, FL 32701
adam@customersthatstick.com
customersthatstick.com

Jeff's Comments

1 I like this title because for me it was vivid and funny, and I thought it captured the stress retailers must feel.

Deb's Comments

a I really like the title. It could also have been shortened to *Crazies at the Counter: Customer Service Techniques from the Retail Front Lines*. I prefer an economy of words when possible.

b This is a nice idea for the cover. These bullets show the author's credentials in an easy-to-digest snapshot.

Jeff's Comments

 This isn't the TOC for the manuscript; it's for this proposal. I encourage this because it helps organize and orient the editor, who will be reading your proposal along with a hundred others during any given week.

 Because the title also essentially clarifies the target markets, I'm fine with including that information in the overview section. This section runs a little long by including several descriptive segments, but because it gets the job done, I allowed it to stay as-is.

Deb's Comments

 This is a good structure for the proposal. I like the idea of naming the first section "Overview and Audience" as it is easy for people to be confused between market and marketing. One is the potential audience, and the other is how you will reach it. This solves this problem. This proposal table of contents is very simple and clear. This won't work for all proposals, but it is always better to go for clarity rather than grandiosity. This author gets right to the information needed by agents or editors so they can make their decision.

Table of Contents

Overview and Audience

Category: Business > Customer Service

Word Count: 35,000–45,000

Estimated Manuscript Completion: June 1, 2014

One of the great myths of retail customer service is that bad service exists because employees are lazy, uncaring, and unfeeling. My experience in managing and owning a business with customer-facing employees presents a different picture. A great deal of bad customer service comes from well-meaning employees who want to do a good job. They simply lack the confidence, tools, and training they need to succeed in the challenging reality of frontline customer service.

I have often wanted to hand my employees a guide that would tell them how to be great at customer service and give them the tools they need to deliver exceptional customer experiences, a book that I could hand to them with confidence, knowing it was teaching them not only the skills they needed to succeed with customers but also the mindset they needed to be great employees. I wanted a book that went beyond basic procedures and pat advice and that would help them successfully address the challenges they faced day-to-day on the front lines, but that book did not exist.

Some books had good information but read more like workbooks. Others had a better approach but dealt with narrowly focused topics such as difficult customers or helpful phrases. Few seemed to talk in a straightforward, relatable way about the experiences frontline employees had in the real world.

Crazies at the Counter is designed to be that book.

Crazies at the Counter shows frontline employees how to succeed and grow in their positions. It will give them the mindset and techniques to start each shift knowing they can handle not only the daily operations but also the crazy, unexpected situations and customers that can derail even the best operations.   **e**

The book differs from competitive books on the market in that it offers better explanations for why certain customer service techniques and procedures are important and shows how to implement those techniques and procedures during day-to-day life   **f** on the front lines.

It's also important to understand who these employees, the potential readers of this book, are. Frontline service jobs are heavily staffed by younger workers, which today means the millennial generation. Millennials learn differently. Their brains have been conditioned for fast, instant information. They want answers quickly, and they do not want to hear how it was done "back in the day."

Crazies at the Counter delivers on both points. First, it is a book about the experiences frontline employees have day to day. Some customer service books treat the front lines like a peaceful fantasyland where, once in a while, there is a problem. Such messages have little credibility with frontline employees because this is not how the frontline operates. The frontline is the real world, not a fantasyland, and frontline employees want to know about what works in that world.

Deb's Comments

d There are differing opinions on this. I prefer to leave out when the book can be completed as this is something negotiable. If the book is available upon request and is complete, you can indicate this.

e The author changes from what the book does to what it will do. I prefer to be consistent and to always speak of the book as if it already exists; for example, "It gives them the mindset" rather than "it will give them." As the author, you want to speak from authority.

f This would be better in the competition section. In the overview you should be focused on what the book does. It should be very concise. The author does a good job with that, but I believe it could have been even more organized, and a shorter version would have been equally effective. The overview is just that. It is meant to give a brief snapshot of what the book is about and what is in it for the publisher and reader. More than that dilutes the effectiveness. I would have liked to have seen an anecdote of a "front line" story. That would have been stronger than a discussion of how the book differs.

Second, the book is easily accessible to millenials. It uses short chapters, a conversational tone, anecdotes, bullets, and call outs to make the information easy to digest and retain. Research or statistics are presented in a sentence or two instead of a paragraph or two. *Crazies at the Counter* gets to the point at once and only once; it does not find six ways to say the same thing. **g**

Crazies at the Counter teaches frontline employees what they want to know about their jobs in a way that makes it easy for them to learn. More importantly, it tells them the why and how behind specific techniques and procedures.

Owners and Managers Need a Simple Solution

The recession changed organizations in a seemingly permanent way. Companies that downsized are, in many cases, not returning to their pre-2008 staffing levels. Companies have seen margins grow and have learned to do more with less. Lean is sticking, and frontline teams are more stressed than ever.

In many cases, frontline service employees have fewer resources and less help to do their jobs. Worse, these reductions in staff create a vicious cycle—fewer staff means more customer service issues, which takes more staff time, which in turn creates more customer service issues. Reduced resources and smaller teams are making frontline employee jobs more challenging and less pleasant.

Executives and managers understand the importance of great customer service to bottom line results, especially in this new reality, but often do not have the budget or time for complicated solutions. They do not need another flavor-of-the-month customer service initiative that will have their employees rolling their eyes and that will wear off after a few weeks. They need a tool that will help them provide sustainable change quickly, efficiently, and cost effectively.

Crazies at the Counter gives them this tool. The book is specifically designed to function as both a primary and an adjunct text. Organizations with frontline teams can use it either as a standalone training tool or as part of a more formal training program. In larger companies with well-developed training processes, the book will help tell the customer service "story" with a new voice. In smaller organizations, the book can serve as the basis for workshops or new customer service training programs.

How The Book Works

The techniques in this book have been honed over decades in business, including over eight years owning a retail business and directly engaging with hundreds of employees, as well as coaching and overseeing a regional franchise network consisting of over 500 frontline employees.

The book is set up in a topical format. Related topics are grouped together to aid in learning and to facilitate the book being used as a reference tool once it has been read.

The book includes nine basic sections.

1. **Great Service Is All in Your Head** sets the stage for the entire book. Frontline employees are shown the ways their own mindsets hold them back from providing great customer service.

2. **The Mind of the Modern Customer** gives employees a glimpse into the expectations and predilections of the modern customer. This section helps employees understand the various ways customers are already preconditioned for a bad experience.

3. **The Seven Service Triggers** explores seven automatic triggers that are responsible for any customer situation taking a negative turn. Employees are taught how to preempt many common customer service issues by proactively avoiding these triggers.

4. **Be a Great Teammate** helps employees understand how their actions impact not only the organization but also their fellow teammates. It walks employees through the basic concepts they need to know to be a valuable part of a frontline team.

5. **Own The Service Floor** focuses on the relationship between day-to-day procedures and the delivery of great service. This section gives employees not only the basic tools they need every day on the service floor but also shows how preparation and proactive effort can create positive customer experiences and preempt bad ones.

6. **Killer Communication Skills** discusses why great communication is at the heart of great service. This section takes an 80/20 approach to customer communication by exploring the verbal skills most frontline employees will need to succeed in their jobs.

Deb's Comments

h Explaining how the book works could have been put in a separate section. Also, buried in the previous paragraph is a good statement that could have been the first line of the overview: "*Crazies at the Counter* is an entertaining and practical training tool for all organizations with a frontline team. Customer Service employees will feel as if they are swapping stories with the only people who truly understand." Always make it clear what the takeaway is for the end user.

i The author is describing how the techniques were derived, but this information should be included in the "About the Author" section instead. Here the discussion is "what are the techniques?"

j This should be titled "Book Structure" or have its own heading. For this type of book it is a good choice on the part of the author to include a reference to the actual book at this stage of the proposal. He has anticipated that the reader of the proposal is likely thinking, *So what is the book?* The information given here is well structured and clear. The author will expand on this in the chapter outline.

Jeff's Comments

④ This bio section is okay. While doing no harm, it has room for improvement. The first thing a publisher wants to know is how many copies the author will sell. For that reason, it often makes sense to "show the money" right away and reinforce it wherever it's relevant. In this instance, I would begin the section by discussing and expounding on the author's websites, blogging velocity, and speaking schedule, to be followed by his credentials.

Deb's Comments

Ⓚ This would be a good place to put the paragraph about how the techniques in the book were derived. The "About the Author" section is not supposed to be a resume. You should use this section to show why you are the appropriate author for the book. Then you should add what you bring to the table in authority and potential platform. This is an author overview, so it should be focused. All parts of a proposal can be entertaining as well, so if the author has his own tale from the trenches it would be fine to include it here.

7. **Those Difficult Situations** dives into the challenging situations that frontline employees deal with every day. This section teaches general principles for dealing with difficult customer issues and shares specific, actionable techniques that can be used in almost any customer service situation.

8. *Crazies at the Counter* tackles the rare situations that leave frontline employees shaken and drained—dealing with crazy customers. Employees are shown how to address unreasonable and irrational customers, how to deal with customer threats, and how to keep it all in perspective.

9. **Your Customer Service Experience** wraps up the book, reiterating the messages learned and inspiring frontline employees to do their best every day.

The sections above illustrate an easy-to-digest, relatable, and actionable customer service book based on the realities of the retail environment. It is what managers and executives need to create well-trained, motivated teams on their own front lines and is what frontline employees need to be successful in their jobs.

About the Author

Adam Toporek is a Customer Experience Strategist and founder of CTS Service Solutions, a customer experience consultancy that helps organizations deliver Hero-Class™ Customer Service through scalable and effective real-world solutions.

Adam has worked deeply in the franchise and retail spaces for the past eight years as a Regional Developer and franchisee for Massage Envy Spa and as a former Area Developer and franchisee for European Wax Center.

Adam's educational background includes a Bachelors of Business Administration from the University of Georgia and a Masters of Business Administration from the University of North Carolina at Charlotte.

As a third-generation retailer and entrepreneur, Adam understands what it means to be face-to-face with customers and the crucial role that the customer experience plays in making organizations profitable and sustainable.

His philosophy of customer experience design and training can be best summed up by his belief that stories are for inspiration, systems are for execution.

Adam has built upon this philosophy, his education, and his experience to become a respected expert in the customer experience and customer service spaces.

Adam is a member of the Customer Experience Professionals Association (CXPA) and part of the Global CX Panel.

Adam is also the founder and principal author of the Customers That Stick™ website. Customers That Stick™ (CTS) is one of the world's most popular resources on the topics of customer experience and customer service. CTS is designed to provide an in-depth resource for all levels of management and frontline employees who are interested in customer service and the customer experience.

Customers That Stick™ publishes two original posts per week. CTS also frequently publishes articles written by guest authors from a variety of specialties and professions.

CTS publishes and shares content across numerous channels including Twitter, Facebook, Google +, YouTube, and SlideShare. Readers and influencers regularly share the content on social media.

CTS also regularly records and publishes video interviews with online influencers and customer service experts like Jeannie Walters, Richard Shapiro, Kate Nasser, John DiJulius (author of *Secret Service: Systems That Deliver Unforgettable Customer Service*), and Matthew Dixon (coauthor of The *Effortless Experience*).

Adam's writing has appeared on popular blogs such as *Spin Sucks, Grow, Velaro, Waxing UnLyrical, Inkling Media, Blue Kite Marketing*, and *Decide 2 Do* blog. CTS is syndicated on *CustomerThink*, a global online community of business leaders focused on the customer experience.

Adam has been interviewed or quoted in the following media: WORL 660 AM, Mix 105.1 FM, WKMG Local 6 (CBS), FOX 35 Orlando, The Daily Buzz (national), Orlando Business Journal, Quintessential Careers, and ISO & Agent.

Jeff's Comments

5 This section could have dug a little deeper by referencing several more pertinent titles and explaining the differences from the proposed work. The expansion would reinforce the real-time vibrancy of the market for these books while giving the author an opportunity to show off his knowledge about what's missing and what works.

Deb's Comments

1 This first paragraph is a bit unclear. Isn't this book also for executives and managers who may use it in their training programs? It might have been better for the author to simply list comparative titles that support the market for the book. After reading the competition, I am less clear about what the book is and what it is not. The purpose of the competition section is not to show that your book is better but rather to show that there is room in the market for your book.

■ The Competition **5**

Most customer service books are written for executives and managers. Those customer service books that have specific frontline application seem to fall into two categories: books that focus heavily on anecdotes and theory and technique-oriented books that read like workbooks.

Crazies at the Counter blends these approaches by focusing on usable, real-world customer service techniques in a readable, relatable style that can be used by executives and managers for training programs and read by frontline employees. The book employs a short chapter style, an attention-getting title, and a straightforward, real-world approach.

Crazies at the Counter would fit in a publisher's catalog most comfortably next to Jeffery Gitomer's book *Customer Satisfaction is Worthless, Customer Loyalty is Priceless*. Gitomer focuses on frontline customer service and uses short chapters, forceful prose, and creative formatting to get his points across.

Aside from Gitomer's work, three other titles are most directly competitive:

- *Customer Service Training 101: Quick and Easy Techniques That Get Great Results* by Renee Evenson. (Amacom, 2011. Paperback: $14.93). This book focuses heavily on customer service basics. It has solid content but reads like a workbook.

- *The Customer Service Survival Kit: What to Say to Defuse Even the Worst Customer Situations* by Richard S. Gallagher. (Amacom, 2013. Paperback: $12.97). This book is closer in style and format to *Crazies at the Counter* but is limited to only handling tough customer situations.

- *Smile: Sell More with Amazing Customer Service* by Kirt Manecke. (Solid Press, LLC, 2013. Paperback: $12.18). This book discusses customer service and sales best practices for customer-facing professionals. This is the most directly competitive title and appears to have been self-published.

The customer service book market is crowded and vibrant. Corporate America needs a book written explicitly for modern frontline employees, and it needs to be written without fluff and filler. In the customer service space, *Crazies at the Counter* fills a gap that is not wide but is deep.

Marketing and Promotion ⑥

Crazies at the Counter is positioned strongly for both the retail and corporate markets. I plan to use my existing platform as the basis for an aggressive online campaign and accompany it with traditional publicity through a professional publicist. I will also pursue a focused strategy of corporate outreach using speaking, workshops, and conferences.

The Platform

Having numerous friends and colleagues who are both bloggers and published authors, I understand how to create a multi-channel ⓝ approach to online book publicity.

I have been blogging continuously for almost three years. Customers That Stick™ is syndicated with average monthly traffic between 10,000 and 16,000 (7k-9k direct, 3k-7k via syndication).

I also have a strong, professionally managed social media presence:

- 4,000 Twitter followers
- 1,800 Facebook fans
- 1,000 email subscribers
- 600 Google+ circles
- 400 LinkedIn connections

I have been building relationships through blogging, social media, and in-person contact and have established a wide network of online and customer service influencers who will extend the reach of my platform and provide a rich resource for high quality book blurbs.

Jeff's Comments

⑥ I would combine this section with the author biography section. The platform description is straightforward and has strong potential, but fails to show any kind of guaranteed track record. This may be impossible since the author has no traditional publishing track record to brag about.

Deb's Comments

ⓜ I would not point out that the market for this book is crowded but rather focus on the merits of this one. It also sounds negative to label other content as fluff and filler. I always recommend pointing out your strengths rather than another book's weaknesses. From the title I am expecting a book that shows me the worst customer service challenges and how to effectively solve them. I want stories. In this paragraph I am left feeling that those might be fluff and filler.

ⓝ I don't recommend referring to friends and colleagues as part of your platform. It dilutes your strength. You can name key influencers who will support your project. Otherwise it is too tenuous a connection. The blog is a strong statement.

Jeff's Comments

 Having a specific retail sales strategy is innovative and a smart idea, especially since publishers still rely on traditional retail distribution. Of course, none of his promised tactics guarantee results, but they do show that he understands what needs to be done to get results, and that he's eager to do what's required.

8 Like above, it's smart to make corporate sales a distinct focus here because it can be a very profitable channel for publishers of business books. Though the author doesn't go into much detail, he shows that his head is in the right place.

Deb's Comments

o This is a strong statement of potential special sales. The agent or editor can interpret this in terms of numbers. This is always a plus.

Retail Strategy

Retail customers will be targeted through a blended campaign that includes online marketing and traditional publicity.

The retail strategy will employ the following online tactics:

- Use the blog to build anticipation and buzz through teaser posts about the book's progress.

- Employ social media channels and email list for direct book promotion and outreach, using contests and other engagement strategies.

- Create a keyword-targeted infographic outlining key points from the book.

- Design a SlideShare presentation focused on a specific topic from the book.

- Produce a number of YouTube videos designed to spark conversation and buzz.

- Write a number of topical guest posts and leverage my existing network of bloggers and influencers to place them on targeted blogs.

I am developing a series of free webinars to build interest, and the first webinar based on a section from *Crazies at the Counter* is already in motion. This free, live webinar, *Mastering the 7 Service Triggers*, is scheduled for January 9, 2014. The webinar will build early excitement for the book within my community and will serve as a "test run" so that I can hone the marketing and content approach prior to any launch campaign.

Corporate Strategy **8**

The corporate market is a strong opportunity for marketing book sales in large quantities, and I will be pursuing numerous opportunities both pre- and post-publication to set the stage for bulk corporate sales.

I will be rolling out a customer experience workshop designed to help business owners and managers. This workshop will serve as a platform for hyping the book, building my list, and creating

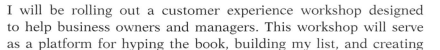

opportunities for the future sale of frontline-oriented workshops based on the book. I will be launching this workshop in Q1 2014 beginning in the Southeast.

I will also begin securing speaking opportunities and building my speaker's kit in Q1 2014.

Customers That Stick™ is a media sponsor for the 2014 XYZ Customer Experience conference in San Diego. This conference is a high quality, high-ticket event designed for C-suite executives from Fortune 500 companies—the perfect target audience for potential bulk sales.

As a result of this media sponsorship, I will be included on the XYZ website, in the conference program, and in emails to the attendees. I will also have a flyer distributed at the conference and am able to deliver a white paper or similar document to the attendees.

These activities will present incredible opportunities for brand building, marketing the workshops, and building buzz for the book.

Book Blurbs

I have developed a list of customer experience experts and online influencers I believe would agree to write book blurbs for *Crazies at the Counter*. Most are colleagues; some are friends.

Because the manuscript is not complete, I have not approached these individuals yet; however, I can give a fair estimation of the likelihood of receiving a blurb from the following individuals.

Very Likely

Fairly Likely

Personal Commitment

I am committed to publishing and marketing this book. I believe in the message of *Crazies at the Counter*, and I believe in the results organizations can achieve by putting this book in the hands of their frontline employees.

My belief and commitment are proven by my work. I have been building my platform consistently for the past three years and have blogged consistently at least weekly or bi-weekly for that entire period.

Jeff's Comments

9 Blurbs can add important energy to sales, so it's smart to specifically promise to get as many effective blurbs as possible by naming the persons you will reach out to. Simply stating the names of people you will contact doesn't bind you or them to actually providing the blurb. Many names were listed here in the actual proposal but were deleted upon the author's request.

10 I have never seen a distinct "Personal Commitment" statement in a proposal before, probably because it can be seen as self-evident by virtue of the fact that the author has gone to the effort of generating the proposal. But I liked seeing it here because it's an original tactic and reflects a positive humility, and it also implies that the author knows it's "on him" to make the book succeed.

My willingness to invest in this book's success has already been demonstrated by my investment in Steve Harrison's Publishing and Publicity Workshop, and my commitment only begins there.

I am willing to travel for book events and signings and will actively pursue interview opportunities, which means relentlessly seeking out media opportunities over a sustained period with targeted pitches and using each successful media exposure to create momentum for the next one. I am also willing to invest funds in a professional publicist.

With the right distribution mechanism behind me, I will make sales happen.

Jeff's Comments

11 Even though it's not long, this is an effective outline because it breaks up each chapter up tiny sound bites that illustrate a "feel-able" thought or concept. The author provided several completed chapters in a partial manuscript, so a more elaborate outline wasn't necessary.

■ Outline

The first draft of *Crazies at the Counter* is about 30 percent complete, and many of the chapters are either drafted or outlined. While changes will occur during the writing process, the outline is representative of the structure and content of the final manuscript.

The chapters in boldface indicate sample chapters included in this proposal to demonstrate how the individual chapters fit into the book's larger structure.

- Introduction
- Are Customers Really Crazy?
- Why Hero-Class™ Customer Service Matters
- Before We Get Started

- SECTION 1: GREAT SERVICE IS ALL IN YOUR HEAD

  - Customer Service Is Not a Two-Way Street
  - How Do You View Your Customers?
  - Viewing Complaints as Gifts
  - Do You Know Your Mental Rules?
  - Be Proud, Then Swallow Your Pride
  - Are You Renting Customers Space in Your Head?
  - It's True: Your Attitude Does Determine Your Altitude

- SECTION 2: THE MIND OF THE MODERN CUSTOMER
  - The Customer's Mental Rules
  - Everyone is Rushed, Everyone is Stressed
  - You Don't Know Your Customer's Story
  - Seek First to Understand
  - Everyone's Been Burned Before

- SECTION 3: THE SEVEN SERVICE TRIGGERS
  - Service Trigger #1: Being Ignored
  - Service Trigger #2: Being Abandoned
  - Service Trigger #3: Being Hassled
  - Service Trigger #4: Being Faced with Incompetence
  - Service Trigger #5: Being Shuffled
  - Service Trigger #6: Being Powerless
  - Service Trigger #7: Being Disrespected
  - Putting the Safety On: Put Yourself in Your Customer's Shoes

- SECTION 4: BE A GREAT TEAMMATE
  - It's Showtime
  - ABP
  - Rise Above, Don't Stoop Down
  - The Opening Shift
  - The Closing Shift
  - 5 Reasons Documentation Matters, A Lot
  - Document Quickly or Document Poorly, Your Choice
  - When to Help a Coworker Struggling with a Customer
  - When Your Manager Says No

- SECTION 5: OWN THE SERVICE FLOOR
  - First Impressions
  - The 10 & 5 Rule
  - How Are You Today?
  - I'm Just Browsing

Sample Chapters (excerpt)

Introduction

My father, who used a successful retail career to become a wholesale distribution entrepreneur, bestowed a few nuggets of business wisdom upon me as I was growing up:

- "A computer person who understands business is worth his weight in gold,"

- "Payroll always comes first," and

- "Never go into retail."

If you are reading this book, you probably understand why he made the last comment.

Retail is a different kind of animal.

If you work in retail, you know what it's like to work short two people, be sold out of the hot sale item, and be slammed ten minutes before closing. You know what it is to be screamed at by a customer for something you did not do, cannot control, and are not empowered to fix.

You also know what it is like to help a customer find just the right gift, assist a new teammate in learning the ropes, and celebrate the joys of a successful promotion. You know what it's like to think outside of the box to find a solution for the customer or to keep the store open five extra minutes to help a desperate customer.

Sometimes, you even know what it's like to change someone's life for the better.

To be successful in this topsy-turvy world of frontline customer service, you have to be able to handle the highs and lows, the joy and stress, and the gratification and fear that comes from interacting with the public each day. This ability requires a very particular set of skills, skills that you can either hone over a long career or can learn through proper tools and training.

If you are like the hundreds of frontline employees I've worked with over the years, the customer service training you have received in the past did not prepare you for the realities of frontline customer service.

I wrote *Crazies at the Counter* to do just that. This book will give you the mindset and the tools to not just survive but to thrive on the front lines of retail.

This book is about customer service in the real world.

Crazies at the Counter moves beyond hollow sound bytes and empty slogans to provide you with tested techniques that work. I can tell you to delight your customers until I'm blue in the face. You're going to look at me and say, "That's nice. Tell me how to do it when I have three lines on hold and Jenny is late coming back from lunch — again."

I've had hundreds of frontline employees look me in the eye and ask me questions just like that. They deserved a better answer than "go the extra mile for the customer," and so do you.

While I was writing this book, I struck up a conversation with a gentleman at a conference. He was a frontline employee, just like you, and when I told him what my book was about, he said, "Oh boy, the world needs that book. I hope everyone reads it. Now, let me ask you a question, 'What do you think of the phrase the customer is always right?'"

I was a little surprised by the question, but I just smiled and said, "I think it's idiotic. Customers are often wrong, sometimes dead wrong."

When I told this gentleman that I was writing a book on customer service, his first question to me had nothing to do with what the book was about or whom it was written for. His first question was about one of the most famous (and infamous) customer service phrases ever.

Why? Because like most people in frontline service, he had been taught a lot of empty phrases that never connected to the reality he faced every day at his job.

Unfortunately, slogans and catchy phrases are often used in customer service as a replacement for actual training and tools. Not all of these phrases are bad; they're just incomplete.

- Service is not something you do. It is something you are.

- Touch a customer's heart, and you touch their wallet.

- When complaints go down, satisfaction goes up.

- A great customer experience is the best form of marketing.

- Service is not something you do; it is something you are.

I agree with the sentiment behind every one of the phrases above, and I share ideas like them regularly on social media. They are great conversation starters and excellent for inspiration. None of them are substitutes for real training and techniques.

When it comes to frontline customer service, I have my own saying:

Slogans are for inspiration; training is for results.

Proposed Title:

WHETHER YOU FEEL LIKE IT OR NOT ❶ ⓐ

How To Make Yourself Do All The Unexciting Things It Takes To Run A Business

By Steve Levinson, Ph.D. and Chris Cooper

Steve Levinson
27405 110th Avenue Northwest
Newfolden, MN 56738
Phone: 218-681-6033
Fax: 651-967-0021
email: slevinson@habitchange.com
http://habitchange.com

Chris Cooper
Newtown Cottage
Botcheston Road
Newtown Unthank
Leicestershire LE9 9FB
Phone: 0845 683 6653
http://bemoreachievemore.com

Jeff's Comments

❶ This working title grabbed my attention. It seemed to reflect my inner voice, that hectoring drone that strains to discipline and hassle me about the invariable cascade of tasks and obligations that forms everyone's existence. How could I not pay attention?

Deb's Comments

ⓐ Although the title is long, I like it. It seems like a fresh take on books for business people. Entrepreneurs especially are often creative and not enthralled with methodical details. This pulls me in from the start.

Jeff's Comments

❷ I generally recommend generating a paginated TOC for the proposal. Anything that helps the editor navigate your proposal will help you.

❸ On a scale of 1 to 10, I give this overview a 10. Why? Because it introduces the essence of the book without taxing my intellect.

Deb's Comments

ⓑ I really like the first line. It is clever, to the point, and captures the essence of the book in an entertaining way.

ⓒ This would be a good place to mention the title and what it does, not what it will do. It also might be better not to limit it to the self-employed. There are people running businesses in upper management who face the same issues. While this is a primary market, it is not the only market for this book.

▮▮ Contents   ❷

▮▮ Overview

If you run your own business, you probably have a lot on your plate. Unfortunately, much of it isn't all that appetizing. Running a business takes more than just doing things you're eager to do. It also takes doing things you really don't feel much like doing. You may truly *intend* to do all the unexciting things that matter to your business, but do you actually follow through? If you don't, you're robbing your business of potential. You could even cause your business to fail.

The purpose of this book is to teach small business owners how to consistently transform their own good intentions into action so they can achieve greater business success. The book will:

- Show readers why the ability to follow through is vital to business success

- Explain why poor follow through is the inevitable result of the way the human mind treats good intentions and the ineffective way business owners think about their own good intentions

- Introduce readers to a new way of approaching their own good intentions

- Teach readers simple but powerful follow through principles and strategies that they can begin using immediately

This will be a very concise, easy reading how-to book that immediately taps into the experience of self-employed individuals, who every day are faced with business chores they don't feel like doing and therefore often neglect. The book respects the realities of readers by promising not to become another chore. Its short length and design will immediately tell the reader "We're going to make it easy for you to solve a big problem." **c**

Market

The primary audience for this book is self-employed individuals who run their own business. Given that there are over twenty million sole proprietorships in the U.S. alone, the potential market is quite large.

We believe that the book will appeal particularly to hands-on business owners who must wear many hats and who lack the formal structure of a job to *force* them to follow through in doing the many unexciting things they know they should do to make their businesses as successful as possible. Included are people who operate full-time or part-time home-based businesses, independent professionals, and those who are thinking about or preparing to someday start their own business. A possible secondary market may be intrapreneurs and others who are not self-employed but who enjoy a high degree of autonomy as employees.

Although the concepts, principles and strategies we will teach can benefit anyone who faces follow through challenges, we are targeting self-employed individuals because they are especially susceptible to follow through problems and they stand to gain a great a deal from learning how to do a better job of following through.

The many business owners we know and have worked with can readily relate to the problem the book promises to solve. Although

Jeff's Comments

4 This is good and it's good enough. Could it have been better? Yes. The authors put themselves in a box by suggesting that the self-employed are the only market segment for the book, and there's no reason to do that. For sure they are probably the primary customers, but you don't have to be self-employed to have a problem doing the things you'd rather not. It would have been easy for the authors to open up the envelope a little by including everyone who works, and even people who don't have a job but have a lot to do in their personal lives.

Deb's Comments

d At this stage in describing the market I would recommend that the authors interject why they know these things. Where are they getting their information? Every section of a proposal is an opportunity to persuade. Even though they list their degrees on the cover page, in the business world it is better to support credentials with direct relevance to the subject matter.

they may come across as ambitious and optimistic, they are troubled by their tendency to avoid and neglect doing the unexciting *uphill* things they know they should be doing—and truly intend to be doing—to achieve their business goals.

Jeff's Comments

❺ The competition section is relatively unimportant, but it is mandatory. If done right, it's an opportunity for authors to show off their knowledge about what's happening in their field while promoting the perception that they are meaningfully distinctive. There are several potential problems with the way the authors handle it here. More titles should be referenced, and those that are listed are old, obscure, and/or unsuccessful. In the first paragraph the authors claim that there are very few books like the one they propose. However, I think they are being too narrow about what *similar* means. There have been many books about overcoming such common maladies as procrastination and lack of motivation. Those kinds of self-help books could arguably be within this book's market spectrum.

Competition

There are many books that promise to help business people become more productive and effective. However, none that we're aware of tap directly into the common experience of self-employed individuals who every day rob themselves of success and satisfaction because they struggle—and often fail—to do things they know they should be doing but simply don't feel like doing. What's more, none of these books promise to teach solutions that are based on the realization that, in light of the way the human mind is designed, you essentially have to *trick yourself* into following through.

Relevant popular titles include:

EAT THAT FROG: 21 GREAT WAYS TO STOP PROCRASTINATING AND GET MORE DONE IN LESS TIME by Brian Tracy

Paperback: 128 pages
Publisher: Berrett-Koehler Publishers; 2nd edition (January 1, 2007)
Language: English
ISBN-10: 1576754227
ISBN-13: 978-1576754221

This 128 page book has sold nearly a half million copies. It promises to teach readers effective personal time management practices.

GETTING THINGS DONE by David Allen

Paperback: 288 pages
Publisher: Penguin Books; First Thus edition (December 31, 2002)
Language: English
ISBN-10: 0142000280
ISBN-13: 978-0142000281

This extremely popular book promises to teach readers how to achieve the clear mind and organized thoughts that the author believes contribute to productivity.

18 MINUTES: FIND YOUR FOCUS, MASTER DISTRACTION, AND GET THE RIGHT THINGS DONE by Peter Bregman

Paperback: 288 pages
Publisher: Business Plus; Reprint edition (September 11, 2012)
Language: English
ISBN-10: 9780446583404
ISBN-13: 978-0446583404

The book promises to teach readers how to maximize efficiency in a world filled with distractions.

THE FOLLOW-THROUGH FACTOR: GETTING FROM DOUBT TO DONE by Gene C. Hayden

Paperback: 256 pages
Publisher: McClelland & Stewart (December 28, 2010)
Language: English
ISBN-10: 0771038178
ISBN-13: 978-0771038174

 This book, which seems to preach more than it actually teaches, promises to teach readers how to set priorities and make commitments.

Authors

The authors are well-versed in the subject matter of this book.

Steve Levinson, Ph.D. is a licensed clinical psychologist who specializes in helping people follow through on their own good intentions. An internationally-recognized expert on the topic of following through, he developed a breakthrough theory that explains why even the most motivated people often fail to follow through on their own good intentions. He was the principal author of *Following Through: A Revolutionary New Model for Finishing Whatever You Start,* which was co-authored by peak performance business consultant Pete Greider and published by Kensington Books in 1998. A second edition of *Following Through,* published by Unlimited Publishers LLC in 2007,

Deb's Comments

e My personal preference is not to tear down other books to support your own. The competition or comparative titles are intended to show where your book belongs and that there is a market. You want to distinguish yourself in a positive way by saying something like, "Our book goes beyond by providing …" If you are sure of your niche and added value to the literature, it will show in a clear statement.

f The authors have very impressive and relevant credentials. The first author has developed the breakthrough theory used for this new application to business. The second author is a living example that the theory works. To strengthen this proposal, I would have recommended working that in right in the overview and then repeating it in the "About the Author" section. Keep in mind the question the agent and editor are asking themselves while reading the proposal: *Who are these authors and why should we listen to them?* Use what you have whenever you can to bolster your credibility.

Jeff's Comments

6 I have no objections to the way this section appears.

is still in print (ISBN-10: 1588321797, ISBN-13: 978-1588321794). Although *Following Through* was not intended to appeal primarily to a business audience, it continues to garner praise from business experts and has become "required reading" for executives of companies like Northwest Mutual Insurance.

Levinson is also the inventor of an electronic device called the MotivAider® that helps users make desired changes in their own behavior and habits, and cofounder and president of Behavioral Dynamics, Inc., the company that developed, manufactures and distributes the MotivAider® and supports its users in over fifty countries.

More information about Levinson and his work on the topic of following through is available at http://habitchange.com/levinson.pdf.

Chris Cooper is as an executive mentor and coach, facilitator/trainer, consultant and keynote speaker who has personally used and benefitted from the principles and strategies revealed in this book. Cooper, who's based in the United Kingdom, created and hosts what may well be the world's most listened to internet radio show for entrepreneurs and business leaders. *Be More. Achieve More. Inspiration for the Entrepreneurial Mind* is accessed up to 100,000 times a month from over 50 countries. (http://www.voiceamerica.com/show/1959/be-more-achieve-more.)

A regular media contributor and regional president of the Professional Speaking Association (UK), Cooper speaks on the topic of following through at events and conferences. He is a true entrepreneur who went from executive positions with Rank Xerox, United Biscuits, Mars, and Punch to start and grow his own now-thriving business, which focuses on talent development and business elevation.

More information about Cooper is available at http://bemore-achievemore.com/about-chris-cooper.aspx

Promotion

Steve Levinson and Chris Cooper are well-positioned to promote the proposed book.

Jeff's Comments

7 This section is dangerously weak and reflects that the authors are unaware of what publishers clamor for from their authors. Fortunately, the authors have a lot more to say about their self-promotional possibilities, so what's here is used as a starting point.

Deb's Comments

g When you include a promotions section, you want to make sure that the agent or editor sees potential sales figures. It would be wise to reiterate here the direct promotions that can occur through the co-author's radio show. Sometimes proposals are divided among several people on an editorial committee, so it is worthwhile to mention the promotions in two separate places so it is noticed. In addition, the foreword is a bonus here because it translates into real, although potential, numbers. It would be good to indicate where they are in the stage of acquiring the foreword and how they are connected to the person they are seeking the foreword from.

Levinson

Dr. Levinson writes articles, does interviews and makes presentations that convey in a compelling and down-to-earth way why even the most motivated people often do a lousy job of following through.

His company's website, http://habitchange.com, which has an entire section devoted to following through, attracts businesspeople and others eager to learn how to turn their intentions into action.

Cooper

Cooper is a natural networker who has lots of high profile contacts in the world of business. In addition to promoting the book directly to a large radio audience made up mostly of business owners, he potentially has access to the networks of the more than a hundred well-known business experts who have already been guests on his show.

Further Promotional Help

Dr. Ivan Misner has tentatively agreed to write a foreword. Dr. Misner is founder and chairman of Business Networking International (BNI), the largest business networking organization in the world. BNI has over 150,000 members and made more than seven million business referrals last year. Dr. Misner's complete bio is at http://ivanmisner.com/bio/.

■ Specifications and Delivery

Specifications

We envision a visually appealing book that by virtue of its short length and design immediately conveys to prospective readers that this will be an easy read. We estimate 150 pages including 6–12 simple black and white cartoons that tap into the experience of readers and echo and reinforce the book's key points (example below), callouts, quotes, and suggested reader exercises (all

Jeff's Comments

8 It is important for the authors to disclose their vision for the book because it strays from what's considered ordinary. If the proposed book doesn't fit average parameters in terms of length, format, graphics, etc., you need to clearly explain what your expectations are at the outset. And you might want to consider how flexible you are; the further a book is from what's standard practice, the more potential there is for rejection. On the other hand, proposing an unusual format might be exactly what the doctor ordered, especially if the subject is exceptionally cluttered with look-alike books.

pending). We expect final word count to be 25,000 words or less. Again, we believe that containing less rather than more text will send the right message to the intended audience.

THE TASK I MUST UNDERTAKE IS TOWERING OVER ME LIKE A GREAT BIG MONOLITH

IT IS TOO BIG TO CONTEMPLATE, SO I THINK I WILL GO AND HAVE A LITTLE LOOK AT THE INTERNET

weblogcartoons.com

Jeff's Comments

 It's not mandatory to state this information in the proposal, though since it will certainly be one of the first questions any interested publisher will ask, there's no reason not to address it in the proposal, assuming you already have the answer.

Delivery 9

First drafts of the introduction and all sixteen chapters have already been written. In sixty days or less, we can make improvements to material that's already been drafted, identify callouts and quotes, prepare suggested exercises, and identify existing cartoons or prepare specifications for simple custom cartoons.

Contents of the Proposed Book

Jeff's Comments

10 This TOC is redundant since the following outline pages repeat it verbatim.

Deb's Comments

h This is a very clear and well-thought-out table of contents. You can visualize the book through the way this is structured.

Jeff's Comments

 This is an excellent outline section with just enough commentary for each chapter. Brevity was called for since a large chuck of the manuscript was available.

Deb's Comments

 Although sometimes you can use actual material from the book, these summaries do the job of explaining the chapters without being too cursory.

▪ Chapter Summaries

INTRODUCTION

We begin with a clear statement of the book's purpose, which is to teach readers how to improve their ability to follow through so they can achieve greater business success. We then set the reader's expectations: "This is not going to be one of those feel-good books that pump sunshine up your butt."

Chapter 1: How Poor Follow Through Can Literally Kill Your Business

In this chapter, we first define poor follow as "the failure to actually do something you've determined you *could* do, concluded you *should* do, and decided you *will* do to make your business as successful as possible." We then show readers how they pose a threat to their own business by failing to consistently follow through in doing the unexciting *uphill* tasks that readers know they should be doing.

Chapter 2: The Benefits of Exceptional Follow Through

In this chapter, we show readers how the ability to consistently transform their good intentions into action can contribute to extraordinary business success. We describe exceptional follow through as having no success-wasting *dead space* between *decision* and *action*.

Chapter 3: Why Business Owners Need Help Following Through

In this chapter, we explain why business owners are especially susceptible to follow through problems despite–or to some degree, because of–their ambition. We show readers how, ironically, the relative absence of the kind of *follow through infrastructure* that employees hate makes it far harder for self-employed individuals to follow through.

Chapter 4: It's Not Your Fault! Meet the Surprising Root Cause of Poor Follow Through

In this important chapter, we give readers some good news: Their follow through failures are not exactly their fault! The root cause of poor follow through is the lousy way the human mind is *wired* to treat good intentions. We argue that recognizing this fact is an important step in learning how to follow through despite the faulty wiring.

Chapter 5: Take Your Intentions Seriously

In this chapter, we show readers how to make their intentions more effective by taking them more seriously. We teach them how to adopt *serviceable* good intentions and how to feel more accountable for behaving in accord with them.

Chapter 6: News Flash: Intentions Are Not Self-Implementing!

In this chapter, we urge readers to set aside the sadly mistaken belief that truly good intentions will implement themselves. We use the alarm clock as a model to illustrate why it's necessary for readers to make sure that they'll be *forced* to behave in accord with their intentions.

Chapter 7: Principle 1: Stay Focused on Your Intentions

In this chapter, we teach readers that intentions are only effective when they're at the top of the mind, and unfortunately, they don't stay there on their own. Readers must therefore find ways to keep their attention focused on their good intentions.

Chapter 8: Principle 2: Don't Rely Unnecessarily on Willpower

In this chapter, we teach readers that it's foolish and unnecessary to rely primarily on willpower to get uphill tasks done. Instead, we urge readers to *leverage* their willpower by using situations to do the heavy lifting.

Chapter 9: Principle 3: Make It Feel like You *Must* Follow Through

In this chapter, we teach readers that a key to following through is to make following through actually *feel* necessary.

Chapter 10: Put Yourself in a Jam

In the book's longest chapter, we use lots of examples to illustrate the various tricks readers can use to push, prod, and force themselves to do what they know they should do.

Chapter 11: Outsmart Temptation

In this chapter, we teach readers that the smartest way to deal with temptation is to create circumstances that make it as difficult as necessary to actually do what they're tempted to do.

Chapter 12: Create Intention-Rousing Cues

In this chapter, we teach readers how to create and use cues or prompts that keep their intentions (and the motives that support them) on *the front burner,* which is where they must be to be effective.

Chapter 13: Detoxify Dreaded Tasks

In this chapter, we teach readers how they can pave the way to tackle an important but unpleasant business chore by first stripping the chore of all its unpleasantness and committing only to doing what's left.

Chapter 14: Don't Hesitate to Pay for Follow Through

In this chapter, we urge readers to not overlook the possibility of paying for a service that makes them feel accountable for following through.

Chapter 15: Stay on Top of Your Intentions

In this chapter, we show readers how to set up a simple system for keeping track of their intentions and their progress in implementing them.

Chapter 16: Never Ever Expect to Follow Through Automatically

In this last chapter, we reinforce the idea that following through must always be a deliberate *manual* process rather than one that readers can expect to happen automatically. The chapter ends with a checklist of new enlightened beliefs about what it really takes to follow through.

■ Sample Chapters

CHAPTER 4

It's Not Your Fault! Meet the Surprising Root Cause of Poor Follow Through

QUOTE

We have some good news for you. Believe it or not, poor follow through isn't exactly your fault.

Forget for a moment that you're a business owner. As a human being, you're largely off the hook for not following through. That's right, poor follow through is caused primarily by the mixed-up way the normal human mind treats good intentions.

You see, although we tend to worship the human mind because of its awesome capabilities, it doesn't do everything right. In fact, when it comes to equipping us to follow through on our good intentions, the mind is actually an abysmal *engineering* failure.

Obviously, we humans have an extraordinary ability to use intelligence to figure out what we must do to get whatever we want and need. We can intelligently decide, for example, to forgo an immediate pleasure or perform an unpleasant task *now* in order to achieve an important benefit later on. But, amazingly, our intelligent decisions do not *automatically* drive our behavior. The same impressive mind that so beautifully enables us to figure out what we must do to succeed, doesn't automatically require us to behave in accord with our intelligent decisions. In fact, to make matters worse, our behavior is often easily influenced by forces that couldn't care less what we've intelligently decided.

Because our behavior isn't *hard-wired* to our intentions, we can—and often do—intelligently *decide* precisely what we should do and then do something far less intelligent instead.

Your intentions don't really drive your behavior

You can intelligently decide, for example, to spend Saturday afternoon tidying up your desk so you can find things more easily, be more productive and thereby be more successful. Your intention, however, will not automatically drive you to tidy up your desk. It won't even make you feel like tidying up your desk. In fact, you may feel strongly like **NOT** tidying up your desk or feel strongly like watching a sporting event on television. What's more, those strong feelings are likely to influence your behavior more than your intention will. In other words, although your intention represents an intelligent decision about what's in your best interest, it simply will not force you to act in accord with it.

Yes, if you look at how the mind actually works instead of how we think it *should* work, you'll see that it's wired to give grease to the squeakiest wheels—not the smartest wheels, which are your intentions.

When faced with the prospect of cleaning your messy desk, there's a good chance that the feeling of wanting to avoid a burdensome task or of wanting to do something fun instead will simply *outsqueak* your good intention. Again, it doesn't matter that what gets the grease is dumb, short-sighted and runs counter to your ambitions.

It's tempting to assume that your extraordinary passion and enthusiasm for your entrepreneurial dreams will allow you to rise above this unfortunate flaw in the way the mind treats intentions. But as long you make that false assumption, you'll be a victim of the flaw. Set aside the assumption, and you can learn how to work around the flaw.

If you simply recognize that the mind isn't wired properly for following through, you'll take a giant step in the direction of improving your ability to follow through.

CHAPTER 9

Principle 3: Make It Feel Like You Must Follow Through

Perhaps, like us, you've been inspired by stories about extraordinary people who faced enormous obstacles but simply refused to accept the odds against them. They just kept pressing forward, often doing extremely difficult things day-in and day-out without getting even the slightest result to encourage them. They went on like this for months or even years. And then suddenly, they achieved success.

What's their secret? How did they make themselves do it?

Well, for many of the super-achievers we've encountered, they did it because, in a sense, they had no choice. They felt like they *had to* do it. They felt driven to do anything and everything they believed they needed to do in order to succeed.

Take Chris' friend, Billy Schwer. He spent twenty years in arguably the most grueling and demanding sport there is—boxing. During his impressive career, Billy won British, Commonwealth, European and International Boxing Organization world titles. His skills, courage, determination and grace in the ring attracted a huge fan base, and his personality made him a favorite amongst other boxers, promoters and the media.

So what was the secret that enabled Billy to stick with the rigorous training regimen that was so critical to his success? Billy's secret is that *he felt like he had no choice.* "If I didn't train in the rain, sleet or snow," he told us, "I knew there was a big risk I would get killed in the ring!" It wasn't just a matter of *thinking* he really should stick with his training regimen. Billy could actually feel it in his gut: *Train or die.*

Then there's Meryl Koslow, a very successful entrepreneur who spent years *wiring* herself to follow through as if she were shot-out-of-a-cannon. "I am always motivated," she told us. "I have firecrackers in me when I wake up. All I want is to make millions of dollars in every given minute, and I feel driven to do it."

Motivation for the rest of us

Most business owners don't have firecrackers in them when they wake up. And most don't feel like they'll literally be killed unless they do what they know they should do every day. For every Billy and Meryl who are fortunate enough to automatically feel like they must do whatever they believe success requires, there are probably tens if not hundreds of thousands of business owners who just aren't wired that way. Although we truly want to succeed, we don't automatically feel like we have to do whatever we decide we must do to be successful.

But just because you're not wired the way Billy and Meryl are, doesn't mean that you can't follow through like a champion. It just means that you have to do something *manually* that they do automatically. It means you have to learn how to become deliberate and creative about making yourself feel like doing what you know you must do to be successful.

Of course, it would be nice if it would just happen automatically. But that's not going to happen, so we suggest that you just get over it. The worst thing you can do is pretend that you're wired like Billy and Meryl if you're not. It's a surefire way of robbing you and your business of success.

The secret to following through is to essentially *trick yourself* into actually feeling—not just thinking—like you *must* do the same thing you've decided you should do.

Alastair Campbell, who is Head of the Ideal Marketing Company, figured out a way to make himself feel like he had to lose weight. He wrote out a check for £500 (about $800) to a political party that he really disliked. He then gave the check to a trusted friend with instructions to mail the check unless Alistair had lost at least 9.5 kilograms (about 21 pounds) by "weigh in" at the end of October. It wasn't just money that Alistair put at stake. He realized that if he didn't lose the weight and the donation was therefore made in his company's name, his company would appear on a list of staunch supporters of an organization he found totally repulsive. Imagine how embarrassing that would be!

So Alistair, who couldn't lose the weight for all the *right* reasons, lost the weight to keep from losing his money and his honor.

Going too far?

Now if you think Alistair went too far, think again.

Just imagine what you could accomplish by creating high octane reasons like this that actually *force* you to do the various things you intend to do. For example, suppose you've intelligently decided that you really should make an important call that you've been putting off, or you really should work on that financial spreadsheet that should have finished two weeks ago. But the good and right and logical reasons for doing these things just aren't working. So truly, why wouldn't you be willing to get yourself in gear by creating the threat of losing money and being embarrassed about officially supporting a cause you detest?

When the right reason for doing something important doesn't work, what's wrong with a creating a compelling reason that does work? You see, if you have the stomach for it, you can always create a compelling reason that's powerful enough to *force* you to follow through.

Ironically, the biggest obstacle you have to overcome in order to put this principle into practice is an irresistibly logical and widely-held belief that that's nevertheless dead wrong. It's the belief that you can and should count only on the good or the right reasons for following through to motivate you to actually follow through.

We urge you to forget about whatever you think *should* motivate you. All that matters is what actually *does* motivate you. A good or right reason that fails to make you feel in your gut like you absolutely must do what you've decided you should do is useless. You're much better off with a bad or wrong or dumb or irrelevant reason that nevertheless makes you feel like you have no choice but to do what you intend to do.

Billy Schwer, who never beats around the bush, put it this way: "Whatever will empower you, you must use it to get yourself off your arse."

Of course, you should always *decide to follow through* for the right reasons. But it's a huge mistake to count on the right reasons to make you actually follow through. To follow through, you need a compelling reason, that is, one that you can actually feel rather than just think. And if you don't have a compelling reason, you have no choice but to create one. That not only takes practice. It takes courage.

CHAPTER 13

Detoxify Dreaded Tasks

QUOTE

Although often the best way to get yourself to follow through is to create a situation that forces you to follow through, there is a kinder gentler strategy that's worth trying. It's one that takes a very different approach to dealing with that awful "I really don't want to do that today" feeling that you have in your gut—a feeling that Levinson and Greider referred to as "The Avoidance Monster."

To understand this strategy, you need to first take a fresh look at what happens when you avoid doing something you've decided you should do.

The first and most obvious consequence of avoidance is that whatever it is that you're avoiding doing, doesn't get done. But there's a second consequence that's easy to overlook, but it's an extremely important one. Avoidance prevents you from building the routine or habit that would eventually make it easier for you to do what you intend to do.

It's this second consequence of avoidance that the *Detoxify Dreaded Tasks* strategy addresses. By stripping away the toxic parts of the task that you're avoiding—the parts that make it feel worth avoiding—this strategy allows you to at least move forward with building a routine.

Tiptoe around the Avoidance Monster

My (Steve's) client Thomas concluded that he really should be reviewing his business's financial performance once a week. Although he had promised himself many times that he'd start doing these reviews "next week," he kept putting them off because he hates accounting.

Disgusted with himself, Thomas finally decided to try to get the ball rolling by tiptoeing around the Avoidance Monster. So first he stripped away everything about these reviews that had been causing him to avoid doing them. Then he promised only to do whatever was left.

By the time Thomas had stripped away everything that had been repelling him, frankly, there wasn't much left. But here's what he promised to do: Every Thursday morning at 10 AM, he would gather up the materials he needed to do a proper review, put them on his desk, and then sit down. That's it. If he did only that much and nothing more, he told himself, he will have fulfilled his obligation, honored his commitment, kept his promise, followed through. Of course, if he just happened to feel like going further, that would be fine.

By stripping the dreaded task of everything that had been making it worth avoiding, Thomas made it possible to move forward. He was able to establish the *shell* of a routine of doing weekly financial reviews. He was now at least *showing up* regularly for these reviews, and was now ready to actually look at financial information when the spirit moved him, which sometimes it did. In fact, more often than not, after doing the minimum he promised to do, Thomas actually did more—sometimes a lot more.

Before long, Thomas had developed a routine of doing substantive and useful weekly financial reviews.

Lower the bar to clear the hurdle

I (Steve) used this same strategy to follow through on my intention to exercise every day. Although my goal was to ride my exercise bike for forty minutes every morning, the very thought of having to peddle and endure boredom for forty minutes was enough to keep me in bed.

So I asked myself what I would have to remove from the routine to make it doable, that is, not at all worth avoiding. In other words, what was the most I could imagine doing every day without thinking "Oh no, not that damned bike again!" The answer turned out to be "not much." I could imagine putting on my exercise clothes, sitting on the bike, and putting my feet on the pedals. No problem! But I couldn't picture myself doing any more than that without taking a chance of waking up the Avoidance Monster. So I promised to do only that much (actually, *that little).*

I kept my promise every day. It was easy. There was nothing to avoid—nothing to dread. What's more, once I fulfilled my obligation to put on my exercise clothes, sit on the bike and put my feet on the peddles, I usually find myself peddling. Sometimes I peddled for just a few minutes. Sometimes I peddled for a lot longer. Before long, I was peddling for forty minutes every day, and doing so had become a self-sustaining habit.

Get the ball rolling

Steve's client Amy got the ball rolling in the direction of following through on her intention to organize her office.

For weeks, every time Amy thought about getting started, she woke up the Avoidance Monster. She felt a big "Oh no, not that!" in the pit of her stomach that kept her from moving forward. Scolding herself only made matters worse, and so did giving herself pep talks about how good she would feel if she finally got the job done.

Amy dreaded organizing because she knew it would be a big and overwhelming task that would force her to make a bunch of little decisions she didn't feel at all like making. She tentatively concluded that if all she had to do is spend a minute or two a day organizing with absolutely no expectation of accomplishing anything, she wouldn't avoid doing it. So that's what she agreed to do—not one iota more.

That changed everything. Once Amy had removed all the *toxins* from organizing, she no longer dreaded doing it. She not only organized every day, she almost always spent much longer than a minute or two. A few times, she got on a roll and spent hours organizing. She even had to remind herself that she could stop at any time without breaking her promise.

What especially impressed Amy is that as her organizing started to produce tangible benefits, she sometimes even looked forward to spending time organizing.

Commit only to doing the easy part

Kathy Tracey, who we mentioned earlier, often relies on this strategy to follow through on her intention to keep herself fit.

"I break down the actions I need to take and commit to doing the first part of it only," she told us. "So for example, if I should go out for a training run after a long day at work but I feel tired, I commit to putting on my running kit and shoes but not to the run."

Kathy, who is also Managing Director of The Learning Company Ltd, uses this same strategy whenever she faces an avoidance-worthy task at work. "I just commit to the first part. Breaking it down like this makes it all seem much more manageable," she explained. "And once you gain some momentum on a task, it's easier to keep going."

Kathy also told us about a friend who uses a similar strategy to follow through on his intention to cook proper meals for himself, which is something he often doesn't feel like doing. He promises only to cut up an onion. "And then the rest starts to happen!" Kathy explained.

Remember, the key to getting good results with this strategy is to never set any requirements on how much you must actually accomplish. If you start to insist on doing more than you feel like doing, you'll wake up the Avoidance Monster, and it will be all over.

PROPOSAL 6

▌ Book Proposal for

Evidence of Eternity
The Psychic Lawyer's Case for Everlasting Life

By Mark Anthony
The Psychic Lawyer™

Jeff's Comments

① This is a nice, clear title.

② The proposal's TOC shows good organization, which helps make the proposal more reader-friendly.

Deb's Comments

ⓐ Love the title.

▌ Table of Contents

Deb's Comments

b This should be titled "Overview."

c This is an interesting quote but seems like a non sequitur. At minimum it should be separated from the content by spacing. It also could have been expanded into an actual anecdote.

d Is the author saying that his goal is to change people? If so, how? It would be more powerful to first state the problem and then explain how the book solves it. For example: "People are frightened of death. The stories in this book taken from my experience as a fourth-generation psychic medium will console readers while entertaining them, inspiring them, and at times making them laugh." The author has focused too much on himself without first establishing what is in it for the reader.

e For a better structure, first state the problem you are solving before you support it with why you are the person to solve it. Publishing is a hard copy business. You and your platform are secondary to a good quality book. There has to be a reason for the book to exist unless it is a celebrity memoir. This second part of the

Overview of *Evidence of Eternity*

"Last night, just before midnight, I was walking alone down Oak Street, next to the old abandoned insane asylum when suddenly—I came face to face with Death herself." **c**

Information doesn't change people, stories do. As a best-selling author, a successful trial attorney, and a fourth generation psychic medium, I know how to tell stories that captivate a reader's interest. **d** *Evidence of Eternity: The Psychic Lawyer's Case for Everlasting Life* is a 66,000 word non-fiction book explaining innovative, complex, and esoteric concepts in easy-to-understand language. Inspirational, gripping, and occasionally humorous **e** narratives support each chapter of *Evidence of Eternity* to educate, entertain, enlighten, and console the reader.

The foreword for *Evidence of Eternity* has been written by New York Times bestselling author and world renowned Near-death experience research expert Dr. Kenneth Ring. *Evidence of Eternity* has also been endorsed by several other New York Times bestselling authors including Dr. Raymond Moody, Dr. Jeffrey **g** Long, who alongside Dr. Kenneth Ring are the three top Near-death experience researchers in the world. It has also been endorsed by New York Times bestselling authors Dr. Joe Vitale of *The Secret*, Dr. My Haley author and collaborator on her late husband Alex Haley's New York Times bestseller *Roots*, Deborah King (Hay House) and William Buhlman of the Monroe Institute. Additional endorsements are forthcoming.

Evidence of Eternity is the perfect follow up to my last book, *Never Letting Go: Heal Grief with Help from the Other Side,* and will capitalize and expand upon that book's success. While healing **h** is an important component of *Evidence of Eternity,* this new book will appeal to an even wider audience, as it is also for those interested in gaining a clearer understanding of the Afterlife and the science behind spirit communication. The appeal of *Evidence of Eternity* extends to anyone who enjoys emotionally riveting narratives, edgy crime stories, and an exciting page turner.

The title *Evidence of Eternity: The Psychic Lawyer's Case for Everlasting Life* ties together and maximizes the benefit of my unique brand "Mark Anthony the Psychic Lawyer™." As an attorney and as a medium, I understand the importance of evidence. In my role as a trial lawyer, I present evidence to a judge or jury to prove my case. As a medium, verifiable evidence received from a spirit is critical proof of the reality of spirit contact. Lawyers are seen as logical—mediums as sensitive. *Evidence of Eternity* bridges the gap between two diverse worlds by combining my left-brained logical approach to a right-brained spiritual activity. The melding of evidence, science, theory, faith and my own research is the basis for the subtitle: *The Psychic Lawyer's Case for Everlasting Life.*

Since the dawn of recorded history, humans have asked these questions: What happens when I die? Is there a God? Is there an Afterlife? Does Heaven exist? Does Hell exist? Is reincarnation real? Can someone really talk to spirits? What do messages from spirits mean?

Despite the prevalence of spirit communication throughout history, many people refuse to believe in it, are skeptical of it, or feel it is somehow evil. These attitudes pose more questions, "Is there any science to prove this, or is it just cold reading? How do you know it's not a demon impersonating your loved one? My son committed suicide, did he go to Hell? The man who murdered my grandfather was found not guilty. If there is a God, how could God allow that?"

Evidence of Eternity tackles many tough questions and concepts anyone interested in life after death is curious about. One of the things which make *Evidence of Eternity* stand apart is the absence of the usual "Psychic 101" chapter of overused and cliché explanations filled with typical terminology such as clairvoyance, clairaudience, and clairsentience, which all too often inundate books in this genre.

My brand, Mark Anthony the Psychic Lawyer™, provides credentials other authors in this field lack. As an Oxford educated attorney with over 25 years of litigation experience, I understand the importance of presenting evidence to prove my case. Quantum physics, physiology, genetics, scientific theory, and theology are woven together in a cohesive and entertaining style which presents the scientific basis and theories concerning life after death, spirit communication, karma, reincarnation, enlightenment, and 'in-lightenment' (each individual's personal connection with God).

As a man of faith, I explore the theological basis and philosophical concepts that address our finite existence here in the material world and our infinite existence as a spirit in the Afterlife. This book takes an interfaith approach and is respectful to people of all faiths. One

paragraph would be more effective before the author's qualifications.

f This author has written a previous book. Before mentioning the endorsements, it would be more logical to add a paragraph fully describing what this book is about and how it differs from the first. Even a short "logline" would benefit the proposal. For example: "The feedback I got from the thousands of readers of my first book, *Never Letting Go: Heal Grief from the Other Side*, was that they wanted and needed more evidence that the afterlife is real." In light of a previous book that essentially competes with the author's new book, it is important to explain right away that this book expands on the ideas in the first and is in response to a need. What is in it for a reader should always be foremost in your mind as you write your proposal.

g It would be more effective to separate the endorsements into its own subheading after the overview has clearly shown what the book is about. You need to think like an agent and editor. Your proposal needs to show clarity of purpose and a clear hook that an agent or editor can explain to someone else. This book did indeed sell. However, the proposal could have been more powerful with a little rearranging of the content and some subheadings to make it easier for the agent or editor to see important information.

(h) This paragraph would be more effective if it immediately stated the concept of the book: that it provides a clearer understanding of the afterlife and the science behind spirit communication. In my opinion the author does not need to have such a long overview, as much of the information could be broken down into subcategories. We recommend the actual overview be a "get to the point" section that is no more than 250 to 500 words. Otherwise you are risking that the agent or editor will skim and miss the important facts.

(i) This section and the previous paragraphs focus on the author's unique brand. However, this could be simplified and bulleted. At this stage the clarity of the book being offered should outweigh the supporting credentials.

(j) I disagree with the author that these terms should be in the overview.

of the key points in *Evidence of Eternity* is that faith and science are not mutually exclusive.

As an evidential medium, I employ evidence from riveting true stories of spirit contact. These stories are about people the reader can identify with, so the narrative becomes personal to the reader.

For example, *Evidence of Eternity* seizes the reader's attention immediately with the September 11, 2001 experience of my cousin Reed who worked in the South Tower of the World Trade Center. When the first hijacked jet struck the North Tower, Reed heard the voice of his deceased grandfather who insisted he leave the South Tower. Reed was the last person aboard a crowded elevator when the second hijacked jet struck the South Tower. The doors of the elevator were abruptly flung open. To Reed's astonishment, his grandfather's spirit appeared, beckoning to him. Reed leapt from the elevator seconds before it exploded in flames. Overwhelmed by the horror surrounding him, he instinctively trusted his grandfather's spirit to guide him through the devastation, barely escaping with his life. In the aftermath, he was consumed by survivor guilt wondering why he was spared.

Many people report seeing the spirit of a deceased loved one during a crisis and can identify with Reed's story. Others, who have lost a loved one or survived a disaster, will relate to Reed's survivor guilt and post-traumatic stress disorder.

Many new terms and innovative concepts to explain communication with spirits and the nature of the afterlife are presented in *Evidence of Eternity*. I've developed these terms and concepts based on credible evidence, scientific theory and in conjunction with my own research. These are introduced in a logical and progressive manner chapter by chapter in order to build upon other new concepts presented in subsequent chapters. Although the chapter summaries address these new concepts and terminology, it is important to **(j)** this overview to briefly highlight them:

Levels of the Other Side describes the multitude of frequencies and dimensions of the Afterlife, which may be thought of as levels. Some levels are closer to the Light, the spiritual energy of God, and other levels are more distant. While many religions discuss levels of the Other Side, *Evidence of Eternity* presents this concept in a logical and easy to understand manner which incorporates both the power of faith, the science of frequency, and theoretical physics.

Collective Consciousness Disconnect builds upon the concept of Levels to the Other Side, and demonstrates the interconnected nature of spirits in the afterlife. In spirituality as in physics, energy is neither created nor destroyed only transferred. As the spirit pre-exists the body, that energy is transferred to the Other Side at death. When the spirit separates from the body, the uniqueness of the person is contained within the spirit and returns to the "oneness" of the Other Side. Even though that spirit merges into oneness with the energy of God on the Other Side, the unique personality of the spirit remains intact within the individual's consciousness. A spirit is able to disconnect from the Collective Consciousness of the Other Side for many reasons. One of those reasons is to resolve issues with people in the material world.

Interdimensional Communication is the logical transition from the Collective Consciousness Disconnect. Interdimensional Communication is an updated and much more descriptive term for communication between our material world dimension and the dimension of the Other Side. This presents the theory that spirit communication is based on the transfer of energy involving frequency and vibration, and makes the comparison between Interdimensional Communication and the use of telephone communication via satellite.

Multiple Meaning Messages occur during Interdimensional Communication when a medium receives a piece of evidence from a spirit which has more than one level of significance. Multiple Meaning Messages are compared to radio transmissions broadcast by the military which when initially received, seems to be just one message, when in fact there are several encrypted messages piggybacked on that signal. Like verbal speech, Interdimensional Communication also contains nuances, subtleties, and words with several connotations. For the client to receive the maximum benefit of Interdimensional Communication, the medium must be able to fully recognize and interpret Multiple Meaning Messages.

The hereditary nature of psychic ability is supported by the science of genetics which has proven that many physical and mental traits are hereditary. To demonstrate this concept, I utilize stories from both sides of my family. To say I have a colorful and interesting family is an understatement. My childhood was a combination of "The Sixth Sense" meets "Everybody Loves Raymond." Since the release of *Never Letting Go*, I've been thronged with letters, emails and requests on a daily basis by readers who want to know more

What would have been more effective is a statement that as a lawyer he is used to jargon and terminology. This could be seen as a benefit for mutual understanding of difficult concepts. Then he could say that he has created a glossary of new terms that he believes will help readers come to a meeting of the minds of what these concepts really mean. The author takes a lot of time explaining that he came up with the terms but that is assumed. These could have been given under a separate subheading in the chapter-by-chapter summaries. Also, agents and editors will skim these if presented in this format. It would be better to create a carefully bulleted list followed by an annotated list like you would do for chapters.

about my family's psychic heritage. This is the perfect way to explain a scientific concept while at the same time placating the existing reader base and to entertain the new and expanding base. The discussion of genetics personalizes psychic abilities to the reader, as the chapter also demonstrates the prejudice, discrimination, and abuse endured by psychics and mediums.

Frequency Beacons builds upon the previously introduced concepts of Interdimensional Communication, the Collective Consciousness Disconnect, and Multiple Meaning Messages. Frequency Beacons explain the energetic connection between people in the material world and spirits on the Other Side. A Frequency Beacon is the energetic impulse created by a person's emotions which are detected by spirits. Spirits can hear us and are aware of what is going on in our lives because of this energetic link. Anyone who has experienced a "visitation" or the "presence" of a deceased loved one will be able to relate to this chapter.

The healing component of Evidence of Eternity delves into excruciatingly painful topics such as homicide, suicide, a child's death and the death of a pet, through a new perspective.

Grief leads to crime which leads to grief is one of the signature theories of Mark Anthony the Psychic Lawyer ™ and is presented in the chapter *Homicide and the Other Side*. This concept has been the subject of many of my TV and radio interviews. This intense chapter begins with an explanation of an 11 year-old boy who loses a brother to measles. His parents ignore him and fail to help him cope with his grief. As a result he becomes aggressive and anti-social. Three years later when the boy is 14 years old, his father dies suddenly. The teen's behavioral problems escalate into a total disrespect for authority resulting in his expulsion from high school. The only loving relationship remaining in this teenager's life is with his mother who dies of cancer when he is 17 years old. The young man's behavior spirals downward into aggression, anger, hatred and violence. His name was Adolf Hitler.

Hitler may be the poster child for my theory that grief leads to crime which leads to grief. The discussion of homicide then leads to the question, "Was the criminal born or was the criminal created?" To bring this concept home to the reader, stories from my years of experience as a prosecutor and later criminal defense lawyer, coupled with my work as a medium are invaluable. Grief particularly for a child or teen which is not dealt with in a healthy manner can lead that person to addictions, impulsive behaviors, rage, anger, and criminal activity. The grief stricken person is often transformed into one who commits crimes which ultimately inflicts harm, and even death upon others. In short, grief leads to crime which leads to grief.

Many of the topics within *Evidence of Eternity* are painful, so tasteful and diplomatic comic relief is used to alleviate the intensity of the subject matter. This is especially necessary in the chapters on homicide and suicide.

Evidence of Eternity presents different perspectives of homicide from the view points of the victim's spirit, the family members of victims, and even from the view point of a murderer on death row. The homicide chapter ends with a message of hope that although the road is not easy, it is possible to find a path out of hell.

Suicide is much more than just self-inflicted homicide—it's an extremely complex and painful act with far reaching repercussions. In the United States alone, more people die from suicide then they do from car crashes, yet it is treated as a social taboo. To personalize this chapter for the victims of suicide, it begins with the account of my childhood friend Billy who took his own life. *Evidence of Eternity* explains suicide from the victim's perspective, which is seen as the *only* solution to an intolerable reality from which there is no *other* escape. This concept is further illustrated by heartrending stories about bullying, mental illness, impulsivity, suicide as a form of revenge, and accidental suicide.

Addressing suicide in a sensitive and diplomatic manner is extremely important and *Evidence of Eternity* educates the survivors about what awaits the spirit of someone who committed suicide. Many religions teach a person who commits suicide goes to hell. This is often a terrible fear which plagues the loved ones of a suicide victim. *Evidence of Eternity* alleviates this fear by explaining there is no hell, nor is there a "one size fits all" fate for the soul of a person who commits suicide. The chapter ends with a message from a spirit of a young man who committed suicide who relays the message, "We are all the children of God and no parent could ever condemn a child to an eternity of suffering, and God is the most loving parent of all."

Reincarnation is the logical discussion to follow the topic of suicide. It also lightens the tone of the book before the following chapter about the death of a child. The explanation of reincarnation combines justice, theology, balance/karma and objective evidence.

Deb's Comments

k Aside from my opinion that this overview is too long and should be at least broken down into subheadings, I believe this author should not have referred to content in his previous book. This book should stand alone. There is no need to make comparisons more than to use the first book as a reason the second book had to be written.

l Now the author is introducing yet another concept in the overview. Keep your description of the book organized and tightly written. Is it about humans? Pets? This chapter about pets should be in the chapter outline. In my opinion there are too many concepts for the agent or editor to digest on a first read.

Deb's Comments

m My concern with this proposal is that the author has so much to say that he did not organize it simply enough. A writer's inclination is not to leave anything out. The greater challenge is to determine what to leave in. The author here is a good writer and the book is certainly well organized and well written. However, the proposal should have been

Although considered by many in the United States and Western Europe to be a primarily Hindu and Buddhist belief, it may surprise many readers when evidence is presented that reincarnation is at the root of both Judaism and Christianity. Further evidence of reincarnation is presented with heavily documented case studies of two women, one from India, and the other from England who recalled specific details of previous lives.

Even though stories about the death of children appear throughout *Evidence of Eternity*, it is necessary to the healing aspect of this book to devote an entire chapter to this topic. It doesn't matter if the child was a fetus or an adult, the bond between parent and child is like no other. *Evidence of Eternity* approaches this very sensitive topic in a tender and diplomatic manner. It offers coping advice and counseling for parents who have siblings who have died. The stories in this chapter address children taken by death through different causes.

It is revealed how the spirits of stillborn and aborted children can and do communicate as fully mature, sophisticated and intelligent spirits. This relates to earlier chapters which discuss the immortal nature of spirits who pre-exist a human body and live on after death.

In my previous book *Never Letting Go*, one of the key points was "Grief can take on a life of its own and become one's life." *Evidence of Eternity* takes this concept further with a story of a Senator who cannot accept the death of his son. *Evidence of Eternity* **k** demonstrates how Interdimensional Communication with a deceased child is an important therapeutic step in accepting the reality of the loss of the child, and through that acceptance finding inner peace with the death.

Pets are part of the family and the death of a pet is extremely traumatic. However, the chapter on the death of a pet is more than just the grief associated with losing a beloved animal. It is about Interspecies Interdimensional Communication and provides a new and credible way of understanding spirit communication between human and animal.

Evidence of Eternity demonstrates how animals manifest intelligence differently than humans. People often wonder how it is possible to communicate with the spirit of an animal. Spirits don't **l** speak any human language; rather they transmit intelligence in the form of energetic vibration. Through this means of communication, the differences in cultures and even species are eliminated. Whether human or animal, once freed from the confines of a finite existence, a spirit communicates through vibrating waves of frequency which contain concepts, images, sensations, and emotions. These waves of frequency emitted by the spirit then interface with the medium's energy, and are translated into recognizable information based on the memories, feelings, and cultural references housed in the medium's brain.

Communication with animals adds a warm and fuzzy element to *Evidence of Eternity*. It concludes with a reading I conducted before a large crowd of people for a police officer named Trevor, who is heartbroken over putting his police dog Ajax to sleep. Ajax provides exact details of his life with Trevor, and then demonstrates how love and forgiveness are not solely human virtues.

In-lightenment is another new term introduced in *Evidence of Eternity*. In-Lightenment is also the final chapter which ties everything in the book together and describes the two way nature of the (m) "Light." However, this begins with a humorous story how in the span of 24 hours, I was called an infidel, a heretic, and a Satanist, by three different people who each believed that their religion was the one and only way to God. The chapter transitions into the meaning of In-Lightenment. In religions and belief systems since the dawn of time, God has been described in terms of Light. However, the Light is both external and internal. Enlightenment is an acknowledgment of one's connection to the love that is God, whereas In-Lightenment is acknowledgement that the love that is God is within each of us.

The book ends with a story of love and In-Lightenment. During an Interdimensional Communication session an elderly man receives a message from his wife who died slowly of cancer. Her spirit tells him, "It's okay to open the window again."

Weeping, he recounts while she was dying her only joy was looking out the window at the garden. He reveals he won't let anyone touch the window because when the light hits the glass at the right angle, he can still see her handprint.

After the reading, he realizes the message wasn't only evidence of his wife's everlasting life in Heaven—it was metaphor for all of us. In our grieving, we may be shuttered behind our defenses and closed in, surrounded only by pain. There comes a time when it is okay to open the window again, and breathe the glorious fresh air of a new phase of life.

(3)

streamlined. This last story could have been the only one included to show how the author uses evidence in the book and how effective it is. Instead, even in this paragraph the author focuses on the creation of a new term. These are common choices we see in proposals when authors are passionate about what they are doing and want to make sure the agent or editor understands their vision. The problem is the end result can be the opposite of what is intended. Clarity and organization are the most important things. I love this last story, but it's buried in the other "sell points."

Jeff's Comments

3 This overview is much longer and more detailed than I would have liked. It might have been more effective to save most of this content for the outline section. However, I was on the fence and decided to concede to the author's preferences because there are no serious redundancies and everything lucidly reinforces what the book will be. Furthermore, this is a crowded book category, so it was important to prove the author's unique and passionate perspective.

Jeff's Comments

4 It's become so common for published authors to claim "bestseller" status that the statement no longer means very much to industry insiders. There's no actual definition for what constitutes a bestseller, so many authors can say it and get away with it. But I've recently encouraged authors to refrain from doing so, unless there's a specific list they can refer to.

Deb's Comments

n The author focuses on his law credentials as what sets him apart. However, it begs the question: Are there other lawyers who are also psychic mediums? What sets this author apart is that he is an evidentiary medium, which is a real term in the field. And having a law degree has helped his practice. But I am not sure if the branding of the psychic lawyer is setting him apart or not. I think his gifts and his writing are what he truly brings to the table. His books are good and well written. The good news is he understands the concept that writers need a personal brand. For that he deserves a bravo!

▪ About the Author: Mark Anthony, the Psychic Lawyer™

Mark Anthony, the Psychic Lawyer™ is a psychic medium specializing in communication with spirits. He is descended from a long line of psychics and mediums that have been helping people connect with deceased loved ones for over 100 years.

Mark is a bestselling author and his critically acclaimed book, *Never Letting Go,* (Llewellyn Worldwide 2011) is the definitive guide to healing grief with help from the Other Side. *Never Letting Go* was **4** nominated as Metaphysical Book of the Year at the 2012 COVR (Coalition of Visionary Resources) Awards at the 2012 INATS (International New Age Trade Show) Convention in Denver, Colorado.

Mark's credentials make him unique among psychic mediums. He earned his law degree with honors from Mercer University in Georgia and studied law at Oxford University, England. Mark **n** holds the prestigious Order of the Barrister Award and is licensed to practice law in Florida, Washington D. C., and before the United States Supreme Court. He has practiced law as a prosecutor, criminal defense attorney, personal injury trial attorney, and certified mediator.

An intelligent, charismatic, humorous, and accomplished public speaker, Mark appears worldwide on television and radio both as a paranormal expert and as a legal expert in high profile murders. In one TV interview, Mark explained, "Being a lawyer and being a psychic are not mutually exclusive. They are both about evidence."

His recent media appearances include: NBC Washington D.C., NBC Miami, CBS Pittsburgh, CBS St. Louis, Fox News Boston, Fox News Network, Coast to Coast AM Radio, CBS Radio, Fox News Radio and Sirius XM Radio. On many shows he connects audience members with loved ones on the Other Side. Using his gift as a spellbinding presenter, Mark explains the scientific basis of spirit contact. He regularly lectures at expos, conventions, and universities, including Harvard, Brown, and Yale.

Videos of Mark Anthony's television appearances, gallery readings, and author video about *Never Letting Go* may be viewed by visiting: www.ThePsychicLawyer.com

Although he has inherited the ability to communicate with spirits, Mark has worked conscientiously to expand his psychic gifts to the fullest potential. This includes study at the prestigious Arthur Findlay College for the Advancement of Psychic Science in England.

As both a criminal defense and prosecuting attorney, Mark has litigated cases ranging from misdemeanors to murders. One of his distinctive theories is that grief leads to crime, which leads to grief. In his dual professions of attorney and medium, Mark has seen how unresolved grief can lead to behaviors which result in the bereaved committing crimes that inflict grief upon others. His professional life has been enhanced by his exceptional intuition. Mark's psychic gifts have provided him with a unique outlook on criminal behavior as well as an uncanny empathy for murder victims' families.

In a recent radio interview Mark was quoted as having said, "I believe communicating with spirits is a very important therapeutic step in the long and difficult journey through grief." It is Mark's life mission to use his abilities as a medium, his experience as an attorney, and his skill as an author to educate people about the scientific reality of spirit communication and to assist and enlighten those suffering from the loss of a loved one.

(5)

Book Foreword and Celebrity Endorsements   **(6)** **(o)**

Evidence of Eternity has already received the endorsement of spiritual leaders and experts in the field of Near-death Experience and Afterlife studies. All of them are world renowned New York Times Best Selling Authors. Additional Endorsements are forthcoming and will be added to this list. The foreword by Dr. Kenneth Ring follows the list of Celebrity Endorsements.

To date *Evidence of Eternity* has been endorsed by:

Dr. Raymond Moody, M.D., Ph.D. is a New York Times bestselling author who has written eleven books which have sold over 20 million copies. In the 1970s Dr. Moody coined the phrase "near-death experience" when he created a new field of study to examine people who

Jeff's Comments

(5) This bio section is a strong roundup of all the author's relevant credentials and experiences.

(6) It was smart for the author to generate these impressive endorsements before pitching the book. That's something all authors should attempt, though some people will understandingly insist upon seeing the full manuscript. A more realistic option might be to simply present a nonbinding list of eligible endorsers that will be contacted once the book is finished.

Deb's Comments

(o) This is where the endorsements belong. A small sentence in the overview would have been fine if it appeared in the right order. I think the long overview sets up the author for some typical disorganization that happens with all book proposal writers. This is why we suggest writers get to the point and organize the pieces of the proposal accordingly. This author has impressive and relevant endorsements. Networking with like-minded people is helpful as you prepare for your own book proposal. It is unlikely they will come to you.

had clinically died and then came back to life. This led to his ground-breaking work, *Life After Life*, which completely changed the way we view death and dying and has sold over 13 million copies worldwide.

"Mark Anthony's Evidence of Eternity *is a truly fascinating account of his dual life as a practicing attorney and a psychic medium. Combining science, theoretical physics, physiology and theology, Mark does an amazing job of dispassionately presenting evidence of an afterlife while sensitively describing the inner world of a person with inexplicable talents. In all honesty, this is the most interesting book about the paranormal I have read in a long time."*
—Raymond Moody, Author *Life After Life*

Dr. Jeffrey Long, M.D., is a New York Times bestselling author and a leading near-death experience researcher. He founded the Near-death Experience Research Foundation (NDERF) which is the largest data base of near-death experiences in the world. Dr. Long also serves on the Physician Advisory Committee of the International Association for Near-Death Studies. According to *Time Magazine*, his book *Evidence of the Afterlife* is based on years of scientific research which unequivocally concludes life after death exists.

I took the liberty of including both Dr. Long's letter which accompanied his endorsement:

Dear Mark,
Thank you so very much for sending me your book! Goodness, I could not put it down! It is an honor and privilege to give this book my enthusiastic and heartfelt endorsement. I would suggest the following as my 'blurb'. Thanks again, and a huge congratulations Mark! I am sure that *Evidence of Eternity* will be widely read and an inspiration to a vast number of people.
Kindest regards,
Jeffrey

"This is one book you won't want to miss! Mark Anthony is exceptionally qualified to write on this subject- he is a renowned psychic, medium, and attorney. He presents powerful evidence for the reality of an afterlife and that our deceased loved ones can communicate with us. This highly recommended and easy to read book contains a treasure trove of stories and insights that are powerful, inspiring, and could change your life."
—Jeffrey Long, M.D., author of the New York Times bestselling
Evidence of the Afterlife: The Science of Near-Death Experiences.

Dr. Joe Vitale is the author of numerous New York Times Bestselling books such as *The Attraction Factor* and *Attract Money Now*. He is best known as the co-author of *The Secret* which has sold over 19 million copies in more than 40 languages. Known as "The Buddha of the Internet," Dr. Vitale is well known for his combination of spirituality and marketing acumen. A featured guest on television around the globe, he is an international celebrity and has an Internet following of millions.

"A riveting book opening your heart and mind to the realities of an invisible world waiting to help us. This book is unforgettable. The stories are astonishing. The message is empowering. Read this right now!"
   —Dr Joe Vitale, author "Zero Limits", star of "The Secret"

Dr. My Haley is the widow of Alex Haley and collaborator on his mega bestseller *Roots*, which was adapted into one of the most provocative and highest rated mini-series in TV history. She is an internationally renowned celebrity and the bestselling author of *The Treason of Mary Louvestre*.

"Few books in the area of metaphysics have I read that are more clear and thorough than Evidence of Eternity. *The book excels in the big task of explaining the nature of things in a scholarly way and, at the same time, engages us in easy conversation on how our present experience can interact with the Other Side in a variety of uplifting ways. It off-loads a host of faith concepts that have been negatively freighted over time and provides a refreshing, de-mystifying understanding of "beingness". Gone is the notion that death is the finish. Rather, we are reminded that energy is never created or destroyed; that our loved ones who were with us before still stand by our sides helping us, loving us, and aiding in our betterment. Moreover, we learn we have others who steadily work to benefit our growth and enlightenment. How amazingly positive.*

Evidence of Eternity *is provocative, stirring, endearing, and hopeful. Mark Anthony goes a long way to help us do what many want and need and that is—try to make sense of it all. For a guide to strong spiritual connection and means to personal discovery, this is a book you want to read."*
   —Dr. My Haley, Widow of Alex Haley and Collaborator of the
      New York Times best seller *Roots* and Author of the Bestseller
      The Treason of Mary Louvestre

William Buhlman of the Monroe Institute is a New York Times Bestselling Author and America's leading expert on out-of-body experiences. His forty years of extensive research have given him profound insights into out-of-body experiences and life after death. William Buhlman appears worldwide on TV and radio to discuss his views on the afterlife. His books have been translated into over 40 languages.

"Mark Anthony is a master in interdimensional communication. In Evidence of Eternity, *he opens the portal to the other side through his actual conversations between those who have passed and the people that care about them. Mark addresses murder, suicide, death of children and unresolved family issues with a mix of passion and logic like no other. We are urged to pay attention to these messages and be aware that spirits are all around us. The anecdotes were so fascinating, that I couldn't put it down."*
    —William Buhlman, author of, *Adventures in the Afterlife*

Deborah King is a New York Times Bestselling author, health and wellness expert, and spiritual teacher. Deborah is featured regularly in broadcast, online and print media. She makes frequent appearances on national TV and if regularly featured in *The Huffington Post* and *Psychology Today.* Deborah is the host of *Live From Hollywood,* a spiritually-based entertainment show, and the host of a popular weekly show on Hay House Radio.

"Mark Anthony has a real gift for Interdimensional Communication. His book, Evidence of Eternity, *logically explains the afterlife all the while demonstrating that faith and science are not mutually exclusive."*
    —Deborah King, Author of *Be Your Own Shaman* and *Truth Heals*

Dr. Kenneth Ring is Professor Emeritus of Psychology at the University of Connecticut and a New York Times Bestselling Author. He is an internationally recognized authority on the subject of near-death experiences who has written five books and nearly a hundred articles on the topic. Dr. Ring is also the co-founder and past President of The International Association for Near-Death Studies (IANDS) and the founding editor of its quarterly scholarly journal, The Journal of Near-Death Studies, now in its thirtieth year. Dr. Ring has appeared on many television and radio programs and been often interviewed in the press in connection with his work on near-death experiences.

"For anyone who wonders whether it is possible to make contact with loved ones who have died, Mark Anthony is your man. A well-known and very gifted medium (and a criminal attorney), Mark delivers the goods—and then some—in his latest book. Evidence of Eternity *is an absolutely riveting book, full of highly evidential and fascinating cases and much spiritual wisdom. I was unable to put it aside until I had read it at one sitting. Five stars plus!"*

—Kenneth Ring, Ph.D., Author of *Lessons from the Light*

Foreword for *Evidence of Eternity* by Dr. Kenneth Ring ⑦

As a researcher of near-death experiences (NDEs), I never wanted to have that much to do with mediums, particularly during the early stages in my career. One may wonder why? My work with near-death experiences and my interest in UFO experiences was outré enough for an academic like me. Besides, I was never interested to try to "prove" life after death, anyway, or even make a good case for survival of consciousness after physical death. I was always more interested to show what we could learn from near-death experiences, and let my students and readers draw whatever conclusions they liked. For an academic, to get too close to mediums and talk about the afterlife was to court banishment from the academy—it was stuff for the tabloids, not for "the halls of Ivy."

However, during my years of researching altered states of consciousness and NDEs, I learned a lot about mediums and had no doubt that some of them could indeed transmit messages from the dead, and could know things about the people they were reading for that it would be impossible to know by normal means. And naturally, I had read about many of the celebrated mediums of the past—Leonora Piper, Gladys Osborne Leonard, and many others. Yet, I never sought out a reading for myself until a couple of years ago when something very peculiar happened to me that, in the end, I could not ignore.

Ultimately, it proved to have something to do with my father.

Jeff's Comments

⑦ Presenting a prewritten foreword by a well-credentialed person isn't expected at the proposal stage, but if you have it, use it.

I was separated from my father when I was very young when he went off to war during the early 1940s. Although he survived the war, for various reasons he never returned home and then he died young, at 41, while working as an artist in New York. As I grew to manhood, I started thinking a lot about my father and began to sense his presence in my life as a kind of guiding influence. As a scientist, my initial reaction was to question this sensation, but on some level I felt the connection was real, so I decided to write a memoir about my father and his putative effect on my life after his death, and called it *My Father, Once Removed*.

Then two years ago, I started to hear from a number of my friends—all of them independently of one another and all of them connected in some way with NDE studies—and all of them telling that recently they had had some kind of fantastic reading from a medium (never the same medium, mind you) and asking me if I ever had considered having a reading myself. Most of them exhorted me to. Of course, I demurred, declined, and generally deflected the conversation to other topics. Except, it kept happening!

After the fourth such occurrence, I finally succumbed and arranged for a reading with one of the mediums who had been urged upon me by one of these friends. Afterward I wrote an article about my reading entitled, somewhat humorously, *"Medium Hot,"* which I eventually inserted as the last chapter into a revised and expanded version of my memoir about my father.

I will spare you the details, but the reading I received strongly and independently corroborated virtually everything I had learned or speculated about my father's life, which the medium could not have known by normal means. And not only that, but his feelings of deep love for me, which I had previously learned from his half-sister, as well as his posthumous role in my life, which I had long sensed, was also stressed by the medium. Moreover, the medium was accurately able to tell me some extremely obscure facts about my family life that really blew me away. It's one thing to read about such things in books—it's quite another when it happens to you! (Partial)

Kenneth Ring, Ph.D.
Professor Emeritus of Psychology
University of Connecticut
Author of the New York Times bestseller, *Lessons from the Light*

Jeff's Comments

8 This section builds a very strong case supporting the fact that many people from various walks of life are intensely interested in the subject.

The Market For *Evidence of Eternity*

The market is ripe for *Evidence of Eternity* and the time for this book is now! Momentum for explaining the metaphysical in rational terms has been building since the time of J.P. Morgan who once said, "Millionaires don't consult psychics—billionaires do."

Evidence of Eternity has mainstream appeal. It is equally important to both the marketing and promotion section of this book proposal to realize one of the key marketing components for the **(p)** mainstream appeal of *Evidence of Eternity* is my unique brand as Mark Anthony the Psychic Lawyer™. The dual roles of attorney and psychic medium seem contradictory to most people. Attorneys are perceived as coldly logical and mediums as mystically sensitive. My brand bridges the gap between the paranormal and the logical. This "controversy" continually generates interviews of me on television and radio. One of the many interview topics for publicizing *Evidence of Eternity* will be revealing my left brained logical approach to a very right brained spiritual activity.

My brand is well ahead of the curve with the evolution of belief systems over the last decade. What has traditionally been considered 'paranormal' is now discussed openly. Surveys demonstrate that tens of millions of Americans not only believe in God, but also in paranormal phenomena such as spirit contact, hauntings, extra-sensory perception (ESP), reincarnation, and the existence of angels. In fact, in 2012 alone, over 30 million Americans consulted psychics—and that demographic exceeds what has been typically coined as the "New Age" movement.

The following data compiled between 2001 and 2013 summarizes statistical evidence that strongly supports a booming and lucrative market for *Evidence of Eternity*:

- Gallup Poll indicated 92% of Americans believe in God.

- *Newsweek*, CBS, and Beliefnet polls show 90% of Americans believe in some form of Afterlife or spiritual realm. **(q)**

- *Time Magazine* reported over 30 million Americans per year consult psychics.

Deb's Comments

(p) In the market section, the focus should be on the reader and therefore what problem you are solving. In my opinion the focus on the author's brand is not answering the question asked by this section in the proposal. Your task in the market section is to determine your demographic: who you are trying to reach. If this author has good statistics from his first book and an extensive mailing list proving that the book has an audience, that can be included. Otherwise it is a bit of a distraction in what is meant to be a highly focused section.

(q) These statistics are somewhat helpful. However, it casts a rather broad net. His book is about *Evidence of Eternity*. The better focus would be on the enormous success of books and movies that are about "heaven is real." He is mixing in everything related to psychics, ghosts, and the paranormal. That is like saying, "Everyone will want this book." Even though you may anticipate a much larger market, focusing on a small one first shows that you have a clear sense of your audience. You don't have to oversell. It is better to stay small if it is clear.

- Gallup Poll stated 75% of Americans believe in paranormal phenomena such as ESP, ghosts, or experiences that can't be explained by normal means.

- The Pew Research Center reported 29% of Americans say they have felt in touch with someone who has died; 18% say they have been in the presence of a ghost.

- Pew also discovered the proportion of Americans who say they have interacted with a ghost has doubled in less than 20 years from 9% in 1996 to 18% today. The number saying they have felt in touch with someone who has died has also grown considerably, from 18% in 1996 to 29% today.

- Harris Poll found 71% of Americans believe in angels, 68% believe the soul survives physical death, and 24% believe in reincarnation.

Mediums who communicate with spirits are one of the hottest trends in popular culture. This definitely enhances the market for this book. There has been a sizable market segment for movies about people who communicate with the dead since *Ghost* and *The Sixth Sense* and more recently, *The Men Who Stare at Goats, The Gift, Hereafter, Suspect Zero,* and *Paranormal Activity.* (A franchise which recently released *Paranormal Activity 5.*)

"Hyper-reality" programs dealing with spirit contact and the paranormal have sparked tremendous viewership in this arena, according to *TV Guide.* Demand for television shows about spirit contact, psychics, paranormal investigations and the Afterlife such as: *The Long Island Medium, Psychic Kids, Paranormal State, Psychic Investigators, Paranormal Witness, Deep South Paranormal, Ghost Adventures, Ghost Hunters, Most Haunted,* and *Sixth Sense and Beyond* (a hit paranormal TV show in the U. K.).

Psychics and mediums are frequent guests on popular television talk shows including: *Oprah's Super Soul Sunday, The Ricki Lake Show, The Dr. Oz Show, Dr. Phil, The Ellen DeGeneres Show, The Katie Couric Show, The View, Maury,* and *The Talk.* Even avowed skeptic, Anderson Cooper, regularly interviews psychic mediums. My publicity team is currently booking me on these shows.

Radio has surpassed television in embracing Hyper-Reality shows and this venue will be another major market for *Evidence of Eternity.* Numerous paranormal themed radio shows currently entertain large audiences on AM, FM, satellite, and internet radio. I appear regularly as a guest on several of these shows including the two largest, *Coast to Coast AM* with George Noory (3 million plus listeners per broadcast) and the immensely popular *Darkness Radio*, broadcast on Fox News Talk Radio from Minneapolis. Like most radio shows today, both stream worldwide on the internet.

As with their paranormal show counterparts, producers of mainstream talk radio programs realize controversy is good for ratings. Edgy topics on the Afterlife and spirit contact are recurring themes. I am routinely interviewed on a number of mainstream radio talk shows for my expertise as a legal analyst in high profile murder cases and for my views as an expert on paranormal phenomena, spirituality, and the Afterlife. This broad-based appeal has provided an extremely effective marketing strategy that continues to expand the sales of my last book, *Never Letting Go,* and the popularity of my brand Mark Anthony the Psychic Lawyer™. I will continue to employ this strategy for *Evidence of Eternity.*

Women age 40 plus are the main demographic for *Evidence of Eternity,* presenting a distinct advantage. The Harris Poll indicates that women buy 78% of books sold, either for themselves or as presents. The poll also stated that 24% of all books read in the United States are about religion and spirituality with women being the largest buyers of these books. According to the data, 28% of women and 19% of men regularly read books about religion, spirituality, and psychic phenomena. Facebook Analytics confirms that my current fan base is primarily made up of women in the 35 plus age range.

Even better news is that men will also be attracted to *Evidence of Eternity*. While on tour of the United States promoting *Never Letting Go,* I observed that my brand as The Psychic Lawyer™ sparked high interest in men as it bridges the gap between the paranormal and the logical. This corroborates data from a CBS Poll that find equal numbers of men and women in the United States believe in psychic phenomena. Another statistic revealed by the poll indicates 20% of women admit to the experience of psychic phenomena such as premonitions, telepathy, or ESP, as opposed to 13% of men. Men aren't less psychic than women; they are more reluctant to admit to a psychic experience. *Evidence of Eternity* presents information in a manner that gives them permission to accept the reality of spirit contact. Although attitudes are evolving, traditionally it has been acceptable for women to embrace and trust their feelings about psychic phenomena, while men have felt stigmatized for doing so.

Evidence of Eternity will appeal to men because it presents psychic phenomenon in a rational manner based on science, theoretical physics, and evidence. It addition, it contains edgy, action-packed crime stories to which male readers are attracted.

Both men and women have questions about the Afterlife and seek an explanation and understanding over and above traditional religious dogma. At the very least, they are looking for confirmation that God exists, that physical death is not the end, and that our soul is an immortal living spirit. *Evidence of Eternity* will appeal to the following readers:

1. People who believe in an Afterlife,

2. Those who believe in an Afterlife and are looking to validate their religious or spiritual beliefs,

3. People unsure of the existence of an Afterlife, but who seek 'permission' to believe in one,

4. Skeptics who do not believe in an Afterlife, but are open to its possibility,

5. Families who have lost a loved one to homicide,

6. Individuals who have lost a loved one to suicide,

7. Parents mourning the loss of a child,

8. Animal lovers mourning the loss of a pet,

9. People who enjoy crime stories, and

10. Fans of Mark Anthony the Psychic Lawyer™.

Many who believe they have sensed the presence of a deceased loved one search for hope and answers outside of traditional religious guidelines. *Evidence of Eternity* provides reassurance, validation of their beliefs, answers to questions of what lies beyond, and rational explanations for Interdimensional Communication with spirits. Although *Evidence of Eternity* is thought provoking and challenges dogma at times, the book does so in a respectful manner, making it of interest to open minded men and women of all faiths.

The Competition

Does *Evidence of Eternity: The Psychic Lawyer's Case for Everlasting Life* have competition? Absolutely it does, but this is a benefit. Polls indicate 75% of Americans believe in supernatural phenomena and are looking for answers beyond the confines of traditional religions. As a result, there is an upsurge in interest about life after death, near-death experiences, communication with the spirit world and mediumship. Interest in life after death has gone mainstream, which is why several of these books have been immensely successful indicating there is a lucrative market for such titles.

Evidence of Eternity has mainstream appeal because it is entertaining and engaging while presenting a case for the afterlife based on science, theoretical physics, evidential mediumship and theology. The other books in this genre tend to be written from either a totally clinical perspective or from a totally subjective singular experience.

Evidence of Eternity stands apart from books about near-death experiences because it written by an author who is not a clinician studying someone else's experience, or a person in the throes of death, but by one who is in control of the contact with the afterlife. It blends objective analysis and a subjective in a way that other books on the topic do not, and is driven by gripping, edgy, heartwarming and inspirational true stories.

The books written by religious people on the topics of near-death experiences and the afterlife tend to be heavily colored by their religious backgrounds. This limits the perspective as they attempt to interpret the infinite through the finite perspective of religion. While religion and God are discussed frequently in *Evidence of Eternity*, it is done through an interfaith approach.

The majority of books written by psychics and mediums are written by people who have spent most of their adult lives as practicing mediums. *Evidence of Eternity* stands apart because it is written by "Mark Anthony the Psychic Lawyer™" an Oxford educated attorney admitted to practice law in Florida, Washington D.C. and before the United States Supreme Court. I have nearly three decades of trial experience as a prosecutor, criminal defense attorney and personal injury litigator as well as being a certified mediator and a legal analyst on TV and radio. This brings credentials to the table no other

Jeff's Comments

9 As previously mentioned, this is a crowded book subject, so it's valuable to take multiple opportunities to restate anything that's unique about yourself and your book, and the author does a good job of that here. He also provides a strong cross section of other successful books while showing crucial differences.

Deb's Comments

r The competitive or comparative titles is better in that it shows a connection to the book he is offering in the proposal. The directly related titles are those that are focused on the afterlife and not on ghosts, the paranormal, and spirit communication. This section would have been more effective without the repetition of the author's credentials. In this section you are showing where your book fits. Use the comparative titles to show the market for your book.

medium does. This fresh perspective incorporates the scientific, evidential, and practical with the spiritual.

Interest in the subject matter of *Evidence of Eternity,* is growing and has become mainstream. Once someone has read one book on the afterlife and spirit contact, it provides incentive to read more books on this subject. That is why the following books although competitive, are actually complementary:

Proof of Heaven: A Neurosurgeon's Journey into the Afterlife (209 pages, Alexander, Eben, price $15.99, paperback, ISBN-13: 9781451695199, Simon and Schuster, October 23, 2012)

The author, neurosurgeon Dr. Eben Alexander, chronicles his firsthand account of what he describes as a near-death experience after he was stricken with a rare brain illness. Although he did not clinically die, he remained in what doctors deemed to be an irreversible coma for seven days. Then miraculously, he returned to consciousness. His book explains his visit to the Other Side, contact with a deceased sister he never knew, and what he describes as the Divine Source.

Paranormal: My Life in Pursuit of the Afterlife (256 pages, Moody, Raymond, price $15.99, paperback, ISBN-13: 9780062046437, HarperCollins Publishers, January 29, 2013) Dr. Moody is best known for his groundbreaking book released in 1975, *Life After Life,* which sold 13 million copies. His new book explains how his pioneering study of the Afterlife began. At age 23 Raymond Moody started an entirely new field now known as near-death experience studies. The book chronicles his youthful struggle with depression and a subsequent suicide attempt. As a result, he was motivated to pursue psychology and the study of the paranormal, which includes the survival of consciousness after physical death, near-death experiences, and reincarnation.

Talking to the Dead (305 pages, Noory, George and Guiley, Rosemary Ellen, price $14.99, paperback, ISBN-13: 9780765325396, Forge Books, October 11, 2011) George Noory is the host of the extremely popular overnight radio show, *Coast to Coast AM* (I'm a regular guest on the show). Rosemary Ellen Guiley is an author who has written several books on paranormal and spiritual topics. Together they chronicle many stories from listeners of *Coast to Coast* during the call in section of the show that claim they have had contact with spirits. The authors present thought provoking questions about the Afterlife, about whether or not spirit contact is based on vibration, and if new technology will allow communication with the dead.

Evidence of the Afterlife: The Science of Near-Death Experiences (227 pages, Long, Jeffrey, price $14.99, paperback, ISBN-13: 9780061452574, HarperCollins Publishers, January 19, 2010) Dr. Jeffrey Long is a radiation oncologist who expanded into the realm of near-death experiences and survival of consciousness studies. He created a forum for people who have had near-death experiences, which led to the creation of a large database for near-death experience survivors. Through clinical analysis, he presents evidence that people who have survived a near-death experience do in fact, travel to another dimension.

Inside the Other Side: Soul Contracts, Life Lessons, and How Dead People Help Us, Between Here and Heaven (259 pages, Bertoldi, Concetta, price $14.99, paperback, ISBN 13: 9780062087409, Harper-Collins Publishers, July 17, 2012) Concetta Bertoldi is a medium who explains that after death, a person's spirit goes to the Other Side. The book references many familiar New Age concepts in her discussions of life after death such as soul contracts, which she describes as agreements made with God before one is born.

Revealing Heaven: The Christian Case for Near-Death Experiences (179 pages, Price, John, price 14.99, ISBN-13: 9780062197719, HarperCollins Publishers, February 19, 2013) Reverend Price has analyzed near-death experiences and states they are gifts from God which are compatible with Christianity and Biblical teachings. The book suggests that near-death experiences exist to demonstrate to us that life continues beyond the physical and to help us cope with the pain of loss.

▪ **Promotion and Publicity** 🔟

Steve Harrison, publicity guru and founder of the National Publicity Summit, has said, "Your book is your brochure because it opens doors." He is absolutely right! Within a year of its October 2011 release, *Never Letting Go* hit number one on Amazon's New Age Channeling best seller list on four occasions: October 2011, December 2011, April 2012, and April 2013. Sales are strong and continue to grow.

As a result of this success, I already have a nationwide promotion platform. My new production and promotion team will expand

Jeff's Comments

🔟 This platform section accomplishes a lot, but it also has a crucial and common weakness. It's clear that the author has the ability and eagerness to effectively promote himself and his books, and he has a bona fide track record promoting his previous book. But what's lacking is information about his social media standing and how he intends to utilize it. Frankly, many qualified authors are not well established in cyberspace. Until recently, publishers were willing to cut writers some slack in this area, but it's quickly becoming unacceptable from a pure marketing point of view. For maximum sales success, authors need to be a visible part of the cyber conversation within their communities, even if they don't directly participate in the conversation.

upon that success to drive sales for *Evidence of Eternity*. Due to the book's broad based appeal, the market for *Evidence of Eternity* will be even larger than that for *Never Letting Go*.

Media coverage to promote a book is invaluable. The publicity bonus for *Evidence of Eternity* is my unique brand and celebrity status as Mark Anthony the Psychic Lawyer™, which has made me a regular subject of interviews. This is especially important for *Evidence of Eternity* because this book, like my brand, has broad mainstream appeal. This new book will appeal to women, the bereaved, New Age enthusiasts and spiritual Christians. However, its appeal will extend to men, skeptics, agnostics, science enthusiasts, people interested in psychology, and readers who enjoy edgy crime stories and a compelling page turner.

As an expert in law and the paranormal, I've appeared on numerous TV and radio interviews over the last 20 years. I am regularly invited to comment on high profile murders and metaphysical topics such as "The Haunted White House," spectral phenomena, when the legal system and the paranormal collide, life after death, and reincarnation. In all of these interviews, my last book has been heavily publicized. Likewise, *Evidence of Eternity* will be heavily promoted. When a major radio/TV program interviews me or a print publication runs a feature story about me, it reaches thousands—even millions of people. This media coverage translates into massive advertising for *Evidence of Eternity*.

When an author says how great he or she is, that's an ad. But when the media says it, it's "editorial". People nowadays are more skeptical than ever, and nothing will help close more sales than showing potential customers what the media says about *Evidence of Eternity: The Psychic Lawyer's Case for Everlasting Life*.

When handled properly, media exposure creates a domino effect. When there is a story somewhere, it leads to another and another. That's because the media like to cover things that everybody's talking about. Not so with an ad. Therefore, with the objective of massive sales for *Evidence of Eternity*, I've assembled an aggressive publicity team with a proven track record of success. My team covers all publicity the bases for book promotion: TV, radio, public appearances, internet and print. The team members are:

Roxanne 'Rocky' Trainer is my Business Manager, Tour Manager, Associate Producer and Media Director. Based in Orlando, Florida, she oversees all national publicity and media events. Ms. Trainer has successfully secured nationwide TV and radio interviews for me, in addition to public appearances and book signings at numerous locations including Harvard, Brown, and Yale Universities. She has worked with Disney and Universal Studios and has broad experience in the film, television, radio, and music industry.

Nancy Gershwin is the great-niece of George and Ira Gershwin. As a member of a famed Hollywood dynasty, she is a highly successful television producer who has worked on shows such as *Today* and *Judge Judy*. Ms. Gershwin, who is based in Los Angeles and New York City, has extensive experience promoting psychic mediums. She spearheaded the TV concept of 'talking to the dead' in the 1990s as the co-creator of the television show, *The Extraordinary*. Nancy recently produced and directed my 'sizzle reel' to pitch TV appearances and for use in the development of a TV show based on The Psychic Lawyer™. Nancy Gershwin and Rocky Trainer will produce the author video for *Evidence of Eternity*, which will be used for promotional purposes on TV and the internet.

Gary Grasso is a high-powered and immensely successful Los Angeles publicist who specializes in securing appearances on TV talk shows such as *Good Morning America, The View, The Katie Couric Show, The Ricki Lake Show, Dr. Oz, Dr. Phil, The Ellen DeGeneres Show, The Doctors, Extra, CBS News*, and many more.

Marianne Pestana is a book publicist and social media expert based out of Denver, Colorado. Ms.Pestana specializes in maximizing exposure for authors and their books on the internet, Facebook, Twitter, LinkedIn, and in print. Part of her promotion strategy includes PRWeb, the world's most socially shared news release service. PRWeb's press release distribution network covers major news sites like Yahoo News, Google, and Bing search engines, and over 30,000 journalists and bloggers. In addition to articles and interviews, this will generate book reviews.

As a direct result of the success and popularity of my previous book *Never Letting Go*, and my unique brand as Mark Anthony the Psychic Lawyer™ I've received national attention which has led to appearances on international radio and TV talk shows such as: (Partial)

- **Washington D. C.:** NBC4 with Barbara Harrison *The Haunted White House*

- **Pittsburgh:** CBS Pittsburgh Today *Live with Kristine Sorenson*

- **Miami:** NBC Miami with Justin Finch *Psychic Scams*

- **Boston:** Fox News 25 with Gene Lavign *Never Letting Go*

- **Boston:** *The Literati Scene* with Smoki Bacon and Dick Concannon

- **St. Louis:** CBS *Great Day St. Louis* with Matt Chambers

- **Worldwide:** Fox News Network with David Asman

- **Worldwide:** *Coast to Coast AM* with George Noory*

- **Vancouver, Canada:** 103.5 QM/FM, *The Dale Wolf Show*

*Indicates I am a regularly appearing guest

In conjunction with my publicity team, I will use my numerous print media contacts to promote *Evidence of Eternity* through Barnes and Noble, Goodreads, *Leading Edge Review*, BookReview.com, *Conversations Book Club Magazine*, *Horizon's Magazine*, Powell's Books, Tower Books, and the Institute For Global Transformation to name a few.

Deb's Comments

S I am not sure about the publicity strategy of applying for a Pulitzer Prize, and I am not sure of the results. It is certainly creative. In my opinion the most important thing about the book in a proposal is what is in it for the reader.

An additional promotion strategy for *Evidence of Eternity* will be its status as "Nominated for a Pulitzer Prize" for best non-fiction book. The book's emphasis on science, theoretical physics, and **S** theology combined with edgy and compelling true stories make this an excellent nominee under the non-fiction category. With a previous bestseller and my credentials as an Oxford educated trial attorney who has lectured about life after death at Harvard, Brown, and Yale, a Pulitzer Prize nomination will boost the exposure and prestige of *Evidence of Eternity*.

To be eligible for a Pulitzer Prize, the author must be a U. S. citizen and the book must be published in the United States. The publisher will not have to submit *Evidence of Eternity* for a Pulitzer Prize; my publicity team will do so.

Many readers will be attracted to a book nominated for a Pulitzer Prize. While Harrison Ford has never won an Academy Award, he does enjoy the status of Academy Award Nominee. Likewise, marketing *Evidence of Eternity* as a Pulitzer Prize Nominee will enhance the attractiveness for media interviews and boost sales.

The internet is a huge promotional vehicle and Mark Anthony the Psychic Lawyer™ has a major web presence. I own several domain names, all of which point to the main web domain name: www.HealGriefWithBelief.com. However, I also own the following domains: www.thepsychiclawyer.com, www.psychicattorney.com, as well as www.NeverLettingGo.com, and several others. I will do the same with www.EvidenceOfEternity.com and other variations on the book's title. Additionally, a landing page will be created for *Evidence of Eternity,* which will make it easy for people to order the book online.

The purpose of the website is to promote *Evidence of Eternity,* my brand, and my work as a medium. This approach has proven immensely successful. I also maintain a growing list of emails through subscriptions to my blog and internet newsletter that will be used to promote book sales.

The website design cross publicizes all promotion related to *Evidence of Eternity.* It is integrated into all my social media sites such as Facebook, Twitter, and LinkedIn. I maintain three pages on Facebook, which include a Like page, a Friend page, and a grief support page. I have over 20,000 fans on my Like page, which grows daily.

Successful publicity and promotion are the result of a carefully planned and executed strategy. With a professional team and aggressive comprehensive promotion plan utilizing TV, radio, print, and the internet including social media, *Evidence of Eternity* is destined to become a major bestseller.

▪ Table of Contents of *Evidence of Eternity*

Deb's Comments

t Once again I hesitate in any proposal for an author to state that the book is destined to be a bestseller. This is particularly so if the author is a psychic. Your job in the proposal is to show the things that will translate in the mind of the agent or editor into books being sold.

u In my opinion this proposal could have been more effective. However, as mentioned, the resulting book is well written.

Jeff's Comments

11 The chapter TOC and outline are exceptional and speak for themselves.

PROPOSAL 7

◼ Proposal Critique

The Trauma Toolbox
Healing from the Soul Out

Susan Pease Banitt

◼ Concept Statement ⓑ

Even the most well adjusted person struggles when encountering an overwhelming event. Coping skills can go out the window. All of a sudden we have trouble thinking clearly and acting effectively. Getting the help we need may feel impossible. In *The Trauma Toolbox: Healing From the Soul Out* trauma expert, Susan Pease Banitt LCSW, presents effective immediate antidotes to extreme stress

Deb's Comments

ⓐ This is a great title.

ⓑ We don't use the heading "Concept Statement," but that is a matter of personal choice. This information can go under overview, but it is a long narrative that should be broken up into small paragraphs and bullet points. Every sentence in a proposal should count. If you are trying to draw attention to certain aspects of your book, make sure your points do not get lost in a sea of words. Remember: agents and editors read a lot and often skim. You want to make sure they see what you want them to see.

Jeff's Comments

1 I'm the first to admit that I miss things that should have been caught and fixed. One of those times is right here in the first paragraph. At best, it's a run-on sentence that was overlooked by publishers in the context of the overall promise this proposal successfully offers.

2 This second sentence would have been a strong opener.

Deb's Comments

c This sentence would be stronger if it was written in a more active voice. For example: "There is one intervention more powerful than any others for the healing of traumatized individuals."

d This paragraph is a bit fluffy. This is not a "woo woo" book. Even though it uses the word *soul*, it is not without concrete takeaways. Unfortunately, that is often the impression of books that are too airy in language. This is where the author is defining the core concept, so using the word *being* several times dilutes the power of this paragraph. It would have been better to state it more authoritatively, like: "There are several layers to one's consciousness." If the author uses some more definitive psychological terms,

and traumatic reactions in mind and body. With stressful events on the rise: home foreclosures, businesses failing, people unable to get access to healthcare, significant rises in child abuse and an unprecedented number of soldiers returning home with severe psychological trauma, this book is timely and fills a growing need. The author draws from her thirty-five years of diverse training, as a Harvard trained psychiatric social worker, a yoga teacher and a lifelong student of alternative healing to map out the most current holistic guide for treating the pernicious effects of overwhelming stress and for getting people back on their feet safely and quickly. She demystifies alternative and mainstream, eastern and western, traditional and modern treatments presenting them with logic and common sense. For readers who like to go it alone, she gives step-by-step emotional first-aid tips that can be safely used in the privacy of one's home or office, using resources readily at hand. A unique, one stop shop guide for laypeople that will also empower practitioners *The Trauma Toolbox* is an essential addition to anybody's self-help library.

Book Overview

After twenty years as a therapist I have been astonished to find that there is one intervention, more powerful than any other for the traumatized individual, the possibility of inviolable wholeness at the core of one's being. Most people experience trauma as a blow to their very deepest sense of self. Trauma shatters the layers of mind and body, creating a sense, in an individual, of being irretrievably broken. Grief is overwhelming as patients keen for the life that once was.

The Trauma Toolbox: Healing From the Soul Out illuminates the layers of the human being down to that core level. Trauma is defined as not only a single horrific event or series of events, but also as the individual's sense of self being swallowed up in the suffering of overwhelming stress and events. When people can understand the layers of their being they can start to understand the power and beauty that form the core of their being, the place from which all healing springs. They can also then begin to select the tools for their healing that reveal this center.

When I interviewed naturopathic physicians for this book, I chose three from New York City because of their work on the **e** 9/11attack, with victims and with responders. After they shared their views with me, they all (separately) made the same addition to their comments. Each noted that prior to 9/11, the bulk of their practice was made up of people in New York City who had been living lives of such chronic and extreme stress that they had suffered breakdowns in their physical and mental functioning. *Many of these people had not yet been exposed to one fantastically horrific event, but they still showed symptoms of PTSD in their mind and body*. They all agreed that overwhelming and unmanageable stress is the disease of our times.

In the year since those interviews, dozens of news reports have been flooding the airwaves weekly about the prevalence of extreme PTSD in our returning military. TIME magazine asked the controversial question in the case of the Fort Hood shooter: is he a terrorist or a vicariously traumatized psychiatrist soldier? Soon after, Haiti exploded from the inside out, shattering a people and creating a national epidemic of PTSD that has only begun to be addressed.

In December 2009, I attended the august Evolution of Psychotherapy conference. The world's most famous teachers and speakers on the mind spoke to over 7000 attendees. Deepak Chopra, Jean Houston, Dan Siegel, Andrew Weil, Bessel Van Der Kolk and **f** Jack Kornfield comprised some of the roster. *They were unified in their call for multidimensional healing models and modalities to address the very serious issues facing humanity today*. Jack Kornfield said explicitly and somewhat synchronistically, "We need a trauma toolbox."

the book will have a better chance of reaching a broader audience. The alternative is to clearly define what is meant as one's "being." Here the word is used several times and in interchangeable ways. The author is a trauma expert and has credentials as a social worker. This credibility gets watered down by the use of unclear terms.

e In explaining the book, this statement should be: "I interviewed [however many] naturopathic physicians for this book." My first question would be whether she interviewed any allopathic (Western) physicians and if they were seeing the same results. This is an effective proposal; however, it could have been better organized. It appears to be stream of consciousness.

f I don't see this paragraph as a plus. It can be used in the preface of the book as a way to describe the inspiration. However, in my opinion, the author weakens her own authority and dates her material by referring to these other luminaries. As an author you hope to become a luminary. Unless one of these speakers is endorsing your book, it does nothing for you to mention them or the conference. It also shows that this was not the author's original idea, but rather was a response to something she heard.

Deb's Comments

g This paragraph contains too many ideas. If it is a statement about how lifesaving treatments can traumatize people, then it should be reversed with the first sentence as: "The very treatments that are lifesaving for patients often end up traumatizing them." It is best to keep one main idea to a paragraph. Or use bullets to show how many types of trauma this author has treated. You want your proposal to be easy to follow, well structured, and logical.

h I find this proposal to be disorganized. It did not do justice to the actual book. As you will see in the sample material, the book has a lot to offer. It sold and still sells. However, when writing a proposal, you do not want to take a chance that yours will be dismissed as too difficult to follow.

i This should have its own header to separate it from the rest of the proposal. This is one of the important pieces that needs to be easy to find. One of the first questions an agent or editor will ask is, "What is it?"

Well, I have such a toolbox. I have been gathering tools over my thirty plus years in human services. From autistic children to women diagnosed with breast cancer; from underage sex slaves off the streets of New York to adults incapacitated by early childhood abuse, trauma has played a central role in my work. Because of my work in child protective services I became aware of the **g** ocean of suffering in adults around this country due to undiagnosed traumatic stress and illness. In working with my cardiologist husband, we discovered how many cardiac patients had a history of traumatic events. Research is now corroborating the very real link between PTSD and heart disease….and the reverse. Sadly, the very treatments that are lifesaving for patients often end up traumatizing them.

The beauty and uniqueness of this toolbox lie in its diversity and accessibility to a large number of people. Not all people can afford a therapist, but they should know what their options are and what part of the healing process therapy can and cannot address. Not all medical insurance covers access to naturopathic doctors, acupuncturists or chiropractors yet people find a way to spend billions of dollars every year to access these important practitioners. **h**

Then there are the modalities that are nearly universally available. Almost anybody can grow some lavender in a pot outside. They can find a dog to walk, a tree to sit under in contemplation, a journal to write in, or buy some Epsom Salts at their local drugstore. They can learn exercises of the mind and breathwork to regulate the body. These things are as free as the air we breathe. If people only know which tools they need and get a little guidance, they can alleviate their intense suffering as well as the suffering of those around them.

Here are some of the tools provided for readers in The Trauma Toolbox: **i**

- Skills to build a first-aid kit to respond to any traumatic event
- Insight into the causes of stress in the mind and body
- Motivation to deal with stress sooner rather than later
- Free self-help treatments and resources
- Insider's knowledge about maintaining health

- Ability to make good decisions for effective interventions

- Increased resilience to overwhelming events

The book closes with a look at public policy, public health issues and the need for new models of healing. Negative and positive incentives (the carrot and the stick) for moving towards diverse modes of healing are presented for those struggling with these issues as well as those who treat them. If trauma is the disease of our time, then healing from trauma individually, locally and globally can truly pave the way for a bright future as yet unrealized in human history.

The Trauma Toolbox: Healing From the Soul Out provides compassionate understanding along with a compendium of tools and sources for those suffering the dark night of traumatic stress. It is a unique guide for our times that many will find helpful and possibly life saving.

About the Author

Susan Pease Banitt, LCSW is a Harvard trained psychotherapist. She has worked in human services for over thirty-five years and has been a psychotherapist for two decades. She has pursued an unusually diverse path via training in yoga, meditation, dance and shamanism.

Susan has often chosen to work with some of the most difficult populations in her field including autism, child abuse and extremely traumatized people. Over the years, some of the settings for her work have included: inpatient psychiatric hospitals, outpatient clinics, medical hospitals, medical clinics, and a child abuse prevention and response center. Most of her extensive training was done in Boston, Massachusetts under the highly trained eyes of analysts, well-known social workers and Harvard affiliated professors.

Writing is a large part of psychodynamic clinical work. Case reports, detailed biopsychosocial assessments, process recordings (verbatim transcripts of sessions along with impressions and observations), hourly notes and writing a handbook have been a part of her repertoire throughout her career. Writing for publication is a fairly new endeavor for Susan, a challenge she eagerly welcomes. Writing

Jeff's Comments

3 There's nothing in this overview that does harm. However, it's about twice as long as it needs to be and includes information that should have been reserved for other sections, such as why the book is needed and who will buy it.

4 It's always great to open your "About the Author" statement with the comment that you are Harvard trained. Warning: Don't say that unless it's true. The rest of this section is fine.

Deb's Comments

j If this author had to do it over, I would recommend a much shorter, more concise, and bulleted overview. This overview has too much to digest. As the author you need to reduce the work for the agent or editor. They make quick decisions. Show them quickly and concisely what they need to know. Don't editorialize unless it is relevant. They want to see your writing style, but the proposal is also a prospectus. It is a business plan. Get to the point and do it clearly.

k The author could have reduced the length and content of the overview and started with the credential that she is a Harvard-trained psychotherapist. This is probably what helped her sell the book. These are the kinds of facts that are relevant in an overview because it immediately establishes authority to write a book. Instead, the author here gave away precious attention to the attendance at a conference of others in the field. Every word counts. Make them count for you. Agents and editors have limited attention spans.

l This proposal is not that old so this is an old statistic. If you are going to quote a statistic, try to get one that is the most recent. Or you can simply quote something that will not be dated at all. You want your book to be "evergreen," with strong backlist potential. Therefore, avoid things that will immediately make it seem like old news.

m The market focus might have been more targeted if it looked at those people who are not responding to traditional treatments. The core hook of this book is that this Harvard-trained psychotherapist has something that no one else has. While these statistics might not be readily available, anecdotal statements would suffice if they are examples

itself, though, is an area of practice in which she has always received highly positive feedback.

Recently, Susan had an article published in Nexus, the local National Association of Social Work chapter's newsletter on the link between psychological trauma and celiac disease. The Oregonian published her op-ed piece on police brutality and mental health this past November. Susan has just launched her website and blog, www.InsightOutHealing.com. She recently joined the Willamette Writers group to network with and get critiques from other writers.

The author thrives in Portland, Oregon with her cardiologist husband, twin thirteen-year-old girls, four dogs, two cats and four horses. She often wonders why she is still living in the city. Her private practice in psychotherapy has been a source of great satisfaction. She is releasing this endeavor, temporarily, in order to move forward with her writing.

A funny thing happened on the way to her non-fiction book. Susan started writing young adult fiction, a modern "Swiss Family Robinson" set in Yellowstone with a family stranded in an RV. Other projects Susan would like to pursue after *The Trauma Toolbox: Healing From the Soul Out* include a book on people growing up with sociopathic parents, and a memoir based on her spiritual life. Susan sees herself joyfully focusing on the craft of writing for the rest of this lifetime.

■ About the Market **l**

"PTSD is a highly prevalent and impairing condition. Only a minority of people with PTSD obtains treatment. Early and aggressive outreach to treat people with PTSD could help reduce the enormous societal costs of this disorder." (J Clinical Psychiatry 2000)

When we talk about who has PTSD, we are talking big numbers. When we talk about who has been exposed to a traumatic event we are talking huge, almost universal numbers. All of these people are possible readers for *The Trauma Toolbox: Healing From the Soul Out*.

According to the latest research up to 12% of Americans will experience at least one episode of PTSD in their lifetime. They will average **three episodes of PTSD lasting an average duration of 3-5 years,** depending on whether they obtain treatment or not, **for a lifetime average totaling 9-15 years of suffering extreme stress**. The majority of Americans diagnosed will be women, and the majority of those who seek treatment and resources (including books) will also be women.

Not all people exposed to extremely stressful events develop full-blown PTSD, but they suffer stress related consequences to these events, and they, too, seek out resources for healing. How many of us will suffer a traumatic stressor sufficient to potentially cause PTSD? Just about 90%! Yes, approximately **90% of Americans will suffer a traumatic event sometime over the course of their lifetime.** But most of us will not experience just one such event. The average exposure comes to **4.8 lifetime traumas**. Who are these people? Let's break down the groups a bit.

We have been at war with Iraq for 8 years now. President Obama just announced a significant increase in the number of troops deployed to Afghanistan in December 2009. To date, 1.8 million soldiers have served in Iraq and Afghanistan. The Rand Corporation estimates that a full third of these soldiers are returning with PTSD, and some professionals think that number is on the low side. Many of these soldiers have family members who will be vulnerable to vicarious trauma—the trauma that occurs when being in close proximity to someone suffering from PTSD- effectively doubling or tripling the cases of PTSD that will result from the war itself. Because these soldiers are young, we can expect symptoms to manifest and worsen over time without treatment or intervention. Currently 70% of veterans that need help **will not seek it from military sources.**

It's difficult to know how many soldiers will reach for a book on alternative healing from stress. Recently I sat next to a young man on his way to basic training and officer's school while I **n** was flying to an international trauma conference. Unbeknownst to me, he leaned over and started reading my section on chiropractic care. He really connected with the information and how it could help the stress injuries some of his soldier friends had from heavy packs and the impact of roadside blasts. I've also had some military spouses contact me around the development of this

of how people do not respond to treatment. This is something that should be able to come right out of the author's case files. Always think of your target market as the direct reader of your book who has the most to gain from the content.

n Here the author refers to anecdotal evidence of a market. This would have been stronger if a clear statement of the audience had been made. What did these people ask and why? Were they trying other things that did not work? What is being offered to them that does not satisfy their needs? Every section of a proposal is an opportunity to show how what you have suits a particular need. This author does this, but some simplification and focus would have made it even more powerful.

book, who want assistance in the reintegration process for their loved ones. While these anecdotes are not "hard data", they do indicate a subgroup of people who are hungry for answers and open to new ideas.

Besides soldiers there are many other professions that lend themselves to disorders of extreme stress due to the nature of the work. These include: first responders (EMT, fire, police etc.); emergency room nurses and physicians; mental health care workers; prison guards; disaster relief volunteers; teachers and crisis workers. Their families suffer stress related illnesses as well. Research shows that after 9/11 first responders' children developed PTSD at the rate of 19%.

Other groups of Americans that suffer high rates of PTSD and stress related disorders include: immigrants, victims of violent crimes, victims of child abuse (adults or children), battered women, college students, those diagnosed with major medical illness, accident victims, caregivers those in divorcing families, those afflicted by chronic poverty and disaster survivors.

As a longtime therapist, I know that my colleagues and I are always seeking out new information to help our clients. We need this information, ourselves, to effectively serve these clients without getting burned out. I am writing the book I have wanted for so long. In getting this book started and doing interviews, I have found that practitioners across many disciplines are enthusiastic about this book. *The Trauma Toolbox* will provide the opportunity for "cross-pollination" among multiple professions. I have no statistics to support this assertion, only a strong gut feeling after years of being in the field as well as the support of many colleagues. I believe they will provide a strong market for this book. The Oregon chapter of the National Association of Social Workers, for example, has strongly endorsed this topic by not only accepting my talk on holistic treatment on trauma shock for the statewide conference this spring, but also by sponsoring my day long workshop in May.

This book will probably do best with a reader with a high school or college education. She will be the survivor of major life stresses, PTSD, or the caregiver or partner for a family member with those issues. (I say "she" because, statistically, the most likely reader for this book is a woman although I know there will be many interested men.) She may have some spiritual leanings or be in the midst of a life transition. She may be one of the thousands of people unemployed or without health insurance who cannot afford therapy yet is looking for answers to difficult and overwhelming issues. She will refer this book to her friends and family because of its inspiring yet practical information. She may live in another country where there are even less services than in the US. She will be very happy to find this book at her local bookstore or online, and she will keep a copy on hand for years to come. This fictional reader represents thousands and potentially millions of readers in the United States of America and abroad.

The Trauma Toolbox: Healing From the Soul Out is a book that answers the needs of our time. It has a large potential market indeed, with the possibility of becoming a bestseller.   **5** **o**

About the Competition (Complementary Titles)

The Trauma Toolbox: Healing From the Soul Out fills a needed spot in the panoply of self-help books. Early on in the self-help genre there were a handful of classics written in self help relating to stress and trauma (The Courage to Heal, 1988; The Relaxation Response, 1976; Waking the Tiger: Healing Trauma, The Innate Capacity to Transform Overwhelming Experiences, 1997). These books were important icebreakers in the topics of stress and abuse and painted with somewhat broad brushes available concepts of treatment.

The books published in the past five years or so have become more specific and tend to take one modality for stress and/or trauma and go into depth with it. These books are hands on and very specific about the intervention being peddled, often an unusual or **p** alternative technique. They are fairly straightforward in their information but narrow in scope. At the same time there have been a number of spiritual self-help books that have been promoted in recent years. Even a couple of memoirs have been published lately addressing trauma. These books address the human condition without directly addressing the mechanisms of stress and trauma.

As a treater of trauma and trauma survivor, I have wanted to find one current overarching book that could give me an idea of all treatments and resources available so the reader could go find **q** the right books or modalities without browsing for hours on end or having to read a number of different books. That book is *The Trauma Toolbox: Healing From the Soul Out*. It combines a number of interventions while placing the utilization of those treatments in

Jeff's Comments

5 The "About the Market" section covers all the bases. However, because there are more than a few subcategories, it would have been helpful to organize the groupings under subheads.

Deb's Comments

o Never state that your book can be a bestseller unless you plan to buy ad space in the *New York Times*. It is meaningless.

p Using the term *peddled* is the wrong message to send. You don't want to disparage other books to elevate yours, particularly if you are writing in the spiritual or mind/body genre.

q This is the first time I realized that the book is a toolkit for readers to find interventions. I find this confusing. A very clear statement in the overview would be helpful.

a spiritual self-help format that is designed to resonate to currents needs and readers. I have not found any other book that meets this criteria. It places spiritual self-help, the latest information on stress and trauma and a compendium of interventions ancient and modern, free or paid services all in one big tent resource.

Specific Trauma Interventions

Here are some self-help books that have helpful interventions for trauma with a narrow focus on one or maybe two modalities. They lack a spiritual self-help focus or diversity in treatments or both.

Healing Trauma: A Pioneering Program for Restoring the Wisdom of your Body by Peter Levine. Publisher: Sounds True, Inc., 2008. Paperback 112 pages. (CD included)

> This book gives a 12 step program to healing from trauma according to the technique of Somatic Experiencing, a modality that Dr. Levine pioneered.
>
> Complaints about this book lay in its brevity and lack of depth.

Acupressure for Emotional Healing by Michael Reed Gach and Beth Henning. Publisher: Bantam, 2004. Paperback, 320 pages.

> This book is a wonderful resource guide for knowing how to do self-applied acupressure, a modality that uses finger pressure to stimulate acupuncture points.
>
> It is an in-depth resource with a narrow specific focus. Towards the end of the book a couple other modalities are mentioned in brief.

Energy Tapping for Trauma : Rapid Relief from Post-Traumatic Stress Using Energy Psychology by Fred Gallo and Anthony Robbins. Publisher: New Harbinger Publications, 2007. Paperback, 184 pages.

> Another self-applied technique, tapping is part of the energy psychology movement. It is a highly effective single intervention book that people seem to find helpful.

Stress Elimination Handbook: A Holistic Self-Help Program to Restore Health, Achieve Balance, and Promote Well-Being by Grandmaster

Adrian Simon Lowe. Publisher: Ibis Press. Not yet released. Date of publishing: August, 1, 2010. Paperback: 160 pages.

> This book is not yet out, but it looks to be a really wonderful in-depth instruction in the art of healing with tai chi and qigong. This book does look like it will incorporate Eastern philosophic underpinnings of healing, with a narrow in-depth focus.

Stress Management: A Holistic Approach by Subodh Gupta. Self-published. Paperback, 80 pages.

> This booklet provides helpful cognitive behavioral techniques.

Freedom From Stress: A Holistic Approach by Phil Nuernberger and Barbara B. Brown. Publisher: Himalayan National Institute, 2007.

> This book explains many stress mechanisms in mind and body. It utilizes mostly yogic techniques of the mind with some forays into breath and diet.

The PTSD Workbook: Simple, Effective Techniques for Overcoming Traumatic Stress Symptoms by Mary Beth Williams and Soili Poijula. Publisher: New Harbinger Books, 2002. Paperback, 237 pages.

> Although this book is more than five years old it is still widely referred to patients by clinicians. This book focuses on practical solutions of the mind in a workbook format to overcome trauma. It is often used in conjunction with psychotherapy.

The PTSD Sourcebook: A Guide to Healing, Recovery and Growth by Glenn R. Schiraldi, Ph.D. Publisher: McGraw Hill, 2nd edition 2009. Paperback: 464 pages.

> This fine book has the largest collection of interventions of any book I have seen along with excellent conceptualization of PTSD. The interventions, however, are American mainstream, lacking information on modalities such as acupuncture, herbalism or even naturopathic medicine. Although he addresses the importance of spiritual life, I would not classify this book as spiritual self-help.

Jeff's Comments

6 This is a strong competition section. The author reveals that she's well versed in the category and offers an extensive list of comparable titles.

7 This shows that the author has a clear vision for the finished book and how long she will need to finish it.

Deb's Comments

r This author did not need to list so many books. In my opinion, if the market had been well defined and the core description of the book had been clear, there would have been no need to list so many books. You don't need to oversell your book. You simply need to show where it belongs in the available literature. You also do not need to list self-published books or books more than a few years old unless they are still on the bestseller list or are considered classics. In either case, the focus should always be on what your book does, not what their books do not do. You especially do not need to list books that are not yet released.

s I never see the need to include production details. You are not self-publishing. You can indicate whether the manuscript is complete.

Beyond Trauma: Conversations on Traumatic Incident Reduction by Victor R. Volkman. Publisher: Loving Healing Press, 2nd edition 2007. Paperback/Kindle, 360 pages.

Again, a monotreatment book to go in depth with one modality. Good, but singular focus, not spiritual self-help.

Healing From Trauma by Jamin Lee Cori and Robert Scaer. Publisher: DaCapo Press, 2008. Paperback/Kindle, 288 pages.

This book is written by a therapist and has much good information, however I found this book to be highly triggering (stimulating of trauma). Some diversity, influenced by Buddhist thought.

Trauma Stewardship: An Everyday Guide to Caring for Self While Caring For Others by Laura Van Dernoot Lipsky and Connie Burke. Publisher: Berrett-Koehler, 2009. Paperback/Kindle: 264 pages.

I have included this book for treaters and responders to trauma, which is another audience for The Trauma Toolbox. Wonderful spiritual tone and helpful mental exercises. Lots of theory and symptom description.

As one can see, there are many books circulating on trauma and stress. While this list is comprehensive it is not exhaustive. Yet, there is plenty of room for a book with provides a more in depth spiritual look at the effects of trauma while providing more comprehensive and up to date resources. *The Trauma Toolbox: Healing From the Soul Out* is that book.

Production Details

Length: 225-250 pages

Delivery: 9-12 months following delivery of first advance installment

Sidebars: 2

Graphs: 2

Permissions: Author will seek permissions for interviews and cases presented as needed, including rights for cartoons, poetry or song lyrics. (see enclosed permission form)

Introduction: Seeking nationally known holistic medicine figure for introduction.

Back matter: Appendix of names/contact information for expert providers who gave information for this book and resources for trauma first aid kit

Index

Marketing and Platform Building

I am aware that the publishing industry is moving through a big transition in how it markets books and authors. I take the need for an author platform very seriously and have spent the last few months moving in that direction and planning for the future. I am willing to go the distance as a practical yet creative marketing partner for my publisher.

In the last few months I have:

- Launched my new professional website: www.InsightOutHealing.com
- Had an op-ed piece featured in the Oregonian (circulation 320,000)
- Published an article with state chapter newsletter for the National Association of Social Work
- Presented a poster at International Society for Traumatic Stress Studies conference (large international conference)
- Given talks at a local hospital and training center
- Grown my social networking sites
- Been used regularly as an expert via HARO (helpareporterout.com)
- Signed on with best-seller Jean Houston to be mentored

Other information such as a special foreword should be listed in the overview if it is relevant, in the table of contents, and then again in the marketing and promotions section of the proposal.

Jeff's Comments

8 I like the way the author has organized the marketing section into many subcategories. It shows that she has deeply researched what publishers want to know and see. None of this alters the fact that the author isn't a celebrity or has any kind of product sales history. But it does show that she is eager to proactively leverage her professional skills and connections in ways that are likely to sell copies.

Deb's Comments

t This type of editorializing about the state of the publishing industry is not necessary. We all tend to say too much. But when you are writing, you have the chance to catch yourself. Simply use this space to talk about what you have in place. Even if you have recently implemented your website, make a statement without indicating that you just put it up yesterday. The fact you have it is enough. You don't need to discuss plans for the future unless they are in concrete terms. Example: "Active social networking, blog regularly."

 This discussion of the blog sounds like it is in the future. If it exists in cyberspace, you have a blog. Therefore, make a strong statement: "I post to my blog every week." If you have syndicated it through various channels, add that, and if you have any subscribers of any type of significant numbers, say that. Agents and editors tend to ignore things in the future.

 This is also future-oriented. If the author has done public speaking, then it is good to mention it. This statement is not meant to offend this author or anyone reading this book, but agents and editors, unless they become personal friends, do not concern themselves with what you enjoy doing. They want to know if you are good at it and if people will come to listen to you, which are the these things that translate into book sales. That is what the people determining whether to back you want to know. This is business.

It is nice to be asked; however, it is more effective to say, "I have developed a training workshop that I

My plans for near future platform building and marketing fall into several categories outlined below.

Articles

I plan to continue to write and submit articles for publication in magazines, ezines and newsletters. These articles will focus on holistic healing from stress and trauma. The targeted audiences include practitioners as well as lay people. In particular, I am aiming for women's magazines, including *O Magazine, Ms., Redbook, Real Simple, Martha Stewart Living* and other "seven sister" magazines.

Blogs

I am committed to my website blog, "Blogging with the Insight Out". Every week to two weeks I will be publishing a 750-1000 blog on a relevant topic. I plan to keep submitting these to *Huffington Post* and other blog outlets for larger distribution. I advertise these blogs on my social networking sites: Twitter and Facebook. I am always looking for ways to expand exposure to my online writings personally and professionally, often through word of mouth or professional presentations. When appropriate I am submitting them as op-ed pieces locally and nationally.

Conferences

I have several upcoming workshops confirmed for the Portland area over the next few weeks. One of these is an international conference for women in psychology. I enjoy public speaking and feel it is the best way to communicate much of the material found in my book. I am always looking for new conferences to submit to. Currently I am applying for two international conferences in November 2010.

Trainings

Due to the amount of trauma responders involved in Haiti at the moment, there is a need for debriefing and helping returning workers. I am currently in talks with Red Cross and Mercy Corps to do trainings for their returning Portland teams.

I have recently been asked to do a relaxation training workshop at a local hospital.

Classes

I am working up 8 and 12-week class proposals for local athletic clubs, fitness centers and neighborhood community centers, many of whom welcome stress reduction classes.

Social Networking

Currently, I post regularly on a Facebook and Twitter account and am looking for ways to expand my audiences there. I am also a member of LinkedIn and Alliance for A New Humanity. I have also begun to find communities through Ning.com and am considering launching a network there.

Regular Networking

I am a member of the Willamette Writers Club in Portland, OR and will be attending monthly events there. At the National Association of Social Workers Oregon Chapter I sit on the newly formed Mental Health Committee. I plan to join a women's business networking group, a writers' critique groups in Portland and City Club of Portland. I have been invited by my children's school community to be a stress reduction expert at various events.

Media

Although I have a great deal of theater experience, I have not so much time in camera. I am now seeking out media training for on-camera interviews. I intend to be the go-to expert on stress and trauma management in the Portland area, later expanding to bigger arenas.

After the book publishing process is underway I will go to a second phase of marketing. Ideally, but somewhat dependant on the advance, I will hire a national caliber publicist to start moving my work out into a wider field. This will include:

Radio/TV Interviews

I believe strongly in the mission of *The Trauma Toolbox* as a vehicle of relieving suffering for large numbers of people. Radio and TV in large markets are a part of that mission, and I will make this campaign a priority.

have taught or will definitely be teaching at the following venues." Everyone who is creative has big ideas. Agents and editors are more concerned with follow-through. They do not want to feel that you as an author are looking to them to create your career. They are looking at what you bring to the table. They will take into account things you are planning if they are supported by things you have already done.

X I don't see the benefits on any of the other ideas listed. If they were written in more concrete terms, they would be great, but all of this sounds like it will occur in the future. It is better to leave this kind of information out if you are going to leave the impression with the publisher that you are not ready. This does not mean you can't make these things concrete-ish. Most importantly, only write in ways that are credible. The agents and publishers are not looking for promotional partnerships. You, as an author, need to take advantage of all that is available to you. You can easily show a greater online or even traditional presence. But the time to do it is not after the proposal.

Video

Many topics in the book lend themselves to visual demonstration, i.e. how to smudge yourself, proper yoga poses for relaxation. I will be uploading short video demonstration clips onto my website.

Featured Blogger

I have my sights set on Huffingtonpost.com but am open to similar forums that attract large viewership.

Workshops

The material in the book lends itself very well to experiential, spiritual self-help workshops. I will be drafting a weekend and weeklong curriculum that helps people transform their suffering via the tools in the book. Ideal places to present these would include the Omega Center, New York; Breitenbush Hot Springs, Oregon; the Kripalu Center, MA; Hollyhock, British Columbia, Asilomar, California and other similar centers which market the workshops and books of their presenters.

After the book is published, I am **all** about the marketing. Have RV will travel… seriously (I have a 31 foot Itasca with all the amenities)! I expect my publisher to be my partner, at least in brainstorming ideas if not actual cash (although that would be great, and I will ask; James Patterson is my hero). Book signings, readings, interviews and all listed above will be continued in the USA and abroad. I have a great advantage as a senior clinician in being able to open doors in both worlds, lay and professional. I have been in the field thirty-five years and plan to call in all contacts and favors everywhere I have been before. I still have connections in the San Francisco bay area, Boston metro, Albuquerque and, of course, Oregon. My neighbor is a member of Congress; maybe I can even do something around stress in Washington, DC.

I'm open. I'm ready. I'm full of enthusiasm. Let's go!

Table of Contents

Deb's Comments

y The table of contents is excellent. In my opinion, the other sections of the proposal could have been shortened with the emphasis on the credentials of the author and the strength of the book being proposed. When it comes right down to it, publishing is a hard copy business. While marketing and promotion is important, you want to focus on your strengths. In this proposal the three things to have emphasized are: the credentials of the author; the fact that PTSD sufferers are not responding to currently available treatments; and the promise that this book shows them alternatives and in fact contains tools that this author in her practice as a Harvard-trained psychotherapist specializing in trauma has determined to be effective. Don't ever lose sight of what you are offering.

Chapter Summaries

Introduction

The introduction encapsulates my story as a survivor of extreme abuse and stress throughout my lifespan. It links my personal story as a survivor and therapist to the larger story of chronic overwhelm and trauma throughout the world and introduces the reader to the layout and scope of the book.

Deb's Comments

z The chapter summaries are very well written. Even though I found organizational and content flaws in the presentation of this proposal, in the end a good book will always have a good chance of finding its way to the right publisher.

Foreword

I am pitching this book to several well-known figures in holistic medicine in order to garner support from one in writing a foreword that endorses this book and these teachings. In June, I will be doing a week-long small group salon with Jean Houston. She or one of her well-known colleagues (Deepak Chopra, Jack Kornfield) may be interested.

Part I: The Trauma Experience

Chapter 1: Devastation

A violinist who lost her career in the moment her car crashed on the way home from the Opera house. A mother who saw her two-year old daughter die in a house fire. A woman who endured 7 deaths in 6 years including her 13 month relationship with her husband dying of cancer. A survivor of childhood leukemia. An adult subjected to severe abuse and neglect as a child. A survivor of Hurricane Katrina. A young soldier returning home from the Iraq war. These are a sampling of the diverse faces of individuals who have encountered overwhelming events. They represent the distinct but often overlapping categories of natural disasters, accidents, abuse, crime, medical illnesses, war, betrayal, and cumulative stresses.

Chapter 1 explores the different kinds of traumatic experiences and explains the current psychiatric diagnostic categories used to diagnose stress disorders: Adjustment Disorder, Acute Stress Disorder and Posttraumatic Stress Disorder. Western Medicine has some efficacy in treating these disorders but often falls short and focuses narrowly on the mind and a handful of psychiatric interventions that fail as often as they succeed. We need a new model for looking at treating survivors of extreme events, and this book will gave patients and practitioners the tools and information they need to get faster and longer lasting relief from debilitating symptoms.

PROPOSAL 8

PROPOSAL FOR

The Successful
Mid-Career Entrepreneur

Leap from the Uncertain Corporate Ladder and Land in the Right Business

By William Seagraves

Need and Contribution

Jim Smith was a well-regarded 20-year veteran of the investment industry when the impact of the 2008 financial meltdown finally reached his mid-sized firm in Jacksonville, FL. Although he thought his company was well positioned to weather the tide of economic hardship, he was caught completely off guard on an unseasonably cold Friday in November of 2009 when his boss tapped on the doorframe of his office and asked if he "had a minute."

Jim immediately knew why his boss had made this unannounced visit even without the security detail waiting outside his door in the hallway. Five minutes later Jim was filling up a cardboard box with his personal belongings under the watchful eye of a stern-faced guard who clearly had an underdeveloped sense of humor. Of course, Jim was only one of many Calisto Investment, Inc. account managers who left the building that day carrying a single cardboard box and a final paycheck in their pockets.

Jeff's Comments

1 This wasn't the author's original title. His first title used words like *baby boomer*, which I usually discourage. Anything that claims to be for people of a "certain age" is unnecessarily risky, for the simple reason that Americans don't like to see themselves as old, which could be anywhere north of thirty. The workplace is rapidly changing, and people don't want to feel like they may have been left behind.

2 This isn't the usual way I would have someone start a proposal; I think it's safest to begin with the overview. But if something isn't broken, I won't insist on fixing it. In a way, the title is already a partial overview, because it instantly announces what the book is about and who should care. I like what the author does here because he strongly illustrates the concept.

Deb's Comments

a I am not sure about the subtitle. The title is great. I am not even sure this book needs a subtitle, but that is something the publisher will ultimately decide. For a proposal this is a winner.

Deb's Comments

b We prefer to title this "Overview" to conform to publishing protocol. That being stated, this is a creative way to introduce the concept. For ease of reading, the author might have italicized the narrative introduction, but that is a choice. Keep in mind that the more your break up the proposal with titles and subheadings, the better. Agents and editors read a lot of these, so you want yours to look professional, and it should be visually pleasant to read.

c This is an innovative way to approach this subject matter. The author clearly explains the structure of the book, then works in his credentials. So far he is pre-selling the book before he even finishes the remaining sections of the proposal.

At first, Jim used the company-provided resources to look for another job, but few companies were interested in talking to an experienced 53-year-old investment expert with high salary demands. Still, Jim took the rejections he got over the next three months in stride and continued his search.

Then, one day his wife came home from work and found him bringing up some of his signature home-brewed beer from the basement. She made a joke about joining him on their patio for "happy hour" then, after a chuckle she said with what she though was good-natured sarcasm, "Hey, I have an idea. You should start your own brewery and forget this job search business."

Jim halted, mid-stride, as if something had physically stopped him. He put the box of full beer bottles he was carrying on the kitchen counter and looked directly at his wife. "You know Sherri, in 20 years of marriage you've given me some really good advice, but this has got to be the best advice ever," Jim said as he walked across the kitchen, arms outstretched to give his wife a hug. "Because, you know what, that's exactly what I'm going to do-----*screech* (the sound of a record scratch)

Jim Smith's mid-career enlightenment narrative illustrates at least two important aspects of this book; first, its principal audience and second, how the "great recession" has created this emerging cadre of motivated and experienced entrepreneurs. What the story does not illustrate is an important part of this entrepreneurial fable: how does Jim Smith, the accidental brew master, accurately determine if a startup brewery is the best path for him, and what are the realistic steps he'll have to take to develop his own vision of financial freedom in an uncertain economy? Fortunately, that's the part of the story answered in this book. **c**

The Successful Mid-Career Entrepreneur: Leap from the Uncertain Corporate Ladder and Land in the Right Business shows its readers exactly how Jim—or anyone else similarly positioned in their life and career—can make the most of their mid-career entrepreneurial pursuits … whether those entrepreneurial pursuits were originally planned for or not.

But why the sudden record scratch? Throughout the book, readers will follow the hero character, Jim Smith, and the story of his entrepreneurial epiphany. At the end of each chapter, Jim will be faced with a decision—one directly based on that chapter's content (or, *lesson*, of sorts). For example, after Chapter 3, which explores the differences between an entrepreneur and a business owner, Jim might just discover that his personality, skillset and business acumen levels are better suited for a craft beer franchise opportunity (those do exist) vs. starting his own brewery from scratch.

Or, after Chapter 5, on charting the best course forward, Jim may discover that he's eligible to use the money in his 401k as startup cash, when previously he assumed he'd have to apply for an SBA loan.

Author William Seagraves, a seasoned and serial entrepreneur himself, carefully deconstructs each part of the business discovery process so that the reader is able to honestly evaluate first, *themselves*, and second, *the unique, mid-career business opportunity at hand*. A wide expanse of practical content vetted by a seasoned financial professional with a proven track record of helping hundreds of clients realize their entrepreneurial dreams make this book the go-to resource for the rapidly growing number of mid-career entrepreneurs.

Primary Audiences

Corporate (or former corporate) professionals (usually in higher, business oriented positions) and specifically:

- **Reluctant business owners** (30% of audience)—these professionals have recently lost their job, aren't sure where to turn, and are not feeling secure at all.

- **Proactive business owners** (40% of audience)—this group still has a job but can see the writing on the wall. They are scrambling to get control of their future before they are forced into the position of being a reluctant business owner. They are better off than the reluctant ones, but definitely aren't feeling secure.

- **Active business investors** (20% of audience)—this group is already in business for themselves but could use guidance on cash flow, management, and exit strategy.

- **Retired and inspired** (10%)—this group is comprised of those who chose to take an early retirement, but don't feel like they're "done." Though they may be financially secure at

Jeff's Comments

3 This section is clearly organized and well said. I like that he separates the primary audience from the secondary audience.

Deb's Comments

d I think this is a good market description. It shows he clearly understands his audience, which will create confidence in the mind of the agent or editor that the author is focused. The next step would be to explain how to reach the audience.

the present, they aren't comfortable with the constraints of a future on a fixed income.

- **Veterans**—although a very small percentage of our audience, Veterans are a group whose unique situation will be addressed.

- Those in this demographic group still "under-employed" due to the lingering impact of the 2008/9 financial meltdown

Secondary Audiences

- Career advisors

- Human resources professionals

Key Uses

Mid-career entrepreneurially oriented professionals considering starting a new business or those professionals closer to retirement age considering a "second act" cap to a successful career will use this book as an essential resource as they plan for and seek out the right business coupled with viable funding options for their new enterprises.

Specifically, this book explores the drawbacks to starting a business under the constraints of traditional business debt. *The Successful Mid-Career Entrepreneur* is a complete guide that explores the full range of questions and concerns voiced by these entrepreneurs, including: how to get started, risks and rewards, potential savings and the costs of this funding strategy. The targeted entrepreneurs will use this resource to:

- Understand why the right business fit is so important

- Understand the tremendous impact that proper funding can have on the future success of a business

- Build a basic framework of understanding and assess the financial risks and potential rewards of funding their business using a self-directed 401(k)

- Gain the needed confidence to act on making their dreams a reality

- Avoid common implementation mistakes by learning through the experiences of others

Jeff's Comments

4 "Key Uses" is a smart section. This isn't an under-published category, so it's effective to reinforce your book's focused "deliverables" while also showing off that you understand what your customers need and want.

Deb's Comments

e This subtitle doesn't mean anything to me. However, the information is useful. It could be used as an introduction in the content part of the book or it could be subtitled "Summary."

Other Potential Titles

Better Late Than Never

Why Now is the Perfect Time to Make the Transition from Employee to Entrepreneur

Make the Leap and Never Look Back

Eliminate Uncertainty and Take Control of Your Entrepreneurial Future

Length

Approximately 200 pages

Table of Contents

Synopsis—This chapter introduces the concept of the mid-career entrepreneur and highlights the unique opportunity for the target audience. While the target audience may not be able to take the business risks of someone in their 20s, the mid-life entrepreneur has a unique set of advantages over their younger counterparts that include: a set time frame with specific, staged goals; greater self-knowledge and awareness of their own strengths and weaknesses. The chapter will help its readers weigh the pros and cons of continuing their career as an employee or striking out on their own as an independent business owner.

Jeff's Comments

5 It never hurts to give alternative titles, though I don't consider either of these to be viable.

6 Providing an estimated word count is more useful than a page count. Few authors, especially first-timers, know how to transfer double-spaced manuscript pages into finished books. Also, if you envision space-eating graphics or illustrations, here's where you say it in detail.

7 I think this is a darn good outline section. Sample chapters were included with the proposal, so extra elaboration wasn't required.

Deb's Comments

f There is no need to show other potential titles. You want to show confidence in and commitment to what you are presenting. You won't be choosing the final title anyway.

g I prefer a TOC before the summaries. Remember to provide the roadmap before the details.

Chapter 2—What Kind of Mid-Career Entrepreneur are You?

- Five types
  - *Reluctant business owner*
  - *Proactive business owner*
  - *Active business investor*
  - *Retired & inspired*
  - *Veteran*
- Forced into freedom

(h) These chapter summaries are well done. The amount of detail you need depends on the subject matter. This author used enough detail to show the agent or editor that the book will be content rich and well organized. As the author, you want to prove that you can execute the promise of the pitch.

Synopsis—Five categories or *classifications* of mid-career entrepreneurs are explored in this chapter including those who were forced into the "freedom" of entrepreneurship due to the economic recession that began in 2008. Various past and current circumstances determine how a mid-life entrepreneur is categorized based on timing, preparedness, personal situation, self-awareness, proactivity, business acumen and attitude.

Chapter 3—Entrepreneur or Business Owner

- The cookie jar
  - *The difference*
- Why it matters
- Essential traits and habits

Synopsis—Not everyone possesses entrepreneurial tendencies. This chapter discusses the particular set of skills and abilities required to succeed as an entrepreneur including business acumen, an ability to see the big picture, and the required people and networking skills. This chapter is connected to a later chapter on the importance of choosing a business type that fits an entrepreneur's individual characteristics and strengths.

Chapter 4—The Way Forward

- The critical attitude shift
  - *Best thing that could've happened*
- Looking forward with a different lens

Synopsis—Regardless of how an entrepreneur arrives at the decision point to strike out on their own (especially if they were "forced into freedom"), it's important to accept the reality of the situation and chart a path toward the future. This chapter will help the reader embrace changed circumstances with a positive attitude and shows the reader how to seize the opportunity in a way that ensures success.

PART II—Embracing Mid-Career Entrepreneurship

Chapter 5—Charting the Best Course *(Creating Your Unique Opportunity)*

- Accelerated 10-15 year timeline
- Advantageous position
  - *Viability of 401k funding*
  - *Business selection*
  - *Exit strategy*

Synopsis—This chapter pushes the new entrepreneur to develop a mindset that will help them seize their best opportunity. It helps the reader appreciate at least three key advantages of starting a business at this point in their lives: the fact that 401k funding could be an option; the fact that they choose when the business begins and the products and/or services it offers; and that they get to choose when the business ends.

Chapter 6—Franchises—A Quick Path to Business Ownership

- Business of your dreams, or ...
- Checking under the hood
- Apples to apples

Synopsis—Chapter 6 is geared more toward those in the "business owner" category of entrepreneurs. Readers learn about the three key elements to watch out for when investigating buying an established franchise business along with other essential tips that determine business fit and provide grounding practices for success.

Chapter 7—Buying an Existing Business

- Pointers
- Pitfalls

Synopsis—Buying an existing business requires more of an entrepreneurial mindset than the less risky franchise ownership. However, there are unique challenges that counterbalance any advantages. This chapter provides pointers on what contributes to success as well as guidance to help avoid the common pitfalls including: correctly judging business maturity and potential for growth; and misreading the outward signs of success that hide fundamental business model flaws.

Chapter 8—Starting Your Own Business

- Risk / reward
- Nailing your business plan
- Planning for the future now

Synopsis—Traditional entrepreneurs are the target group for this chapter. It includes both discussion and guidance on creating an airtight business plan and the creation of realistic risk and reward scenarios.

Chapter 9—Ensuring Entrepreneurial Success

- Why people fail
  - *Success counterpoints*
- Taking control
- Why the time is right

Synopsis—No matter the chosen entrepreneurial path, a common set of pitfalls exist that often lead to failure. One of the most consistent issues in every failure scenario is debt. This chapter explains how traditional debt scenarios often drive a business to make the least advantageous decision or distract its owners from focusing on the best business strategies.

PART III—Building a Long-Term (10–15 Years) Action Plan

Chapter 10—Launch Phase: 0–6 months

- Business funding
  - *401k funding*
- Business selection
- Business planning

Synopsis—The first phase of launching an entrepreneurial enterprise includes business research, planning and selection. This chapter explains the vital steps and considerations that must be part of this six-month decision phase. It includes the key activity of setting up funding for a new business or entrepreneurial venture.

Chapter 11—Operational Phase: 6 months—10 years

- Growth strategy
  - *Employee considerations*
  - *Marketing*
- Business investment
  - *Impact of 401k funding*
- Maintaining balance
  - *Personal*
  - *Professional*

Synopsis—The operational phase tests an entrepreneur's professional and personal mettle and it is where planning meets the reality of the marketplace. This chapter emphasizes in more detail why operation as a debt-free, cash-rich enterprise allows new enterprise owners to focus on business success and enables them to deal with the inevitable challenges of business operations from employee issues to growth and marketing challenges. The chapter emphasizes the importance of a positive, solution-oriented attitude.

Chapter 12—Transition Phase: Exit Strategy
Planning your exit

- The emotional disconnect
- The ultimate return
  - *Watch your nest egg pop*

Synopsis—Mid-career entrepreneurs have the advantage of controlling both their entrance and exit from a business or entrepreneurial venture. The chapter focuses on this full circle strategy and the advantages of front-end exit planning. It discusses various exit strategy options and shows readers how to sell a business and return the profits back to their 401(k) and other investment options.

Chapter 13—Conclusion

About the Author

Other Resources

Competing and Related Works

The mid-life/mid-career audience segment has certainly not been neglected in the marketplace. While much attention has been dedicated to this group, often times the messaging is rather narrow in scope, presenting theories or ideologies without actual applicable knowledge. In fact, a number of titles focus on one of two recurring themes: *a professional crossroads* or *entrepreneurship*. While either topic on its own wouldn't be considered competition, a handful of these books contain language and themes that are complementary. Those titles have been listed separately.

As for those published titles that more closely echo the core topics in *The Successful Mid-Career Entrepreneur* (a professional crossroads *and* entrepreneurship), there tend to be varied levels of urgency. Short synopses for these titles and the other ways they differ, have been included below.

Competitive Titles

Title—**The Second Chance Revolution: Becoming Your Own Boss After 50**

> *Author*—Edward G. Rogoff, Ph.D. & David L. Carroll
>
> *Paperback*—178 pages
>
> *Publisher*—Rowhouse Publishing (2009)
>
> *ISBN*—978-0-9791522-9-0

Analysis—This book also addresses the entrepreneurial issues of those in a similar demographic. While an entertaining and informative read, the piece this book is missing is the "urgency, time and can't screw up" mentality. Mid-lifers are not being coached to take advantage of their unique opportunity but rather fed the information without an inspirational, how-to, take-action spin.

Title—**Second-Act Careers: 50+ Ways to Profit from Your Passions During Semi-Retirement**

> *Author*—Nancy Collamer
>
> *Paperback*—263 pages
>
> *Publisher*—Ten Speed Press (2013)
>
> *ISBN*—978-1607743828

Analysis—This book explores "second-act careers" and the idea of semi-retirement, insinuating that the reader has a choice and is in total control over the situation. There is no urgency in the matter i.e., the impending threat of a layoff to spur this new career choice. While the idea of a "second-act" is congruent with *The Successful Mid-Career Entrepreneur*, it's circumstantially different.

Title—**What Color Is Your Parachute? 2014: A Practical Manual for Job-Hunters and Career-Changers**

    Author—Richard N. Bolles

    Paperback—368 pages

    Publisher—Ten Speed Press (2014) In print since 1970 and revised each year since 1975

    ISBN—978-1607743620

Analysis—As the title indicates, this book is more focused on job hunting than the pursuit of an entrepreneurial dream. However, it was one of the first books published in what we'll call the "professional crossroads" genre and it's still heralded as one of the best and most relevant. The New York Post refers to it as the "go-to guide for everyone from midlife-crisis boomers looking to change their careers to college students looking to start one." Those so-called *midlife-crisis boomers* are the target demo.

Title—**Jump Ship: Ditch Your Dead-End Job and Turn Your Passion into a Profession**

    Author—Josh Shipp

    Hardcover—240 pages

    Publisher—St. Martin's Press (2013)

    ISBN—978-0312646738

Analysis—This book is very similar in messaging and context with one glaring difference—its audience is young adults—young adults who have more time to "experiment" with their careers but not necessarily the resources, knowledge or skillset to do so on the same level. And again, while the core messaging is similar, its origin stems from a different need—one more of restlessness or discontent than a serious need.

Title—The Economy of You: Discover Your Inner Entrepreneur and Recession-Proof Your Life

> *Author*—Kimberly Palmer
>
> *Hardcover*—256 pages
>
> *Publisher*—AMACOM (2014)
>
> *ISBN*—978-0814432730

Analysis—This book is all about creating a safety net via entrepreneurial side venture, or what the author refers to as "side gigs." The root motivation is largely the same—fear of being laid off—but *The Successful Mid-Career Entrepreneur* takes the theme further into a full entrepreneurial transition, not just a part-time venture. The notion of "recession-proofing" your life is congruent.

Title—The Eventual Millionaire: How Anyone Can Be an Entrepreneur and Successfully Grow Their Startup

> *Author*—Jaime Tardy
>
> *Hardcover*—272 pages
>
> *Publisher*—Wiley (2014)
>
> *ISBN*—978-1118674703

Analysis—This book is closely related as it communicates that business ownership is the only path to true, financial independence. The advice seemingly comes from other millionaires who have "been there and done that" and are looking to impart their personal wisdom. *The Successful Mid-Career Entrepreneur* is a bit more formulaic and timetable-driven. In other words, "eventual" does not have a place in the context.

Related/Complementary Titles

Title—Own Your Future: How to Think Like an Entrepreneur and Thrive in an Unpredictable Economy

> *Author*—Paul B. Brown
>
> *Hardcover*—224 pages
>
> *Publisher*—AMACOM (2014)
>
> *ISBN*—978-0814434093

Jeff's Comments

9 Timetables are not required in the proposal, but can add value if the author is positioned for a relatively fast turnaround, which six months is. However, I have discovered that first-time

Title—**Start Late, Finish Rich: A No-Fail Plan for Achieving Financial Freedom at Any Age**

    Author—Paul B. Brown

    Paperback—368 pages

    Publisher—Crown Business (2007)

    ISBN—978-0767919470

Timetable

Final manuscript to be complete within 6 months

Author Background

Having been dubbed the "Mid-Life Entrepreneur Advisor," William Seagraves specializes in helping aspiring business owners make the leap from the restraints of corporate America to discover the freedom that small business and franchise ownership can provide. With more than 20 years of experience as an entrepreneur and financial funding guru, Bill is expertly positioned to offer sound advice that has seen hundreds of small business owners not only succeed, but flourish during the mid-life entrepreneur stage of their lives.

His insight, coupled with the knowledge of sound business practices, has given him a solid reputation among other funding and business coaching companies. In addition to running three of his own companies in the computer services and small business financing arenas, Bill has helped clients establish themselves, growing businesses in retail, restaurant, entertainment, manufacturing, business consulting firms and many other industries.

Bill Seagraves started his career as a successful Product Development and Sales Manager in 1984 in the defense industry. Bill had extensive success in large-scale engineering projects and with sales and marketing to the U.S. government. As an entrepreneur at heart,

writers tend to underestimate how much time they will actually need, so I often encourage them to add an extra three months. Better to be early than late.

⑩ This is well said, but I generally prefer to place this section at the front of the proposal because it's often the first thing publishers want to know.

Deb's Comments

ⓙ I don't see the need for a timetable unless the manuscript is complete. Then you can indicate "completed manuscript available by request." The publisher and agent will determine when the book is appropriate for a particular list. There may be changes and editing needed, and you will have a negotiable deadline. This information in my opinion does not add value to the proposal.

ⓚ The preferred subheading is "About the Author," but anything is fine. Keep in mind this is not a resume. This author does a good job of listing the most relevant credentials. This is an effective match of career and concept. That is what the agent and editor are considering: Does the author have credentials strong enough to carry the book? In this case the answer is yes.

however, Bill moved from California to the Denver area and purchased a small business providing Information Technology consulting and services. Bill's company provided services to small and large businesses for eight years, until he successfully transferred that business to one of his employees.

In 2004 with a partner, Bill co-founded a successful company providing self-directed 401k and other lending services. After helping to establish that company, Bill decided to pursue a broader vision of business services, funding and entrepreneur education. Following this vision, Bill founded CatchFire Funding, in 2008.

Despite the timing of CatchFire's launch (just six weeks before the stock market crash of 2008 which saw the credit markets dry up) Bill and his nimble team were able to rapidly grow the company into a market leader—basically beating the recession against tremendous odds.

Bill continues to manage this growing staff of extraordinarily capable small business experts, many of them having startup business or franchise experience of their own. Everyone on the CatchFire Funding team is passionate about helping mid-life entrepreneurs grow to be just as successful.

In addition to managing daily operations at CatchFire, Bill is a member of a private, international roundtable of highly successful entrepreneurs. As a recognized expert in the field of small business funding and financing, Bill is regularly invited to share his insights as a speaker and panel presenter at franchise and financing events. Bill's company specializes in not only sharing information about wealth building with funding and financing strategies, but also in educating his clients on the best practices for building their own businesses.

Benefits

This book offers:

- Clear insights and guidance from a seasoned financial professional/mid-life entrepreneur/coach and advisor on a rapidly emerging business/professional market segment

Jeff's Comments

11 The "Benefits" section is always a nice touch. In this case it's somewhat redundant, but it never hurts to continually reinforce your strongest points through the proposal; editors often jump around when reading.

Deb's Comments

1 This subtitle doesn't seem to belong here. This could be part of the content section or part of the market section. But the subtitle is unclear. Benefits for whom? The reader? The publisher? Make sure all your subtitles are meaningful and organized for the proposal. This is why we typically use standard headings in a particular order. The agents and editors know what to expect and where to find the information they need.

- Advice specifically targeted to this audience of motivated, well-positioned entrepreneurs who are ready to take action

- An accessible business funding roadmap that puts the topic in big picture perspective

- Action oriented worksheets and decision-making checklists

- Specific strategies that help the reader gain the confidence to act

- A comprehensive long range plan to help mid-career entrepreneurs launch, operate and finally transition away from their successful business

In the end *The Successful Mid-Career Entrepreneur* is a book that challenges a large group of entrepreneurially oriented professionals to seize the opportunity offered by the current economic environment to consider a "second act" cap to a successful career. *The Successful Mid-Career Entrepreneur* speaks directly to both the confident sprit and the calculated concerns of its target audience of business professionals. After all, entrepreneurs inside and outside traditional business seek answers to the same questions when evaluating a potential investment or business opportunity; what are costs, risks and rewards of moving forward. *The Successful Mid-Career Entrepreneur* answers these questions and much, much more.

Market Environment for *The Successful Mid-Career Entrepreneur* (12) (m)

The Successful Mid-Career Entrepreneur is positioned to take advantage of the social, economic and demographic confluences in American society that are pushing the target audience—successful mid-life or mid-career professionals—to make fundamental changes in their expected career and life trajectory.

This claim is supported by a diverse set of recent statistics including the following indicators:

Jeff's Comments

(12) This too might appear to be a bit redundant, but it's solid reinforcement minus distraction, so it got my vote.

Deb's Comments

(m) I prefer the simple "Market."

General Interest and Motivation Toward Entrepreneurship

- Approximately 25 million people—one in four Americans ages 44-70—are interested in starting their own businesses or non-profit organizations in the next five to 10 years.

- Aspiring entrepreneurs have an average of 31 years of work experience and 12 years of community involvement. Five out of six (85 percent) report significant management experience—15 years on average.

- Encore entrepreneurs have modest financing needs. Two out of three (67 percent) report that they need $50,000 or less to get started and only one in five (20 percent) said they need more than $100,000. A large group (47 percent) expects to tap personal savings to launch ventures.

- About half (52 percent) say they have delayed launching ventures because they do not feel secure enough financially and nearly as many (47 percent) say they believe they would not be able to obtain adequate financing. But nearly six in 10 encore entrepreneurs (58 percent) say the current economic climate makes them more likely to start their own businesses or non-profit ventures. (2)

- The demand for franchise business growth far outpaces the ability of franchise businesses to access financing (3)

- According to the Bureau of Labor Statistics, the current pre-retirement market is about 65% bigger than what is was 20 years ago. (4)

Difficulty Obtaining Traditional Financing

- Between 2007 to 2013 bank loans guaranteed by the U.S. Small Business Administration have fallen 60%

- Four of the five major banks in the U.S. have decreased the amount of conventional small loans made in 2012 by two-thirds as compared to 2007

- Individuals seeking small loan amounts ($150,000 or less) are having greater difficulty getting funds. The average Small

Business Administration 7a loan tripled in size from $165,723 in 2007 to $498,971 in 2013.

- The use of personal savings to fund a startup business jumped from 66 percent in 2012 to 86 percent in 2013. (5)

- Credit card use to back a startup enterprise was the leading funding source in 2012 according to one survey (2)

Author Marketing Strategy

The author is committed to exploiting a full range of traditional and social media based marketing channels including industry conference presentations, public workshops, press releases, and radio and television interviews. In addition, the author will take full advantage of his large customer and qualified potential buyer database to directly market the book along with a coordinated YouTube informational video campaign tied to all popular social media platforms including Facebook, Twitter, LinkedIn, Google+ and others. Specifically, these marketing efforts are as follows:

Email Database

As of late-July our database includes an audience of 18,690 opt-in email addresses that grows daily through the use of direct contact strategy that engages this audience at least once a week. We will introduce the book into this ongoing communication stream to promote sales and awareness among this highly targeted group of potential book customers. NOTE: We will continue to run a substantial Google AdWord campaigns that directs 150 users per day to a 401(k) landing page.

YouTube Video Promotion

Since January 26, 2014 we have been running an aggressive Google VideoAd campaign that has garnered 200,000 views as of late-July. This popular 401k funding tutorial has nearly doubled our online lead flow. We plan to leverage the popularity of the video by editing

Jeff's Comments

⓭ As said elsewhere, my natural inclination is to front-load this information. Other than its location in the proposal, this section does an excellent job communicating how the author will leverage everything he's got to promote the book. This is an ideal way to organize this crucial section. My only caveat here is that when specific promises are made in the proposal, the publisher might actually add them to the final contract, so don't say anything you're not serious about.

Deb's Comments

ⓝ This is a good marketing section. Ordinary people can have effective marketing strategies, but you need to begin the minute you think of your book topic. Any author can create an effective online presence. What you don't want to do is fill this section with a bunch of "I will do" after the book is sold. Your book will not make you have a platform. If you understand your audience, there is no reason you can't find ways to start reaching readers prior to the completion of your proposal.

the ending to include an offer to buy *The Successful Mid-Career Entrepreneur*.

Monthly PR Press Releases

Recent public relations efforts resulted in a mention in *Forbes* magazine on the topic of using a 401(k) to fund a business (http://www.forbes.com/sites/tomtaulli/2014/02/09/using-your-401k-to-fund-your-business/) as well as a write-up in *Financial Advisor* magazine (http://www.fa-mag.com/news/retirement-money-used-for-business-start-ups-17575.html). These efforts will continue through marketing channels such as ereleases.com (http://www.ereleases.com/).

Social Media Promotion

We have identified Facebook audiences through the use of the marketing tool, Nielsen P$YCLE Lifestage Groups. We have been aggressively marketing to these targeted segmentations since April 2014, and as of late-July, have garnered over 3,200 likes. This is the same audience that will be interested in the book.

In addition, we will implement a year-long strategy directly based on the contents of the book to build our social media presence on all other social media platforms including LinkedIn, Twitter, Google+ and others.

Presentation and Workshop Activity

The author speaks frequently on the topic of entrepreneurship and alternative funding sources at a variety of related professional conferences (listed below). The author will seek out all other appropriate professional organizations and formally apply to present at annual or semi-annual meetings and conferences while the book is being written and moves through the production process. The author will also design and launch a new public workshop directly based on the book and market through his various customer channels. The top potential related professional organizations include:

- International Franchise Association
  - 1,275 franchisor members, 12,500 franchisees and 660 suppliers
  - Annual Conference: Feb 5-8, 2015 in Las Vegas

- FranChoice Conventions
  - Organization reaches 100's of franchise consultants who sold more than 2500 franchises in 2013
  - Each January and July, annually

- International Business Brokers Association (IBBA)
  - More than 1,000 business brokers engaged in business brokerage and mergers and acquisitions.
  - Fall Conference: Nov 17-22, 2014 in Austin
  - Spring Conference: May 4-9, 2015 in Atlantic City

- American Society of Pension Professionals & Actuaries
  - More than 16,000 career professionals actively engaged in the retirement planning industry
  - Annual Conference: Oct 26-29 in Maryland

- Colorado Association of Business Intermediaries
  - 150+ business brokers in the local Colorado market
  - Fall Conference: Sep date and CO location TBD

Author Buyback Commitment

The author will commit to an initial buyback of 3,000 to 7,500 books depending on unit cost for our own inventory and lead generation.

(1) http://www.statisticbrain.com/startup-failure-by-industry/

(2) http://www.encore.org/EncoreEntrepreneursRelease

(3) http://emarket.franchise.org/LendingMatrix.pdf

(4) http://www.immersionactive.com/resources/50-plus-facts-and-fiction/

(5) http://blog.iese.edu/bizknowledgewatch/2014/who-started-new-business-in-2013-in-u-s/

Jeff's Comments

14 Putting a numerically specific author buyback promise in the proposal can be a decisive value-added incentive, because it provides a way for the publisher to underwrite its upfront investment. However, the publisher might want to hold you to this commitment in the final contract, so don't tender any promises unless you're really willing to do it.

◼ COVER

The Successful Mid-Career Entrepreneur

Leap from the Uncertain Corporate Ladder and Land in the Right Business

By William Seagraves

◼ TABLE OF CONTENTS

Chapter 4—The Way Forward

- The critical attitude shift
  - *Best thing that could've happened*
- Looking forward with a different lens

PART II—Embracing Mid-Career Entrepreneurship

Chapter 5—Charting the Best Course *(Creating Your Unique Opportunity)*

- Accelerated 10–15 year timeline
- Advantageous position
  - *Viability of 401k funding*
  - *Business selection*
  - *Exit strategy*

Chapter 6—Franchises—A Quick Path to Business Ownership

- Business of your dreams, or …
- Checking under the hood
- Apples to apples

Chapter 7—Buying an Existing Business

- Pointers
- Pitfalls

Chapter 8—Starting Your Own Business

- Risk / reward
- Nailing your business plan
- Planning for the future now

Chapter 9—Ensuring Entrepreneurial Success

- Why people fail
  - *Success counterpoints*
- Taking control
- Why the time is right

PART III—Building a Long-Term (10–15 Years) Action Plan

Chapter 10—Launch Phase: 0–6 months

- Business funding
  - *401k funding*
- Business selection
- Business planning

Chapter 11—Operational Phase: 6 months–10 years

- Growth strategy
  - *Employee considerations*
  - *Marketing*
- Business investment
  - *Impact of 401k funding*
- Maintaining balance
  - *Personal*
  - *Professional*

Chapter 12—Transition Phase: Exit Strategy

- Planning your exit
- The emotional disconnect
- The ultimate return
  - *Watch your nest egg pop*

Chapter 13—Conclusion

- About the Author
- Other Resources

■ SAMPLE CHAPTER

Chapter 3—Entrepreneur or Business Owner

Up to this point, we've been throwing around the term *entrepreneur* an awful lot. While this is a good, overarching term that helps us draw a line between those who are the right audience for this book and those who are not, the term itself—in this context—is not entirely accurate.

The truth is, from what I have observed throughout my life and career, there is a great distinction between whom and what I deem to be an *entrepreneur*, versus whom I would classify as a *business owner*. Some might think the terms are interchangeable, but after consulting with nearly one thousand aspiring individuals who are looking to cut the cord from the corporate world and set out on their own—I can tell you differently. There are distinct characteristics and tendencies that belong to each group, so I'll do my best to explain what those are.

I'll start with an analogy I learned from a mentor of mine. Well, to be more exact, from the mentor of a friend of mine, who was kind enough to share his insight. It's called the "cookie jar" analogy. The gist is this: an entrepreneur is a person who can reach their hand into a cookie jar, grab a cookie and remove it from the jar, all without breaking the jar, the cookie or their hand. I'll explain a little further.

Picture two cookie jars, side-by-side—one made of glass and one ceramic. Which one do you think the "business owner" is more likely to gravitate toward? If you answered *glass*, you'd be correct. The simple reason is that the glass jar reveals what's inside, letting the business owner know what he or she is getting into. This isn't to say there won't be any surprises (hey, what appears to be a nut could wind up being a peanut butter chip) but the overall chance of a curve ball is significantly decreased.

Now the ceramic cookie jar...*that* one holds a degree of mystery. In fact, it may not even resemble a traditional cookie jar—it may be oddly shaped, strangely colored, and may even appear out of place. Even still, the "entrepreneur" is intrigued, recognizing that this jar might just represent a great opportunity...even if he or she has little idea what that might be.

With curiosity piqued, the entrepreneur's tendency won't be to immediately open the jar to found out what's inside. Instead, he or she will first mull it over and consider whether there is sufficient benefit to doing so. There may be an amount of *perceived* value, but entrepreneurially-minded individuals are often less concerned with popular opinion and more apt to be independent thinkers.

Making the decision to open the lid requires the vision to see how doing so could meet a need—how it could help a customer, how it could be beneficial to the entrepreneur, or how it could be monetized. I have noticed that there aren't many rash decisions to be made as an entrepreneur. However, once an opportunity to grow a business or positively alter it in some way has been identified, things can move very quickly.

To rope the business owner back into our analogy, at this point, both the business owner and the entrepreneur have removed the lid from their respective cookie jars. Now is the time to reach in and grab the cookie itself, or essentially, to begin to execute on the opportunity at hand.

Who do you think is in a better position to reach in and take hold of the cookie without breaking it? First, you have the business owner, who took one look at the delicious-looking cookie through the glass, swiftly made up his mind to go in and get it, and now has some pent-up adrenaline coursing through those fingers.

Second, you have the entrepreneur, who wasn't exactly sure what he was dealing with, but based on the characteristics he could assess, determined there were likely ensuing benefits that could move his business forward. Armed with the knowledge that his lengthy thought process afforded, his hand is now steady and dexterously poised to grab that same cookie.

Given the two different approaches, it would appear that the entrepreneur is better equipped at this point. While that may be true, let's envision that both of them are able to grab hold of the cookie. The business owner was a bit more aggressive in his approach and therefore a significant amount of crumbs fell to the bottom of the jar—but the majority of the cookie is still intact. The entrepreneur rather delicately picks up the cookie, using only his thumb and forefinger. No crumbs, no mess, and the full integrity and structure of the cookie are unchanged.

Although the business owner and the entrepreneur prepared differently, they are now both at the same stage. This is where the differences become more evident.

The last step in the analogy is successfully pulling the cookie back out of the jar. Remember, cookie jars often have openings that are much smaller than the jar itself. The act of removing the cookie is what we'll refer to as the execution of the idea.

You see, the reason it took the entrepreneur longer to get to the same stage as the business owner is because he thought through the idea at the forefront. He carefully assessed the possible benefits and drawbacks and weighed those things into his decision-making process. Essentially, by the time he grabs the cookie, he has envisioned the execution scenario—from beginning to end—countless times in his mind.

The result is a well-executed business opportunity and thus, he's able to pull out an unscathed cookie.

The business owner? Well, frankly there wasn't near the amount of time spent thinking through the opportunity. He saw something he assumed he wanted, rushed to reach in and grab it, but then pulled it out in a sloppy fashion, hitting the sides of the jar on the way back up, eventually crumbling the cookie and losing sight of the would-be benefits to himself and his business.

~~~

At this point, I hope you're not sitting there confused and salivating for a chocolate-chip cookie. Here is why the cookie jar analogy matters. In demonstrating the differences in how business owners and entrepreneurs approach business-related opportunities, it can help you to start self-categorizing your own personal business style and current preferences. I used the adjective "current" in that last sentence for a reason, which I'll come back to in a moment.

Every person who picks up this book has a unique mindset (which we touched upon in Chapter 2). Some of you have already embraced the idea of business ownership, some of you realize that you're *likely* going to have to embrace it in the near future, and others of you are reluctant to even consider the idea...but yet, you're reading this book—therefore you know that change of some sort is on the horizon.

The point is that no matter what your current professional mindset, you can always grow to change it over time. This also applies to business owners vs. entrepreneurs—I would venture to say that a very rare few of us are *born* entrepreneurs. The vast majority of people who decide to own a business for the first time go into it with the mindset of a business owner. They don't know what they don't know, therefore a revealing glass cookie jar is that much more attractive—the less surprises the better. However, this doesn't mean they can't grow into a more entrepreneurial mindset down the line. I'll give you a personal example.

When I first left my job as a test engineer in the early 1990s, I knew that I wanted to own my own business, however, that was all that I knew. I wasn't sure what kind of business or in what industry, but what I did know was that I wanted the freedom to spend more time at home with my young family and less time on the road crammed in planes and conducting dangerous chemical tests day-in and day-out.

I searched for six months, investigating mostly various franchise concepts before I finally decided to buy an existing computer repair business. Why? The work fit my skillset, the flexible schedule was something I desired, and, perhaps most importantly—there was a bit of a road map. I had spent a decent amount of time talking with the previous owner about how he ran the business, what his biggest challenges had been, and why he was selling the business. Armed with this knowledge, I didn't feel I was going in blindly to figure everything out on my own. The cookie jar was what we'll call "frosted"—I had a fairly good idea of what I was getting myself into.

Fast-forward to today. As the owner of my own funding business, I could never envision buying that same, existing computer repair business. Over the years, I can say with certainty that I have transformed into an entrepreneur. Instead of shying away from business challenges and opportunities, I now seek them out and I embrace them. The ceramic cookie jar no longer terrifies me—it fires me up.

Later in this book we'll explore the various avenues of going into business for yourself and which are best suited for your current professional mindset. I just want you to leave this chapter knowing that regardless of where you start, there is always room to grow, and if your eventual goal is to be an entrepreneur, you *will* get there.

~~~

Let's look back at Jim, and his own cookie jar—the possibility of turning his beer brewing hobby into a legitimate business. He and his wife have a lot of decisions to make, such as how they would produce the beer on a larger scale—would they first do it out of their home kitchen, or would they go full-bore and rent commercial kitchen space and hire an employee or two? But wait, how would they test the market to gauge whether there would be the demand to mass produce right away? What about distribution? Could Jim walk into a grocery store and have any chance of getting his beer put on the shelf? Would he have better luck at a local bar? Were there city or state regulations that would prevent local relationships like that? And forget about city and state—what about any national regulations on producing and selling the beer in the first place?

As all of these scenarios bounce around in Jim's mind, the entrepreneur in him might see each of these things as challenges—mere hurdles that he'll have to find a way to clear in order to see his dream through.

However, what would the business owner inside Jim's head think? He might take one look at that "to-conquer" list and realize that he does not feel equipped, nor does he really want, to go down that road by himself. Where would he even start? With some research, he could find that there are such things as beer brewery franchises. Imagine a franchise system that has already paved the way for people like Jim. All the regulations have been met, all of the business plans laid out, the systems in place—in fact, all that Jim would have to do is make an investment in the franchise.

Sure, he would be giving up some creative license as far as the actual beer brewing goes, but what would be the tradeoff? At the end of the day, perhaps he would find the work fun and fulfilling without the added strain on his checkbook and stress on himself and his family.

Further, he could go a completely different way and just buy the bar down the street. Say he knows the owner and that guy's about to retire to Florida. This could be Jim's chance. Maybe it's not the beer brewing he's after, but rather the romantic notion of running a bar that perhaps he can pass down to his son? It would be a different type of stress and challenge, but at the root of Jim's desire, perhaps that is exactly what he's after.

～～～

Those are Jim's cookie jar options, and we'll follow his journey and his decision-making process throughout this book. But what about your journey and your cookie jar at this point? What opportunities are you prepared to take a chance on? What amount of time, dedication and money are you willing to spend? What circumstances may influence your decisions?

These are all questions I hope to help you find an answer to by the end of this book. I'll continue to relay to you the personal and professional lessons that I've learned along the way—both through my own trial and error and from the wise guidance of the mentors I've sought out along the way.

In my personal experience, the sooner I let go of the *I can do this on my own* mentality, the sooner I was able to receive the direction to help me steer my own entrepreneurial journey. In order to plant this seed a little deeper, I've listed below what I refer to as my "Entrepreneurial Doctrine"—10 essential traits that every entrepreneur has, or adopts over time.

■ Bill's Entrepreneur Doctrine

1) Practice making money.

> This is the #1 skill of a successful entrepreneur. We all know that great ideas do not always translate into large sums of money. At the same time, working hard will not necessarily make you wealthy. Personally, early on in my entrepreneurial career, I felt I had to give myself permission to make money. Making money is not about greed; making money is a skill, and it needs to be practiced. As they say, practice makes perfect.

2) Do the important things first.

> Procrastination is the enemy. There is a reason you always hear about successful entrepreneurs being a step ahead...you can't get ahead if you're always playing catch-up. The faster you learn to suck it up and tackle the big things on your to-do list, the faster you'll get where you want to go.

3) The 80/20 rule drives your business.

It is absolutely true that 20% of your customers will drive 80% of your business. It's also true that 80% of your success will be determined by 20% of what you do. Therefore, it is even more important that you do the important things first.

4) Take advantage of unfair advantages.

Part of mastering this skill is developing the vision to identify the advantages for the taking. Don't be afraid to accept advice and guidance from those who know more than you do. Don't be afraid to exploit your own skillset—own it and benefit from it. Don't take anything for granted and use everything you possibly can to your advantage.

5) Know your customers.

Everyone thinks they know their customers' wants and needs, but do you really? Even if you know what your customer is thinking today, how will that change over time and how will their emotional well-being affect their buying habits? The ability to step out of your box and into someone else's shoes is a skill that will always serve you well.

6) Become known as the go-to expert in your market.

Notice the word "known." Perception is everything. Even if you don't know everything about your product or space, make sure you know a LITTLE bit more than everyone else. The sooner you start acting like the authoritative expert, the sooner your customers and your sphere of influence will believe it.

7) Develop and leverage systems to automate your business.

The term well-oiled machine is popular for a reason. If you have to spend more time in your business than on your business, something is fundamentally wrong. Successful entrepreneurs spend time growing their businesses, not making sure their businesses survive day-to-day. Put in the effort up front to develop systems, purchase software, whatever you have to do in order to get to autopilot faster.

8) Build a kick-ass team.

> The long-term cost (both mentally and monetarily) of hiring a bad employee can never be underestimated. If you take the time and effort to hire the right people, they will make your life easier than you can imagine (and make you look good in the process).

9) Surround yourself with smarter people.

> Smarter than you are, that is. Every entrepreneur I've ever known has had a mentor—in fact, many mentors. Seek people who excel in areas where you do not—find them, shadow them, become a human sponge. Realize that you don't know what you don't know. Find those who do know.

10) Determination, persistence and execution.

> At the end of the day, none of the above habits amount to anything unless they are practiced, applied and refined over time.

PROPOSAL 9

Book Proposal

"The Definitive Guide to Advertising on Google"

Overview

This is a hot topic, and there's a huge market for Google advertisers —people who spend real money advertising online:

- Google is the #1 search engine on the Internet

- Google AdWords is the #1 advertising medium on the Internet, representing about 1/3 of all online ad spending

- Google's advertising sales is $5 billion per year, putting them in the same league as media giants ABC, NBC and CBS.

- Google has well over 200,000 advertisers, from small businesses to Fortune 100. With the possible exception of the Bell Yellow Pages, Google has more advertisers than any other company in the world.

Hundreds of Thousands of Businesses Want to Get More Customers via the Internet

Right now there is a Gold Rush to advertise on Google. Google has over 200,000 advertisers and the game has become very, very competitive. It's very frustrating—it's not as easy as it looks, and people are looking for answers! The Los Angeles Times described

Jeff's Comments

1 The title is strong and clear, so a subtitle wasn't absolutely necessary.

2 Actually, nothing here is a conventional overview, which is supposed to be a clear and concise concept statement. What's here belongs in the market ("Who Will Buy This Book") section. We permitted this to stand as is because it's effective information and the concept is self-evident.

243

paid search as the "most complicated form of advertising." Someone needed to make this simple, so that anyone could do it.

So I wrote the first online version of *The Definitive Guide to Google AdWords* two years ago, *after* I had spent a full year figuring it out. It quickly became a hot, well-known e-book online and since then more than 50,000 people have used my book, my courses and teleseminars to improve their online advertising.

What's in this Book?

The online version already has a 2-year sales track record, and is 217 pages long, with several additional 'handouts' on specialized topics, adding up to over 250 pages of solid content. I expect to revise it for the bookstore version, but the foundation has already been laid. It walks the reader step by step through the setup process and then explains in detail the techniques, strategies and psychology of online advertising.

At the end of this document, I provide a Table of Contents for the existing online version of the book.

What's Unusual About This book?

If all you teach people is Google AdWords per se, all you've done is taught them how to spend money, not how to make money or get new customers. What's unusual about this book, compared to almost every other (both online and offline) is that it places Google advertising in the context of successful selling too—from market research and testing to user-friendly web design and results-oriented, return-on-investment thinking. It uses Google as highly effective a tool to teach essential direct marketing skills to ordinary business owners, marketers and sales people.

Biographical Information

Perry Marshall is president of Perry S. Marshall & Associates in Chicago, which consults businesses in over 100 different industries on e-commerce strategies. Perry is author and self-publisher of *The Definitive Guide to Google AdWords, The Perry Marshall Marketing System, The Definitive Guide to Writing and Promoting White Papers*, and several advanced Google AdWords courses. He is also author of

Jeff's Comments

3 This is actually closer to an overview statement, but could create confusion since it overly refers to the self-published edition that is to be superseded by the proposed edition.

4 Again, much of this information should have been stated in the overview section.

5 Everything stated here is fine, but a lot more could have been said, including links to the author's Internet highlights. In fact, additional author information was presented to publishers in a separate document.

Industrial Ethernet published by the Instrumentation, Systems and Automation Society and co-authored by John Rinaldi.

Perry harmonizes a rare combination of writing, technical, and sales skills. An engineer by education (BSEE), he went into sales and marketing ten years ago and is now recognized worldwide as a very talented copywriter and direct marketing consultant. He has been a featured speaker at marketing seminars from Arizona to Australia, his rate for consulting is $725 per hour, and he maintains a waiting list of 2-3 months for project work.

Bryan Todd, the co-author of this book, is employed by Perry and also has a diverse background. He consults with dozens of clients in dozens of industries, from self-help to high-tech. He has degrees in history and theology, and even taught English as a second language in China for four years.   **6**

This Book is Already Extremely Successful Online

This is the best selling book on Google AdWords on the Internet. My *Definitive Guide to Google AdWords* has sold over $533,000 in the last 24 months (e-book + hard copy, at $49, 97 and $197). It shows advertisers how to buy Internet traffic and build their online sales through smart advertising strategy, and the list of people who endorse me and my book reads like a Who's Who of direct marketing. I have more than 20 pages of testimonials and rave reviews from customers. Here's just one example of the kind of reports we get from customers every week:

 Dear Perry,

Our company just finished our first 24 hours using Google AdWords and I've made the entire firm a believer in you and your system.

I had tried Google AdWords before in the past with a home business I ran on the side and spent $300 without a single sale. I was amused to look at your "wrong way" to set up a campaign and see that it was exactly how I had done it. I knew this was going to be good.

I set up the campaign over this past weekend after completely reconstructing our website using your guide and we launched it Monday afternoon. I've been doing tweaking here and there

Jeff's Comments

6 Here's a good example of how a successful self-published book can be effectively transitioned and presented for traditional publishing. What a publisher will want to know is that the sales are not "flash in the pan" and that the book will continue to succeed into the future.

7 It's okay to insert this testimonial in this context. But in retrospect, I would have saved this for a dedicated "Testimonial Addendum" section and even included many more, similar to what Amazon does.

and the result—$1600 worth of business in the FIRST DAY and I only spent $5.51 in Google advertising. And this is in an industry where the best (or at least most obvious) keywords literally go for $15.00 per click.

I can't believe it. My business partners and I are super-charged with excitement that we haven't felt in many months (months spent cold calling over and over and over). I've become a part of the Perry Marshall Cult. I've bought your White Paper course as well, and will be proposing to my partners very soon to get the high-end programs.

Which strikes me with the ultimate epiphany about using your marketing systems—YOU don't have to sell your products any-more, I am so convinced that I am selling it for you to the people with buying power. Imagine if I can do the same with my business.

I look forward to giving you an update when I can tell all of my sales people that they don't have to cold call anymore, I just want them to sit in their desk and wait for people to call them.

That's success.

Thanks Perry, I owe you a beer if you are ever in Denver.

Best Regards,
Joshua Hartley
Colonial Tax Consultants, Inc.

P.S. Feel free to use this on any of your website/material. Please leave out my last name and company name - we're the small fish in a cutthroat industry and I'd hate for my biggest competitors to figure out what we are doing. :)

The competition is not very thick:

There are relatively few trade-published books on this topic:

- Andrew Goodman's *Winning Results With Google AdWords* (not yet in print)
- *Google Advertising A-Z* by BottleTree Books
- *Building Your Business with Google for Dummies* by Brad Hill

Jeff's Comments

8 In retrospect I would have removed the comment "competition not thick." In fairness, when this proposal was written, there was a relative dearth of competition, but I'd have emphasized that this book is a little ahead of the curve. You don't want to inadvertently give the impression that a lack of similar titles might be due to a lack of interest in the subject. Also, while you want to show your work's distinctions, you don't want to be negative about the other titles' sales success, since that might give pause to a publisher's confidence in the subject in general.

To date none of these books have been heavily promoted. There are several books available online, the most prominent being Andrew Goodman's *21 Ways to Maximize Your ROI on Google AdWords* and Chris Carpenter's *GoogleCash*. There are quite a few others as well, but the rest are fairly obscure. My work is distinctively different from all of these, as evidenced by my reputation online. (Just search *perry marshall google* adwords on Google and you'll get an idea.)

■ Promotion

I am, by definition, an experienced marketer and promoter, having sold over 1 million dollars of my own self published information in the last four years. This promotional effort will continue, bringing name recognition, publicity and sales. I've done a limited amount of radio interviews already (including Matthew Walker's Small Business program on KLSX in Los Angeles). In fact, one of my ads was pictured on the front page of *USA Today* in February 2004, on their cover story on Google AdWords.

To date I have not pursued publicity opportunities in the print media (i.e. Wall Street Journal etc.) simply because I have been too busy to take the calls. In a previous life I wrote many dozens of magazine articles for trade journals like *Machine Design, Sensors Magazine, Control Engineering* and *Intech*. I do know what editors and reporters like and dislike. Already knowing what it takes to court the media, I will take those steps if we reach an agreement, and will likely hire an expert publicist.

The biggest lever I bring to the table with respect to publicity is my email list, which consists of more than 70,000 active business people who are accustomed to hearing from me 1-2 times per month. I have further access, through my affiliates, to over 300,000 people. My plan is to execute a modified version of what has become known as the "Amazon Affiliate Sales Day" model, pioneered by Randy Gilbert, in which people get bonuses and additional services for purchasing the book on Amazon at a specified date. This often pushes a book to #1 status and opens up other distribution channels. I can get 500 to 1000 people on a live teleseminar, and I do speak at a half dozen or more seminars every year.

Jeff's Comments

9 The first change I'd make is calling this the "Author Promotions" section, because publishers want authors who can and will sell themselves. The second change would be to make it third person instead of first person. It's much easier and more powerful to be self-boasting when done in the third person because it has the illusion of objectivity. What's here is fine, but it could have been better organized by using subheads or bullet points.

However there are some things I won't do. Won't do book signing tours and all that; I think it's just a waste of time. I'll use the tools I have in my hands; I'll court the press with magazine articles and interviews (I think print media is a good target) and I'll use my affiliates. Bryan is co-author and he will be fully available to help with this.

Mutual Expectations

What you can expect from me is a combination of expert author and seasoned marketer who already knows what it takes to sell books online, and a proven product that you are simply bringing to a new distribution channel. Let me be forthright about my expectations and concerns:

Should I choose to sign a contract with a book publisher, I am knowingly committing a considerable amount of time and energy, given that I've already got many strings pulling on my time. I will have to take time away from a lucrative consulting practice to publish and promote this book. I am not fully convinced that this is a good investment of my limited time. So I have concerns and questions:

- Will the publisher will be easy to work with? Will the project get bogged down in red tape, such as my rival Andrew Goodman's forthcoming book appears to have been?

- Can I include bounceback offers, links and web resources in the book, which I will do tastefully? I would like to offer follow-up bonuses, if possible on the corner of the book cover.

- If I get you a finished manuscript by, say, the end of July, how fast will this be in bookstores? I've done this once before (my book on Industrial Ethernet) so I'm not a rookie, but I wasn't dealing with a big publisher. I want this to go smoothly with minimal delay.

Jeff's Comments

10 This is an unusual section to include and could have easily backfired by coming across as arrogant and self-important. In fact, I would rarely permit it. But in this case the author had a proven sales record and genuine leverage. He came across as a hard-nosed, self-confident businessperson, not a pain in the ass.

Appendix: Current book Table of Contents

Table of Contents

The Definitive Guide to Google AdWords

By Perry S. Marshall

Jeff's Comments

11 Because the manuscript already existed (was self-published), an expansive chapter outline wasn't necessary.

Deb's Comments

If there is something close to a perfect book proposal, this one is it. However, it was for a book that was already self-published. It was also a book with a track record. Sometimes less is more, but sometimes less is too little.

I have nothing to add to this critique.

Proposed title: THE DEFINITIVE GUIDE TO ADVERTISING ON GOOGLE (no subtitle)

Published as: ULTIMATE GUIDE TO GOOGLE ADWORDS, How to Acess 100-Million People in 10-Minutes (4th Edition, 2014, by Perry Marshall, Bryan Todd, Mike Rhodes, Entrepreneur Press.

This title was originally published in 2006 and is now into its 4th edition due to rapidly changing techniques. It has sold several hundred-thousand copies in total in both print and digital formats.

This is a short proposal because the book had already been self-published.

Proposal Critique for Screen to Screen Selling by Doug Devitre

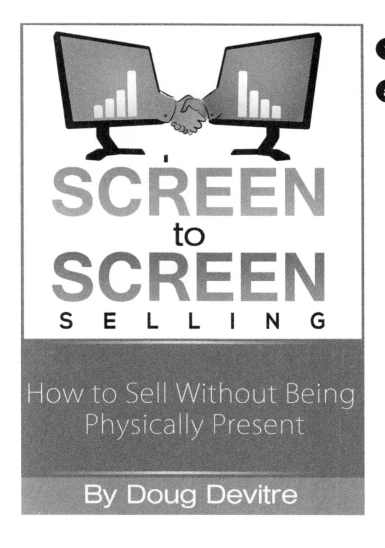

Jeff's Comments

1 I immediately liked this title because it struck me as a novel way to introduce a sales book, and seems to promise a fusion between tactics and technology.

Deb's Comments

a This title with the cover page is very effective. It removes any doubt what the book is about. If you can create a cover like this, it is worth doing but is not required. This looks very professional.

Jeff's Comments

Jeff's Comments

 Right from the start, this proposal possesses a positive uniqueness by the way it was designed, like a true brochure. This can sometimes backfire if the editor thinks you are trying to distract from having nothing much to say, but that isn't a problem here.

 This is my kind of overview, less than one hundred words and paints one thousand pictures.

4 Once again, brevity is a sharp sword. It easily anchors who the customers are.

Deb's Comments

b This is an ideal overview for a book like this. It is clear and to the point. This book relies on the content so it's unnecessary to clutter it up with more support. When writing a proposal, try to think about your strongest selling point. If you are filling a much-needed gap, highlight that.

c This is a strong statement for the first line. Typically, blanket statements are ineffective. Things like "everyone needs this book" miss the mark. Here, due to changes in technology, a bold statement works. Then he breaks it down even further to support his claim.

Screen to Screen Selling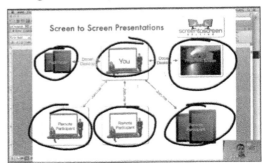
How to Sell Without Being Physically Present

http://screentoscreenselling.com Doug@DougDevitre.com

By Doug Devitre

Overview

Screen to Screen Selling is THE way to sell products and services without being physically present.

This isn't about repurposing old technology. It is about solving real problems faster using visuals that engage the customer in real time so sales professionals can make more sales faster, connect with more customers, and decrease operational costs.

The Market

Every sales professional needs this book if they want to outsell **c** their competition.

Screen to Screen Selling is especially valuable for those who share visuals to enhance their sales presentations. These include:

- Financial services sales professionals (4.6 million)
- Professional services sales professionals (1 million)
- Real estate sales professionals (442,000)
- Insurance sales professionals (443,000)
- Advertising sales professionals (155,000)

Source for estimates http://www.bls.gov/ooh/sales/home.htm

Table of Contents

Chapter 1: I can't be there. Why Screen to Screen Selling is THE new way to sell your products and services.

- I'm stuck. What to do when traffic sucks and the flight is cancelled.

- The world is rectangle. How international buyers are making decisions from your screen.

- Costs of transportation recovered. The money you will save by not showing up.

- Is this for me? Who can use screen to screen selling?

- A disaster waiting to happen. Mistakes you can avoid by learning from other screen to screen selling mistakes.

Chapter 2: Selling isn't telling. Problems with MOST sales presentations

- Blah blah v. ah ha! Prescriptive vs. Diagnostic Sales Presentations

- Hypothermia to hot flashes. Measuring the motivation by taking the customers temperature.

- Your relevance in the research. Knowing your customer's hot buttons.

- Questions vs. Questionable. Who controls the conversation?

- It's your own fault. Stop blaming the customer for technology problems.

Chapter 3: Tech tune up. The tools you will need for screen to screen selling.

- The chicken or the egg? How to prioritize the technology you need for screen to screen selling.

- Your screen to screen air supply. The Internet connection you must have in order to share your screen.

- Keep it on the download. Software you will need for screen to screen selling.

- App packed and tablet tethered. Which apps to use during your screen to screen conversations.

- Pull my stylus. Why the stylus is better than using your finger.

Jeff's Comments

5 If I didn't already like this author, I would have had to now. He presents a brief yet detailed outline. The existence of several sample chapters supersedes the need for more editorial expression in this section.

Deb's Comments

d I prefer to separate a table of contents in simple title form before creating an outline. This combines the TOC with descriptive subtitles. That's fine, but for some books it skips an important step of orienting the agent or editor to the book structure.

Chapter 4: Do we really need an appointment? When preparation isn't as necessary as you might think.

- Archived vs. Access. Retrieving the digital library of your mind.
- But I'm not ready yet. Why you don't need to prepare for every meeting.
- Stop everything now. What to do when the phone rings and the customer needs you now.
- Impromptu meetings and how to prepare in a minute's notice.
- Labor intensity to create presentations.

Chapter 5: Let's put a date on the calendar. Prospecting for the screen to screen appointment.

- Digital disasters. Avoid these mistakes before you starting dialing.
- Should I share or should I go. How to decide when to share your screen with a prospect.
- The customer will thank you later. How to save time scheduling the appointment.
- Phone, Skype, or Hangout? Logistics of the screen to screen meeting.
- Multiple decision makers. Scheduling screen to screen meetings with teams and international customers.

Chapter 6: It's almost show time. How to prepare the screen to screen meeting for maximum impact.

- Avoiding device dysfunction. How to set up your technology on time.
- Hold the phones. How do we conference call everyone in?
- Let's chat about it. How online chat saves everyone time.
- The first impression. The opening slide sets the tone.
- What if someone arrives late and can't join. How to get latecomers on the call with minimal effort.

Chapter 7: It's show time! What to say when the customer picks up the phone.

- Ready, set, flow! How to avoid mistakes before the conversation begins.

- You are someone I can trust. How to build rapport with your customer with visuals.

- Hello, my name is... How to take control of the conversation.

- Whose turn is it anyways? When to draw and when to listen.

- The next visual depends. What they say isn't what they want.

Chapter 8: Decisuals. The diagnostic tool for the dynamite.

- What is a decisual? How a decisual is different than a visual?

- Do it yourself decisuals. Tools to create decisuals for maximum impact.

- Fill in the blank. How screenshots save everyone time.

- See the end in mind. How before and after images show results.

- Charts, diagrams, and graphs, oh my! The details are in the data.

Chapter 9: Wow! That was cool. Presentation shortcuts you must master.

- Keystrokes are better than clicks. Why the keyboard trumps the mouse every time.

- Collaborative web surfing. How to collectively surf the web to solve real problems.

- Mobile device display. How to mirror apps on multiple screens.

- Rapid image retrieval. How to organize visuals and decisuals for rapid delivery.

- Mind maps that mesmerize. How to collaborate with customers using mind map software.

Chapter 10: Hold the phone John! Don't end the call until you do these things.

- Clarification or confirmation. How to tell if you met the customer's expectations.

- What next? How to affirm the next steps in writing to advance the sale.

- To ask or not to ask. When to ask for the sale or set another appointment.
- Let's meet again. The next screen to screen meeting.
- End with a smile. How to leave a lasting impression that humanizes your persona.

Chapter 11: They said yes! How to save time filling out the forms.

- If only John Hancock could see this now. How online signatures save you both time.
- Paper or plastic? How online forms are replacing paper and ink.
- Faster than fax. Which tools can you use to save time filling out forms online.
- Stop the scrolling madness. How screen share saves time filling out complex forms.
- The back up to the back up. When printing paper agreements is absolutely necessary.

Chapter 12: Visual summaries. What your competition never does that gives you the edge.

- The digital napkin. How to create a visual summarization of the call.
- Chicken scratch or handwriting match. What to do when you can't read your own handwriting.
- Whoops I forgot to say that. How to strengthen your argument with visuals you didn't use during the call.
- The missing visual. The last step before you hit send.
- Lightning fast delivery. The fastest way to send your notes using the right channel.

Chapter 13: For quality and training purposes this call will be recorded. Every conversation makes the next one better.

- Did I hear them right? How to make sure the customer told you what you needed to know.
- Did you speak your mind right? How to ensure your language matched the message you were trying to communicate.
- Did I show that right? How to record and watch a video of the call for future playback.

- Did I smell that right? How to know when the customer understood the points you were trying to make.

- Did the transitions feel that right? How can you improve your presentation skills for the next call.

Chapter 14: Screen to Screen from the Mobile Device: How to initiate screen to screen meetings from anywhere.

- Beam me in Scottie. Visual teleportation to show up in real time.

- That's not a hummingbird, it's a drone. How drones influence how purchase decisions are made and why you need to know how they work.

- Can you show me that property? How to sell objects and spaces from your screen while on the go.

- We bring virtual things to life. Tips and tools to showcase your product or service.

- Be resourceful. How to make the most out of the screen share options you have.

Chapter 15: Screen to Screen Presentations: How to engage your audience to solve real problems quickly.

- To draw or not to draw. When and how to draw on your slides during your talk.

- Real time slide manipulation. How participants create your visual in real time.

- The voice of God. How to bring in third parties to participate who are not physically present.

- The A/V help you will never get. Barriers to meeting spaces in remote locations.

- The back up to the back up. What to do when screen to screen doesn't work.

Chapter 16: Screen to Screen Webinars: How to engage participants to buy using webinars.

- Webinars on steroids. Why your PowerPoint alone is the kiss of death.

- I can't wait to see what you draw next. How the whiteboard keeps attention throughout the webinar.

- The webinar backchannel. How to use Twitter hashtags to keep the discussion going.

- Whoops! Massive mistakes to avoid on screen to screen webinars.
- Going the extra mile. How to draw on your apps using screen share.

Chapter 17: Screen to Screen in the Boardroom: How to influence decisions during live meetings.

- I can see you now. How the boardroom is different from remote presentations.
- The technology setup. How to set up the technology in the boardroom for maximum impact.
- The room layout. Where do you and is everyone else seated?
- Stop, start, and sprint. When to listen, when to talk, and when to control the screen.
- Final words. How to end the meeting so the next steps are finalized.

Chapter 18: Screen to Screen Marketing: How to leverage the time spent during conversation to use to create marketing.

- Conversations captured. How to stage and repurpose new conversations for content marketing.
- Video interviews. The steps to record conversations videos for YouTube, blogs, and social media.
- Whiteboard videos. The step-by-step process that more than your Mom gets to see.
- Podcast with your people. How to create a podcast from conversations so others can listen to from their car.
- Blogs you didn't have to write. How to quickly make a transcript of the conversation to use in blog posts.

Chapter 19: Cross sell, up-sell, and digging up the well. How to visually enroll customers in multiple products and services.

- Amazoning your presentation. Demonstrate multiple options that help the customer make better decisions to solve their problems.
- Path of the purchase. How to decrease buyer's remorse by making the transaction transparent.

- You would do all that for me? How to increase the tangible, intangible and peripheral benefits of your offer.
- Can my friend buy too? How to increase the number of referrals during screen to screen calls.

Chapter 20: Screen to Screen Metrics. The numbers you need to know, improve, and master.
- More revenue. Increase the conversion on sales appointments and presentations.
- Money saved. Decrease the operational costs by selecting affordable tools that work and travel costs.
- Time saved. Decrease the decision making time for team members and customers.
- Time saved. Decrease the customer service response time.
- Customer satisfaction. Increase the number of referrals, repeat business and customer satisfaction.

■ Introduction

Imagine if you could jump through your computer screen to help your customer. How much time could you save? How much time would you save them? How much money would you save by not having to travel?

There are more cars on the road than ever before, the price of airline tickets are higher, and travel budgets are shrinking, not to mention the acts of God prevent us from being face to face with our customers. As much as we want to it just isn't feasible to see every customer as much as we like anymore.

So what do you do then if you are serious about helping your customers make better decisions and can't be physically present?

New technology allows us to connect with customers in a way that was never possible before. You can Skype in to see your customer face-to-face, host a webinar to present your products and services, or use the trusty telephone to communicate. The problem is many sales professionals do not know how to use the technology, start the

Jeff's Comments

6 This is a good sample introduction to the book, but it's misplaced in the body of the proposal and could cause a measure of confusion. An easy fix would be to simply move it to the "Sample Chapters" section.

Deb's Comments

e This could be a general description of the book. By titling it "Introduction," I assume it is sample material. It does a good job of continuing the persuasive aspect of why the book should exist, but if it is the intro to the book, it would be more directed to the actual reader.

conversation wrong, or rely upon old systems and tools that simply don't work anymore.

The customer wants their problems solved and don't have time to fiddle with the technology that you use. They don't have time to sort through pages on the Internet to find information they need. And because you couldn't be there for whatever reason they don't have time to redo the same thing twice.

The biggest trend in sales is the decrease in the sales lifecycle.

The sales professional who is orchestrating the transaction can save their customers a significant amount of time navigating the important steps by using new technology that costs less, works on multiple devices, and simple to use.

Screen to Screen Selling teaches sales professionals how to sell without being physically present using the new technology everyone already has access to and what to expect in the future.

Deb's Comments

f In the actual intro to the book, this might read, *"Screen to Screen Selling* teaches you, the sales professional, how to sell …"

g This is a highly effective example of how to handle competitive works. In each instance, the author distinguishes his own book without disparaging the other books. He shows clearly where his book fills the gap.

Jeff's Comments

7 This gets my vote for a "model competition section." Importantly, the author shows that he has actually read and understood these books, and has a clear vision for where he fits into the information puzzle. What is often a throwaway section becomes an extra sell in this instance.

Competitive Works

(1)

Whiteboard Selling: Empowering Sales Through Visuals by Corey Sommers and David Jenkins

Published by John Wiley and Sons

http://www.amazon.com/Whiteboard-Selling-Empowering -Through-Visuals/dp/1118379764

This book provides a good introduction to using visuals to explain advanced concepts however it is doesn't share how sales professionals can convert prospects using interactive dialogue. One must assume that the visual is created ahead of time before the meeting or after the meeting to summarize the conversation whereas screen to screen selling involves the interactive element of converting prospects to sales.

(2)

Slide:ology: The Art and Science of Creating Great Presentations by Nancy Duarte

Published by O'Reilly Media

http://www.amazon.com/slide-ology-Science-Creating-Presentations /dp/0596522347

Nancy's read is a very visual appealing book which influences decision makers by creating simple but effective presentations. A drawback to this presentation style is that it is prescriptive rather than diagnostic. In other words the order of the slides make assumptions that the presenter knows the order of the conversation when in fact it is the prospect who has their own needs that can only be uncovered using questioning.

(3)

80/20 Sales and Marketing by Perry Marshall

Published by Entrepreneur Press

http://www.amazon.com/80-20-Sales-Marketing-Definitive-ebook /dp/B00CGNRVHE

Perry's is similar to the Pareto principle examples we have seen in the past and he applies his own real life examples on how to earn more and make less. The challenge with this book is that it doesn't cover the conversation with clients when making the sale. Screen to screen selling covers the missing piece when there is a serious prospect and you need to convert them without being physically present.

(4)

Visual Leaders by Dave Sibbet

Published by John Wiley and Sons

http://www.amazon.com/Visual-Leaders-Visioning-Management -Organization/dp/1118471652

Visual leaders is a well done literary art that shares who targets leaders of organizations to create visual representations to decrease decision making time around strategy and operations. Where it falls short in my opinion is how these visuals are shared with teams who are not physically present. Large organizations who have leaders separated by large geographic regions need to be physically present and screen to screen selling fills that void.

(5)

New Sales Simplified by Mike Weinberg

Published by Amacom

http://www.amazon.com/New-Sales-Simplified-Prospecting -Development-ebook/dp/B0094J7S9Y/

Mike's practical book breaks down the sales process in an easy to read format that any sales professional can apply. Screen to screen selling is similar in nature however by adding the technology component to sell virtually makes it a winner.

(6)

Spin Selling by Neil Rackham

Published by R.R. Donnelly and Sons

http://www.amazon.com/SPIN-Selling-Neil-Rackham /dp/0070511136

Neil's book is a classic and must have for any sales professional, which breaks down process and psychology of selling. I believe that screen to screen selling is the evolution of this book that integrates the latest technology to sell services to big and small companies.

(7)

The Art of Explanation by Lee Lefever

Publsihed by John Wiley and Sons **(h)**

http://www.amazon.com/The-Art-Explanation-Products -Understand/dp/1118374584

Lee's book is a favorite for making advanced concepts simpler using drawings. The drawback to this work is that it doesn't encompass live interaction. The drawings have been created in advance and there is no instantaneous visual creation based on the prospect's needs to be served.

Deb's Comments

(h) Everyone can miss a typo: "Publsihed." But don't let it be you. And don't do it often.

Doug Devitre: Biographical Sketch

I was not a computer geek as a kid. Other than Atari and Nintendo, I didn't develop his passion for technology until college. In 2000 I won the Entrepreneur of the Year award at the University of Missouri for an innovative application approach to resumes. You could say the mouse had gotten the taste of cheese. Then I started to explore how to take a techno-approach to selling real estate.

I started my professional career in my Mom's basement studying, learning and soaking up whatever I could. In my first three months in business I sold a million dollars of real estate with 9 transactions. In my first two years in business, I earned 10 professional certifications including his CRS, ABR and GRI.

In 2006 I started to give seminars at the St. Louis Association of Realtors® because others wanted to learn how I was applying technology in my business and in 2008 I dropped my real estate enterprise to go full time in professional training, speaking, and consulting.

Since, the National Association of Realtors® inducted me into the Real Estate Buyer's Agent Council Hall of Fame and the National Speakers Association awarded me the Certified Speaking Professional Designation which is the top credential for those who get hired to speak across the world.

Now, in my spare time I take long walks with my fiancé, play the guitar, piano, harmonica, and feed four dogs.

Business and Marketing Plan for Book

The marketing plan is broken into several key activities prioritized based on which will sell the most amount of books based on proven methods by other successful authors.

Targeted customer segments include:

- Financial services sales professionals (4.6 million)
- Professional services sales professionals (1 million)

Deb's Comments

i This "About the Author" section, which is what we prefer to title it, is short, to the point, and entertaining. It shows the author's personality, which can be important when the publisher is considering how well the author can promote him or herself. It never hurts to be likeable, even in your proposal.

Jeff's Comments

8 I like this bio. The author's career history isn't dense or long, mostly because he's relatively young. However, he shows himself to be the proverbial overachiever, fire-in-the-belly type, and youth is an asset when it's associated with emerging technologies. This isn't to say that middle age is a handicap; I'm simply showing how to turn a possible deficit (lack of experience) into an asset.

9 This section is okay. Nothing said here guarantees that even a single copy will be sold. Frankly, the author doesn't have a product sales track record to boast about, which isn't an uncommon deficit. But he effectively leverages and communicates what he does have: innovative and pragmatic ideas that he will implement. The enumerated "Tactics" approach is very smart, and all of them sound plausible.

- Real estate sales professionals (442,000)
- Insurance sales professionals (443,000)
- Advertising sales professionals (155,000)

The speech, online learning system, and bonus resources are all additional value that support buying the book.

The revenue streams that come from the book include: corporate sales, bulk book buys, back of the room sales, foreign distribution rights, and audio version of book.

My goal is to sell 10,000 books before the official publication date. I will buy 1,000 copies at a discounted price upon the shipment date to deliver to my preferred customers, corporate clients, bulk sales, and as a marketing tool to get more speaking and consulting assignments.

The following are the other high impact tactics that I will use to sell more books.

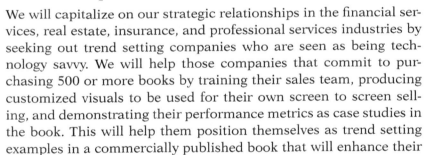

Tactic #1 Corporate Sales

We will capitalize on our strategic relationships in the financial services, real estate, insurance, and professional services industries by seeking out trend setting companies who are seen as being technology savvy. We will help those companies that commit to purchasing 500 or more books by training their sales team, producing customized visuals to be used for their own screen to screen selling, and demonstrating their performance metrics as case studies in the book. This will help them position themselves as trend setting examples in a commercially published book that will enhance their brand visibility, improve image, and improve company morale.

St. Louis is one of the top <u>financial services markets</u> in the United States making it more convenient to meet with executive level decision makers who want to stay on the top of their game. These companies include Edward Jones, Scott Trade, Wells Fargo, and AE Edwards.

I already have connections established with the <u>major corporate real estate brands</u> in the world for which are current clients making it easier to sell this concept company wide. These include Century 21, RE/MAX, Coldwell Banker, Keller Williams, and Leading Real Estate Companies of the World.

Deb's Comments

j Study this book marketing plan. The content may not be relevant or possible with your particular book. However, the presentation is clear. The author shows what connections he already has, how he will leverage them, and what he will add. It is not overloaded with the "I wills," but has some clear "I am already doing these things."

Also, depending on the volume of books purchased we may be able to print a customized copies for their organization for orders of 5,000 or more.

Tactic #2 Books in Lieu of Fee

I'm prepared (fiancé approved) to do a minimum of 50 high profile speaking events in 2015 and 2016 in order to sell more books in lieu of my speaking fee or as a value add to increase my speaking fee. My track record as earning the Certified Speaking Professional designation last year proves I can fill a calendar if that is what it takes to sell more books. My calendar seems lighter in the past because I haven't been as aggressive lately due to planning a wedding, last minute bookings by clients, and taking on more consulting projects. Once the book contract is signed then I will be more aggressive in putting dates on the calendar and negotiating book sales into the contract.

Tactic #3 Back of the Room Sales

My goal isn't just for everyone to have one book. This book ideal for gifting because of how versatile the application of the book is for both business and our personal lives. My speaking program will include business application and also how I use to communicate with my parents, 5 year, 3, year, and .1 year old nephews to drive the emotional hook to buy more books. Even though an event planner buys books in lieu of the speaking fee I will have enough books on hand to sell them back of the room at a discounted price.

If you would like a copy of my CSP application to see my past events for the last 6 years I'm happy to provide it. Also, my Linkedin profile shares many client testimonials that support my work.

Current Speaking Calendar

- 12/08/13—Global Speakers Summit
- 01/24/14 - Florida Realtors® Convention
- 02/12/14 - Maryland Heights Chamber of Commerce
- 03/04/14—Ontario Real Estate Association
- 03/10/14—Miami Realtors®
- 03/11/14—Miami Realtors®
- 03/18/14—Montana Association of Realtors®
- 03/23/14—Florida Realtors®

- 03/19/14 - Montana Association of Realtors®
- 06/03/14—Citrus Valley Association of Realtors®
- 07/06/14 - National Auctioneers Association
- 08/15/14—Florida Realtors
- 10/16/14—Naples Board of Realtors

Tactic #4 Bulk buys

For those companies who buy 20 or more books for their sales teams I will offer to host a one-hour remote coaching call for their team to show them how they can specifically apply the concepts in the book to increase more sales.

Tactic #5: Media Boost

We will target the following organizations in order to sell more books. We will develop relationships with their publications departments, serve as a contributing author for articles, and be a resource for media opportunities using their channels.

Financial services sales professionals

- http://www.afponline.org
- http://www.afajof.org
- http://www.americanbanker.com
- http://www.insidebanking.net
- http://www.internationalfinancemagazine.com
- http://www.financialexecutives.org
- https://www.cfa.com

Professional services sales professionals

- http://www.nasp.com
- https://www.psaworld.com
- http://www.tsia.com
- http://www.ifac.org

Real estate sales professionals

- http://REALTOR.org
- http://inman.com
- http://rismedia.com

- http://crs.com
- http://crb.com
- http://rebac.net
- http://wcr.org

Insurance sales professionals

- http://www.aiadc.org
- http://www.gfiainsurance.org
- http://www.naifa.org
- http://www.aria.org
- http://www.internationalinsuranceprofessionals.org

Advertising sales professionals

- http://www.aaaa.org
- http://www.smei.org
- https://www.ama.org

Note about **REALTOR® Associations**

My strong relationships inside the real estate industry give us an edge over other industries in order to plug into their media channels. I currently write the Weekly Book Scan for the National Association of **REALTORS®** http://theweeklybookscan.blogs.realtor.org and have been writing reviews on other sales authors to build strategic relationships with them in order to cross promote each other's work.

- The National Association of **REALTORS®**. Reach 1,000,000 members. I have strong relationships with the Publications Department that have used my articles and ideas in the past. Potential spotlights include interviews, pre-release campaign, and webinars for their members. They have agreed to allow me to guest post while I produce the manuscript to promote the concepts in the book.

- Each State Association has a communications department that serves 118,000 members to 1,000 members. I have written articles for these publications in the past. Please request examples.

- Real Trends. Real Trends represents the top brokers and managers for the industry. I've written articles for them in the past.

- Inman news. This is one of the largest independent media channels besides the National Association of REAL-TORS®. I've been featured in their articles in the past.

Note National Speakers Association Members and Authors

My contributions to the National Speakers Association by speaking at the national conferences, winter labs, and volunteering have allowed me to build some incredible relationships with *New York Times* Best Selling Authors and other professional speakers who are established in the industry who have big lists. I will be able to ask them to:

1. Write guest blog posts to drive traffic to the book sales landing page.

2. Co-host video interviews on Google Plus Hangouts with sales thought leaders to cross promote books and concepts that drive SEO and links to sales pages.

Tactic #6: Ground Attack

When I travel to cities in which I am there for work I will be face-to-face cold calling fortune 500 companies, Inc. 5000 companies, and local media channels to set up meetings with decision makers.

Tactic #7: Online Sales Funnel http://screentoscreenselling.com

Screen-to-Screen Selling isn't just a book. It is a practical how to guide that involves many steps in the process in order to sell their services to clients. I will be offering my Screen to Screen Selling learning management system for those who want more how to advice and offering for $97 per person. Every person who buys access to the learning management system will receive a hard cover book for FREE in which I will mail to them directly. For example if the book retails for $34 and the LMS is $97 they will save $34 if they act now (to create urgency).

The order of the funnel will include:

1. Build an evergreen webinar system http://screentoscreenselling.com/webinars that introduces the mistakes people make when trying to sell over the phone and online to build the list and cross sell the book promotion and the screen-to-screen selling learning management system.

2. If they don't buy the LMS they will then be inserted into a 10 email follow up series that remind them of the key concepts in the book. Each email will include an email to buy the book.

Tactic #8: Sales page

The mobile responsive sales page will allow customers to buy the book on Amazon, through my shopping cart, or any other recommended sales channel.

Pre-sell Website http://screentoscreenselling.com/order-2

Tactic #9: Email Promotion, Content Marketing, Social Media, PPC, and SEO

Activities include but limited to:

1. Email list of 5,000+ sales professionals who have attended my 200+ live presentations in the past 6 years.

2. Send SEO optimize press release to high authority news services for link building to sales page and media requests.

3. Promote book sales using Linkedin ads, professional sales Linkedin groups, and share updates with 3,426 Linked in connections.

4. Create YouTube videos that demonstrate how to integrate the software together, role-play conversations, and other how-tos, which drive traffic to the book-landing page.

5. Create Slideshare/PowerPoint presentation that reinforces the process and links to the book sales page.

6. Engage Facebook Friends (3,300+) plus Facebook fan page followers (2,100+) with educational content to encourage to buy the book

7. Implement link-building strategies in order to drive traffic to sales page.

8. Implement Targeted Facebook Ads to sales professionals and sales groups.

9. Write blog posts that drive traffic to sales landing page.

10. Engage 4,000 plus followers on Twitter with questions and content to make purchases.

11. Generate sales using secure online shopping cart in order to receive orders.

12. Amazon profile and ebook releases for list building and book promotion.

13. Leverage existing relationships with other "sales" professional speakers with existing platforms and lists with high visibility.

14. Write blog posts for sales thought leaders and existing authors to increase visibility to the book and promote book sales.

15. Host teleseminars with sales thought leaders and existing authors to increase visibility to the book and promote book sales.

Bonus Resources to influence book sales

Book customers will receive complimentary elite membership to access bonus resources.

These include:

- http://screentoscreenselling.com/recommended-tools/
- http://screentoscreenselling.com/recommended-books/
- Screen to Screen Philosophy (26 page PDF) https://www.dropbox.com/s/hzd2ksbovcqrwa0/Screen_to_Screen_Selling_Philosophy.pdf
- Evernote download for checklist
- Recorded webinars

We are also offering an **elite membership** to persuade others to buy more books. For example elite members can receive 5 books and additional resources (this is subject to change).

These include:

- How to videos
- Step by step workbook
- Bonus interviews with expert screen to screeners
- Plug and play resources (Example on right)

Role play exercises, videos, and templates will be created for the following professional profiles.

- Consultants
- Real estate sales professionals
- Mortgage originators
- Insurance
- Financial services
- Website/app designers and programmers
- Accountants
- Attorneys
- Professional speakers

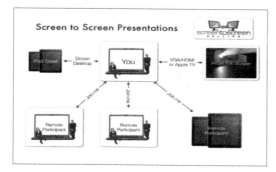

CPSIA information can be obtained
at www.ICGtesting.com
Printed in the USA
BVOW09s1214140218
508131BV00022B/1171/P